Y0-BIM-449

Materialising Roman Histories

WITHDRAWN BY THE
UNIVERSITY OF MICHIGAN

Edited by
Astrid Van Oyen
and
Martin Pitts

OXBOW | books
Oxford & Philadelphia

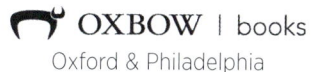

Published in the United Kingdom in 2017 by
OXBOW BOOKS
The Old Music Hall, 106–108 Cowley Road, Oxford OX4 1JE

and in the United States by
OXBOW BOOKS
1950 Lawrence Road, Havertown, PA 19083, USA

© Oxbow Books and the individual contributors 2017

Paperback Edition: ISBN 978-1-78570-676-9
Digital Edition: ISBN 978-1-78570-677-6 (epub)

A CIP record for this book is available from the British Library and from the Library of Congress

All rights reserved. No part of this book may be reproduced or transmitted in any form or by any means, electronic or mechanical including photocopying, recording or by any information storage and retrieval system, without permission from the publisher in writing.

Printed in the United Kingdom by Latimer Trend
Typeset in India by Lapiz Digital Services, Chennai

For a complete list of Oxbow titles, please contact:

UNITED KINGDOM
Oxbow Books
Telephone (01865) 241249, Fax (01865) 794449
Email: oxbow@oxbowbooks.com
www.oxbowbooks.com

UNITED STATES OF AMERICA
Oxbow Books
Telephone (800) 791-9354, Fax (610) 853-9146
Email: queries@casemateacademic.com
www.casemateacademic.com/oxbow

Oxbow Books is part of the Casemate Group

Front cover: Terra sigillata dish. Image courtesy of Judith Bannerman and Jacq Christmas (University of Exeter).

Contents

Preface v
List of figures vii
List of tables xi

INTRODUCTION 1

1. What did objects do in the Roman world? Beyond representation 3
   Astrid Van Oyen and Martin Pitts

PART 1: REPRESENTATION RECONSIDERED 21

2. Writing power. The material culture of literacy as representation
   and practice 23
   Hella Eckardt

3. Soldiers in life and death. Material culture, the military, and mortality 31
   Rob Collins

4. Gallo-Belgic wares. Objects in motion in the early Roman northwest 47
   Martin Pitts

5. Discussion. Reflections on the representational use of artefact evidence 65
   Martin Millett

PART 2: STANDARDISATION 73

6. Standard time. Typologies in Roman antiquity 75
   Alicia Jiménez

7. Different similarities or similar differences? Thoughts on *koine*,
   oligopoly and regionalism 85
   Jeroen Poblome, Senem Özden Gerçeker and Maarten Loopmans

8. Rethinking standardisation through late antique Sagalassos ceramic
   production. Tradition, improvisation and fluidity 101
   Elizabeth A. Murphy

9. Discussion. Material standards 123
   Robin Osborne

PART 3: MATTER 131

10. Finding the material in 'material culture'. Form and matter in
    Roman concrete 133
    Astrid Van Oyen

11. Design, function and everyday social practice. Artefacts and
    Roman social history 153
    Ellen Swift

12. Object ontology and cultural taxonomies. Examining the agency of
    style, material and objects in classification through Egyptian material
    culture in Pompeii and Rome 169
    Eva Mol

13. Discussion. Object-scapes. Towards a material constitution of Romanness? 191
    Miguel John Versluys

PART 4: REFLECTIONS 201

14. On theory-building in Roman archaeology. The potential for
    new approaches to materiality and practice 203
    Andrew Gardner

15. Roman things and Roman people. A cultural ecology of the Roman world 211
    Greg Woolf

Bibliography 217

Preface

This volume explores the role of material things in shaping Roman histories. Different conceptual and methodological tools can be brought to bear on this question, but no example proves the basic point as well as the story of the genesis of this book. At first sight, the key ingredients for a project like this appear to be limited to people and ideas: one needs a stimulating question, a line-up of bright scholars, and a toing and froing of new ideas. These elements were definitely part of the cocktail of the 2015 Laurence Seminar at the Faculty of Classics, University of Cambridge, and of a session at the Theoretical Roman Archaeology Conference (TRAC) at King's College London two years earlier, both organised by the editors. And yet, no seminar or volume was ever made from the mere combination of the aforementioned ingredients. What is missing?

Minds alone do not speak to one another directly, and not even the digital revolution has done away with the need to bring people together physically. Agendas need to be aligned, trains booked, and rooms reserved. These are not just practical trivia, subordinated to the real business of intellectual exchange. For true discussion to be had and intellectual progress to be made, the atmosphere needs to be at once collegial and critical, and imbue participants with the right state of mind. Indeed, the setting directly acts on the mind. In a similar vein, ideas need to be fed, hydrated, and rested. We can therefore state that without the generous financial support of the Faculty of Classics and the McDonald Institute for Archaeological Research, University of Cambridge, not only would this volume not have been made, the ideas expressed in it would not have taken shape.

The fundamental role of the material setting and its inherent contingency mean that the development of ideas is never a case in which one plus one equals two. Instead, as the trajectory of this book unfolded, starting assumptions were challenged, new questions emerged, and routes mapped out in advance were travelled only in part or diverted. These transformations not only affected ideas, but also the very line-up of participants. The original TRAC session included a paper by Ros Quick, and seminar contributions by Hilary Cool, James Gerrard, and John Robb did not end up in the volume, but have nevertheless shaped it in no small measure. Conversely, Astrid Van Oyen's chapter was written after the seminar, and while Elizabeth Murphy was not present at the Laurence Seminar, her contribution to the volume adds a much-needed micro-scale perspective to the whole.

For the eventual publication of this volume, we are grateful for the financial support of the McDonald Institute for Archaeological Research, for the editorial guidance of Clare Litt at Oxbow Books, and for the comments of two external peer-reviewers. For all its emphasis on things – redressing a long-lost balance – this volume emphatically does not deny the essential contribution of human agency. Our biggest thank you, in the end, goes to the participants in the seminar and the contributors to this volume, for expanding our horizons and those of Roman archaeology, and to the reader who has picked up this volume, for joining the exciting dialogue that is Roman material culture.

List of figures

Fig. 2.1	Inkwell of Type Biebrich.	26
Fig. 2.2	Inkwells from the graves of men and women (total 48), where gender was ascribed on the basis of grave goods or osteological sexing.	28
Fig. 3.1	A 3D scan of the tombstone of Flavinus, found in Hexham Abbey (RIB 1172). The iconography and text share Flavinus' identity as a *signifer* (standard-bearer) of a Roman cavalry unit.	32
Fig. 3.2	Grave 7 from Scorton, Catterick. An example of a soldier burial from fourth century Britain.	33
Fig. 4.1	A selection of Gallo-Belgic pottery types from Britain. Codes are from the Deru (1996) type-series.	48
Fig. 4.2	Map showing the location of selected cities and sites.	54
Fig. 4.3	The relative proportions of Gallo-Belgic tablewares at selected sites in NW Europe. Top tier: sites in Britannia with pre-conquest origins; middle tier: civilian centres in Gallia Belgica; bottom tier: military/colonial sites in Britain and sites in NE Belgica.	56
Fig. 4.4	The relative proportions of the most common butt-beaker (and related beaker) types at civilian sites in Britannia and Gallia Belgica, using the Deru (1996) type-series.	57
Fig. 4.5	Common Gallo-Belgic butt-beaker types from north-west Europe.	59
Fig. 4.6	The relative proportions of the most common platter types at sites in Britannia and Gallia Belgica, using the Deru (1996) type-series.	61
Fig. 7.1	Coin minted at Sagalassos, during the reign of Valerian I. The reverse publicises Sagalassos as friend and ally of the Romans as well as the first city of Pisidia.	85
Fig. 7.2	Sample 9. SRSW type 1B191, CaO rich group of non-Sagalassos provenance.	92
Fig. 7.3	Sample 15. SRSW type 1A150, CaO rich group of non-Sagalassos provenance.	92
Fig. 7.4	Sample 20. SRSW type 1B190, MgO poor group of non-Sagalassos provenance.	93
Fig. 7.5	Sample 28. ESD, Hayes form P40, MgO poor group.	93

Fig. 7.6	Dish with off-set rim typical for Boeotian fabrics with attested production at Koroneia and Thespiai, and morphological parallels in ARSW, Eastern Sigillata B and Athenian products.	97
Fig. 8.1	Example of a clay disc applied across the exterior base of a jug that had been cut too thin.	109
Fig. 8.2	Drawings of an 'anomalous' SRSW 1C000/1B000 form, demonstrating similarities to 1C140, 1C180, and 1B220 forms.	112
Fig. 8.3	Vessel mould depicting a smiling face (left) and moulded cup formed in a similar mould (right). The notch in the upper edge of the mould was used to cut the neck-hole for juglet forms.	115
Fig. 8.4	Plan of a late antique workshop complex in the eastern suburbium of Sagalassos that manufactured moulded wares. The north-east areas of the complex have been only partially excavated, and the dotted lines indicate walls inferred from geophysical prospections.	117
Fig. 8.5	Examples of three lamp moulds found on the floor of a workshop. Interior of the mould (left). Exterior of the mould with incised tag (right).	118
Fig. 8.6	Mould and figurines with post-moulding adaptations: figurine mould (a), rider figurines with pinched faces and incised detailing (b–c), and horse figurines with stamped and incised detailing (d–e).	120
Fig. 8.7	Examples of post-moulding appliqués: rider figurine wearing an appliqué helmet (left) and figurine helmet that popped off during firing (right).	121
Fig. 10.1	Schematic representation of different masonry types of concrete walls.	136
Fig. 10.2	Comparison of volcanic ash from the area around Rome (left) and from the Bay of Naples (right).	142
Fig. 10.3	Baths of Caracalla, Rome: concrete wall and dome with brick facing (bottom), tufa *caementa* (middle), and lightweight pumice *caementa* (top).	143
Fig. 10.4	Aula, Trajan's Markets, Rome: a new type of vaulted space enabled by concrete.	148
Fig. 11.1	Bezel from finger-ring with representation of Chi-rho motif (shown backwards), Portable Antiquities Scheme LEIC-5FC533 (Worrell 2008, cat. no. 10).	156
Fig. 11.2	Examples of amber and crystal dice, British Museum acc. nos. 1772,0311.224 (amber) and 1772,0311.220 (rock crystal).	157

List of figures

Fig. 11.3	Examples of bone one-to-six flats, Petrie Museum, acc. nos. UC59202 and UC59217 from Egypt.	160
Fig. 11.4	Examples of five-to-six flats in materials other than bone, Petrie Museum, UC59244 (stone), UC59226 (ceramic), UC59240 (stone), and UC59236 (stone), all from Egypt.	160
Fig. 11.5	Examples of dice broken and renumbered, National Museum of Ireland, acc. no. 1904.548 from Oxyrhynchus (one uppermost), and Verulamium Museum, acc. no. 2002.25 (broken and renumbered) from St. Albans (six uppermost).	161
Fig. 11.6	Example of oval plaque, from Wanborough, Ashmolean Museum acc. no. AN1955.260 and parallelipid die from Knowth, Ireland.	163
Fig. 12.1	Modern semantic network of the concept 'Egypt'.	175
Fig. 12.2	Marble Sphinx from the Casa di Octavius Quartione (II 2,2), Pompeii. Soprintendenza Pompei, Inv. 2930.	177
Fig. 12.3	Painting of a marble sphinx statue from the north wall of the peristyle of the Casa del Peristilio (VII.6.28), Pompeii.	178
Fig. 12.4	Bronze table support in the form of an Egyptian sphinx. From Casa dell'Ara Massima (VI 16,15), Pompeii. MANN inv. no. 130860.	180
Fig. 12.5	Terracotta sphinx from the Iseum of Pompeii, found in the Sacrarium. MANN inv.no 22572.	181
Fig. 12.6	The Egyptianising paintings from the villa at Boscotrecase. Top: Black Room (19), upper section, left panel north wall, in Boscotrecase. Metropolitan Museum of Art, inv. no 20.192.2. Bottom: fragment from the Mythological Room (15), upper section west wall. Inv. Metropolitan Museum of Art No 20192.13.	184
Fig. 12.7	Greek archaising scenes in the two white-coloured panels, from the Villa della Farnesina.	185

List of tables

Table 3.1	The number of soldier burials, as determined through grave goods, indicated in terms of real numbers and as a percentage of the total burials per cemetery.	38
Table 3.2	A selection of soldier burials by site, separating the contents of the grave. An asterisk (*) indicates a cremation; all other graves are inhumations. The date of burial has been given as a TPQ based on the chronology of artefact typologies, unless a C14 date is also available.	39
Table 11.1	Oval plaques with numbering.	162

Introduction

Chapter 1

What did objects do in the Roman world? Beyond representation

Astrid Van Oyen and Martin Pitts[*]

The problem with representation

Archaeologists often remark on the massive and widespread changes in the material environment in the Roman imperial period. There were more 'things' around, which impacted on the lives of the many as well as the privileged few. The volume of traded goods increased, networks of circulation expanded, and local production intensified (e.g. Greene 2008; Bowman and Wilson 2009). With quantitative increase came qualitative innovation. Objects became ever more differentiated in terms of style and function. For many communities, especially in northern and western Europe, the Roman period heralded the first appearance of genuinely standardised material culture, as opposed to objects that belonged to a more generally shared stylistic continuum. Despite the deep and far-ranging implications of these observations for current understandings of the Roman past, there have been relatively few attempts to explain or come to grips with their implications (a notable exception is Wallace-Hadrill 2008). Inquiries into the *causes* of such profound material changes have often involved methodological leaps of faith, connecting the plethora of new objects and styles to top-down models of imperialism, economic growth and Romanisation. But behind these empirical observations lurks another historical question: what were the historical *consequences* of these changes in the material environment? Did these changes actually alter people's relations to things, and through this, to each other?

In order to address these questions, we believe it is necessary to free up conceptual space to reconsider the issue of how we write history from artefacts. The culture-historical equation between pots and people that underpinned (for example) the earliest models of Romanisation is now rightly frowned upon. From changes in artefacts and assemblages we cannot confidently deduce the arrival of new people

---

[*] Department of Classics, Cornell University; Department of Classics and Ancient History, University of Exeter.

(e.g. Eckardt 2014). We argue that in the wake of the discredited culture-historical paradigm, Roman archaeology has neglected the opportunity to rethink its model of material culture. Instead, it has merely refined a representational approach: if objects no longer represent people, they have come to stand for or reflect motives external to them, such as status or other facets of group identity.

What we describe as a 'representational approach' is firmly ingrained in the ways that artefacts figure in major narratives in Roman archaeology and history. To illustrate this further, let us take the example of pottery – the most ubiquitous and numerous class of artefacts that survives from the Roman world. If pottery plays a role in Roman history at all, it does so in an intrinsically representational manner. This practice is perhaps most explicit in studies of the Roman economy. Since the absence of equivalent data means that the Roman economy cannot be directly measured in ways analogous to modern economies, pottery falls into the category of 'proxy data', in which distribution patterns allow otherwise archaeologically invisible economic phenomena to be studied, such as market integration or economic growth (e.g. Brughmans and Poblome 2016b). Despite the general success of this approach, Kevin Greene (2005, 43) has drawn attention to problems associated with a representational way of thinking:

> The 'Roman economy' is not a natural phenomenon or set of variables analogous to climate. Unlike weather and tree-ring growth, no *direct* causal connection exists between the workings of an economy and the deposition of potsherds on archaeological sites. Thus, the term 'proxy evidence' may promote an unduly optimistic expectation that material evidence can be used *directly* for 'reconstructing' the economy.

Greene's cautionary observation highlights the essential disconnection in representational thinking between the specific circumstances of individual artefacts and the bigger ideas they are often made to stand for. In addition, extensive data-mining to illuminate understandings of Roman trade entails problems of biases in large datasets, uneven quantification, and comparing data recorded and classified according to different regional traditions (Wilson 2009, 245–6). Nevertheless, the core assumption that artefacts may stand as proxies for economic activity remains unchallenged (but see Scheidel 2007). Let us be clear: there is nothing wrong with this method *per se*. Studies of pottery as proxy evidence offer much potential for insights into ancient economies. Reduction is inevitable in an approach that largely divorces pottery from the specific contexts in which it was produced, consumed and discarded, so that it may stand for overarching phenomena such as 'trade'. Likewise, it is commonplace in such studies for important characteristics of the data to be ignored, such as stylistic innovation and functional variation. The problem is not that the use of pottery as proxy data is reductive, but that it silences alternatives. Indeed, the fundamental question of why some pottery travelled long-distances when it could be produced locally in most areas of the Roman world is seldom considered in Roman economic studies.

To continue our example of pottery, its representational treatment in historical narratives of the Roman empire is not limited to the field of economics. The representational lure of pottery for cultural and social analysis is neatly summarised by Greg Woolf (1998, 186):

> All but the very poorest had access to some kind of pottery, and those who could expressed their social position and tastes through selection within the variety of ceramics available. Pottery thus makes manifest a series of social categories and claims about status that are inaccessible through most other sources.

Here pots are not so much equated with people, but are viewed as conduits to revealing conscious choices made by different Roman socio-economic groups. In other words, pottery may be used as 'proxy evidence' for social differentiation and cultural process. At one level, this realisation is to be welcomed since it has encouraged wider consideration of pots and potsherds as social and cultural indicators, in addition to their well-established use in charting economic patterns and as a dating tool for archaeological structures. There are, crudely speaking, two kinds of major study that have harnessed this approach – the big picture historical narrative, and the more specialist account of consumption patterns. Both tend to be implicitly representational in their treatment of artefacts, which introduces similar problems to those associated with the use of material culture within economic history.

For an example of the study of pots and culture in big picture Roman history, the elegant discussion of Italian-style *terra sigillata* in Andrew Wallace-Hadrill's *Rome's Cultural Revolution* provides an excellent example (Wallace-Hadrill 2008, 407–21). In many ways this is a rare case in which pottery is given treatment beyond fleeting reference to the archetypal distribution map. Wallace-Hadrill gives detailed thought to the cultural influences acting on Italian-style *sigillata*, its material properties (e.g. colour and decoration), its origins and the reasons for its boom in the Augustan period. However, his conclusion focuses on a representational issue – what was the *meaning* of *terra sigillata* to the consumer? Wallace-Hadrill answers this question by equating the circulation of Italian-style *terra sigillata* with the blanket concept of 'luxury'. While this achieves a satisfactory outcome for the reader in connecting the origins of *sigillata* to other important innovations of the Augustan age, there is an uncomfortable gulf between this high-level generalisation and a lack of detailed consideration of *sigillata* across various contexts of production and consumption.

If bigger picture historical studies can lack the space to do justice to the complexities of artefactual data, this is less a problem for more dedicated syntheses of Roman pottery. Successful approaches in this vein have connected pottery to its role in the social practices of eating and drinking, as everyday arenas in which routine use informed the formation of changing and contrasting cultural identities (e.g. Cool 2006; Roth 2007; Dietler 2010; Perring and Pitts 2013). However, despite the rejection of blunt representational analyses of ceramic changes under the umbrella of Romanisation, and the increased sensitivity of these studies to sample size and context, most studies continue to use an implicitly representational approach. For example, changes in ceramics and cuisine are variously attributed to internal community dynamics (Cool 2006, 168), an emphasis on local identity (Roth 2007, 201), the presence of 'native wives in the households of early settlers' (Dietler 2010, 253), and participation in 'Gallic styles of consumption' (Perring and Pitts 2013, 245). While analysis of material culture has become more nuanced, what appears to be most at stake is what ever more complex patterns *represent*.

At the root of the problems with this representational model is the partial methodological engagement with pottery (and other artefacts, for that matter) as material culture. Attributes of data not deemed essential to reconstructing social and cultural phenomena are often excluded at the outset of analysis, since the primary objective tends to be to understand an abstract concept or process (e.g. cuisine and identity formation) that is external to the object of study (pottery sherds). Crucially, little energy is expended on tracing the broader range of genealogies, associations, continuities and changes in the collective histories and biographies of Roman pottery. For example, in the tradition of Romano-British archaeology, the construct of 'imported pottery' forms a familiar and seemingly well-understood category that tends to be used as one of a suite of materials to shed light upon themes ranging from economic networks to urban/rural relations or eating and drinking. In this way, research jumps straight from labelling something as 'imported' to broader themes, rather than directly questioning the roles of 'imported pottery' as material culture itself. While such leaps were necessary in order not to lose sight of the big picture, archaeology now has tools to build a more continuous path from objects to historical process. A thorough consideration of 'imported pottery'– including thinking about its associations, genealogies and biographical pathways in neighbouring parts of the Roman world – has considerable potential to inform representational readings at local and pan-regional levels (see Pitts, this volume, for further discussion).

So far, we have made the case for why the representational model of material culture can be problematic for bigger picture narratives and synthetic artefact research in Roman archaeology, in large part by failing to get to grips with objects' context and stylistic and material specificities. But what of the implications for the study of Roman finds more generally? In a sense, traditional specialist artefact reports are better placed vis-a-vis synthetic studies to deal with such problems. Compared with the writing of big picture history, experienced artefact specialists often have a greater depth of knowledge of their material gained through routine handling of artefactual assemblages. Here, however, the problem of representation is less concerned with issues of interpretation and research questions (although the same issues are present in specialist reports), but rather with the descriptive languages used to categorise and classify artefacts.

To explore further, let us resume our consideration of pottery. Representational models of material culture are implicit at multiple levels of the description of ceramic wares. At a general level, descriptions of pottery fabrics and vessel shapes are frequently equated with inherently fuzzy cultural concepts, such as 'Roman', 'Romanising', 'Romanised', 'Belgic', 'native', etc.; the terminology of long since discredited archaeological cultures is persistently used, e.g. site-type names such as La Tène and Aylesford-Swarling; wares may be described in terms of historically attested regional groupings (e.g. Durotrigan ware) or modern administrative boundaries (e.g. South Devon ware, North Kent grey ware) with equal likelihood; and in some cases be associated with specific social groups, e.g. Legionary ware. In the majority of examples, these labels no longer carry explicit representational meaning among the practitioners that use them – they are instead a form of short-hand that has been retained for practical reasons (i.e. the need to ensure compatibility with older reports). Nevertheless, the problems caused by retaining such labels arguably go beyond those associated with mere clumsy terminology. These include the perpetuation of hierarchies of preconceived value and importance (from widely circulating 'Roman' *terra sigillata* and 'imported pottery' to inferior 'Romanising' coarse wares), which runs the risk of conditioning interpretation at the level of individual site narratives and regional studies. Categories of objects are treated as known quantities or passive indicators, so that all the analyst needs to do to scrutinise a social process in a given period and region is to build up a big enough database of objects.

Confronting representation

A representational model of material culture is not inherently wrong. This is true especially since material culture's representational role is increasingly accepted as complex, context-dependent and fragmented. Concepts like 'discrepant identities' have proven useful in their emphasis on the multivocality and situatedness of material culture (Mattingly 2004). Moreover, a representational reading of artefacts can be an appropriate strategy in response to certain questions. There is no doubt that a tombstone communicates and reflects at least some aspects of identity (if not of the deceased, definitely of those commissioning it), or that statues rely precisely on a representational mechanism (although this may be more complex than hitherto acknowledged, see Trimble 2011). Our charge against representational approaches is not that they are methodologically unsound, as can be argued of the culture-historical approaches, but that they are partial. The mechanism of representation does not exhaust how material culture works. Study of artefacts centred on representation tends to privilege *certain* things in *specific* contexts: often the special, the new, or the visible; and mostly focused on distribution patterns and consumption practices, which, on analogy with our modern experience of being cut off from production, seem more directly 'expressive'. If, for instance, a certain type of artefact has its 'core' distribution area in the Danube region, and one example is found in a burial in Britain, then this seems like a particularly 'meaningful' case in representational terms.

But even a tombstone or a statue does not *only* act as a signifier for an identity, value, or memory. Both tombstones and statues are also visible, solid, relatively durable, difficult to move around, etc. These aspects are the kinds of information that artefact specialists master so well. Specialists see, handle, measure, weigh, and touch artefacts in all their detail and specificity. Materials are provenanced, their properties noted and even experienced 'first-hand'. Those material properties tend to be approached with a largely implicit, 'common-sense' instrumentalist model of material culture, according to which artefact properties are marshalled by people as befits a specific goal. Someone could for instance choose to harness the hardness of a particular rock in order to use it as a grinding stone. But when it comes to writing historical narratives, a representational model is used, in which artefacts' material qualities do not contribute to historical interpretation. At their best, representational readings are cursorily informed by artefacts' material properties. For example, the rarity of a particular resource may be seen as linked to a certain object's exotic value. But reconstruction of the regime of value in which this object was set to work tends not to be based on the object's material properties. For example, when Dressel 1 amphorae are lined up in a Welwyn tomb in Britain, their interpretation as prestige goods draws first on their scarcity and that of their assumed contents (wine), and much less on their attendant material properties and contextual associations with other objects (Millett 1990, 29–33; but see Poux 2004; Pitts 2005; Dietler 2010).

In order to escape the culture-historical model archaeologists felt the need to break the *direct* representational link whereby 'pots' stand for 'people'. The alternative, however, has not been to rethink representation as the sole mechanism for linking artefacts and historical process, but to turn to a more complex kind of representation on the model of text (Hodder and Hutson 2005; Buchli 1995). The relation between a textual sign and its meaning is arbitrary and depends entirely on its position in a grammatical and semantic structure. The word 'dog', for instance, has no *a priori* relation to the concept 'dog' – hence the great variety in vocabulary between languages, so that words with spelling and sounds as different as 'dog', 'hond', and 'chien' can all refer to the same concept. On those premises, there would be nothing intrinsic to a particular artefact that would steer its meaning. Things accordingly get divided into physical matter *plus* social meaning (Van Oyen 2013, 87–8). Following this model, the 'meaningful' aspects of material culture are located outside the objects themselves, and added to their passive, stable, in itself 'meaningless' physical substrate. To repeat, our aim is not to disprove this model on theoretical grounds (for which, see Hicks 2010). Instead, we want to focus attention on what falls through the cracks of a representational reading of artefacts.

The denying of historical significance to artefacts' material qualities is an important issue, not only because it impoverishes historical interpretation, but also because it severs the link between artefact studies and bigger narratives. The textual model of representation does not grant conceptual space to the specificities of objects, and, therefore, to the key parameters of artefact study. In the linguistic analogy, neither the spelling or typography nor the pronunciation of the word 'dog' steer meaning in any way (except through their arbitrary relations with other words). Moreover, texts are on the whole not handled, measured, weighed and touched as part of their interpretation process in the same way as archaeological artefacts. As a result, it is hard to find a space for the contribution of specialist artefact analyses in historical narratives predicated upon a representational template. The continued labelling of objects along categories and principles long critiqued on theoretical grounds is a case in point of the resulting incompatibility.

In its search for a more complex representational model than 'pots equal people', Roman archaeology thus turned to a textual analogy loosely inspired by post-structuralism. Structural concepts like socio-cultural 'identity' or economic 'growth' became the mould wherein artefacts are analysed and made to speak – e.g. the 'expression of social identity' (Eckardt 2002, 26). The reification of such postulated invisible phenomena has been repeatedly critiqued on theoretical grounds in the last decades (most notably by Latour 2005). While anchored in a more general tendency in social theory, the issue reveals itself particularly acutely in representational studies of material culture. If objects are assumed to represent external meanings, these meanings have to be attributed to and grouped by some external causal force. This leads to a form of reverse engineering by the analyst, whereby 'structural' categories are inserted at the start of research instead of being the outcome of analysis, e.g. 'elite' (Millett 1990), 'Italians, soldiers, Gauls' (Woolf 1998), and 'the military community, the urban population, and the rural societies' (Mattingly 2011, 223). This is not to say that 'elites' or 'soldiers' were not historical realities. Rather, it is an urge not to reify such postulated structural phenomena *a priori*, but to dissect what they were made up of and how they worked in order to avoid the danger of circularity.

Closely related to the reification of social categories is a final issue with the representational approach to artefacts, which is about the kinds of causal forces it invokes in history. The problem is neatly demonstrated by the perpetual bone of contention of how to make historical inferences from distribution maps: does the presence or absence of a certain artefact on a certain site reflect supply mechanisms or choice (e.g. Gardner 2007, 91)? In the former case, big economic structures seem to take over in history-writing, whereas the latter interpretation creates a past made up of human agents making conscious choices along the lines of popular discourse about identity today. While few scholars are fully invested in either model, the problem lies in the difficulty of choosing between them. This is not merely an issue of the limited detail of our data; instead it is symptomatic of how a curtailed concept of how artefacts work forces the analyst into an unrealistic choice between two extremes. Simplification of how material culture works, then, is likely to result in a reductive causality in history-writing. To avoid this, rendering the mechanism of representation more complex is only one step, which needs to be paired with an acknowledgement and exploration of other possible ways in which things can be said to be involved in history.

What is a thing and what does it do?

The last decades have seen a surge of interest in material culture across disciplines as varied as literature, history, art history, anthropology, and sociology. Given its particular expertise and long history of dealing with objects, archaeology could have a major contribution to make to this material turn (Olsen et al. 2012). While each discipline comes to material culture studies with its own historically constructed goals and questions, all emphasise that material culture does not just work in a representational way.

In order to balance the dominance of the question of what objects mean or represent, the recent material turn has focused on asking what objects *are* and what they *do*. Historians and anthropologists have shown that the distinction between humans and things, or society and nature that seems self-evident in the modern West is a historical construct, and is not universally shared (Fowler 2004). Meanwhile, cognitive and ecological studies emphasise the difficulty in pinning down the boundary between humans and their environment: brain, body and world do not just 'collide' (Clark 2008), but may well turn out to be inseparable (Malafouris 2013). Human perception cannot exist except through material mediation (Gibson 1979; Ingold 2000). These insights challenge our ontological categories of 'humans' and 'things', and push for an inquiry into what exactly things bring to the ontological scene. Ingold's call for not writing away the material qualities of objects strikes a chord with the above analysis of how representational approaches risk neglecting the specific properties of artefacts (Ingold 2007; Murphy, Van Oyen, this volume).

The question of 'what objects are' is answered more radically by studies subscribing to the so-called 'ontological turn' (e.g. Henare, Holbraad and Wastell 2007; Holbraad 2007; Viveiros de Castro 1998; critique by Heywood 2012). Anthropologists recounted how in some societies rocks can be people, or jaguars can be people. The traditional response of the western analyst is to revert once again to a representational model, ascribing these different categorisations to culturally specific, constructed meanings overlaying a universally shared and singular reality in which people, jaguars, and rocks are ontologically distinct. In this view objects may well *represent* people, spirits, or immaterial things, but this is not really what they *are*. The ontological turn questions this representational solution on political and methodological grounds and urges the analyst instead to turn to the fundamental ontological categories in her research. In contrast to our Western ontology in which nature is stable and culture varies, in other ontologies the same essence can be shared by different natural forms (e.g. Descola 2013). However, the ontological turn in archaeology has yet to transform from a critical into a constructive project capable of generating new knowledge (for steps in this direction, see special issue of *Cambridge Archaeological Journal* 19.3, 2009).

A more productive alternative seems to be to move from the question of what objects are to what objects do. As agency is no longer considered an inherent propensity, be it of humans or of things (Robb 2010), some other criterion has to be defined for 'what things do'. This criterion can take different forms, but one of the most workable variants proposes that agency (*sensu* what things – or humans – do) be linked to effects on the course of action (Latour 1999; 2005, 71). Ontological status then features at the end rather than the beginning of the analysis, and is predicated upon the shape and modality of these effects (cf. Van Oyen 2015). The link between effect and agency is only one possibility, and different criteria have in the last decades led to a whole spectrum of views on material agency, some more ontologically radical than others (Van Oyen 2016a, 1–3). It is important to note here that, while many frameworks start from the ontological uncertainty just identified (i.e. not *a priori* assuming that things are what we understand them to be from a modern Western perspective), none so far has argued for a resultant material agency imbued with intentionality and reflexivity, and most stay close to fundamental principles of Western ontology in their interpretations (cf. Robb 2004). Concerns about the terminology of material agency, as raised for instance by Andrew Gardner at the seminar that led to this publication, are valid, but they cannot always be taken to indicate fundamental incompatibility (e.g. compatibility between a Latourian material agency and the dialectical framework of Bourdieu has been suggested in archaeology by Maran and Stockhammer 2012).

The question of material agency and its modalities is therefore not the main concern of this volume. Instead we are interested in how the creation of interpretive space for mechanisms other than instrumentalism (things as tools) and representation (things as signifiers) in dealing with things can improve historical narratives and can lead to new insights into the Roman world. The adoption of ontological uncertainty as a starting point for research cautions that the way humans relate to things is not uniform across time and space. Different kinds of persons and different kinds of things emerged from different ways of structuring this engagement (already in Foucault 1975; cf. studies on personhood, Brück 2001; Fowler 2004). By challenging the boundaries of bodies, identity, and memory, Emma-Jayne Graham (2009), for example, has shown how M. Nonius Balbus, major benefactor of Herculaneum, emerged as a literally larger-than-life person through social commemoration after his death. His personhood was no longer defined by the boundary of his skin, but dissipated across the city's monuments and topography, including memorials literally and metaphorically indexing his transformation from patron to ancestor. An answer to the question 'what did things do in the Roman world?' promises to inform at the same time on the specificity of human-thing relations and on the kinds of persons in that world.

Such inquiries should, in turn, shed new light on that other aspect of how material culture works: what and how things represent. Current Western society, for instance, in which few people produce objects themselves yet many consume large quantities of objects whose links to production have been obliterated, creates certain kinds of things and specific kinds of people. As a result, some objects are more predisposed than others to representing for instance status, value, or power. We have already noted that consumption is traditionally considered an area in which the expressive role of material culture is particularly salient. While this may well be the case today, it is the historically specific result of a particular rendering of the human–thing relation, and cannot *a priori* be extrapolated to other times and places.

What different kinds of historical narratives can we expect to follow from a move beyond instrumentalism and representation as the sole modalities of human–thing relations? Starting from ontological uncertainty, the boundary between description and explanation becomes more porous. The case is well illustrated by considering the role of 'practice' in historical explanation (Bourdieu 1977; Giddens 1984; Ortner 1984). Ever since the development of post-structuralist practice theory, 'practice' has been a staple term in archaeology (Dobres and Robb 2005; Dornan 2002). In practice theory, it features as the intermediate-scale dynamic driver of the dialectic between structure and agency. In analytical terms, it is the 'how' of agency, but in Roman archaeology, it is often thought along functional categories, e.g. practice of 'eating', 'cooking', 'constructing', etc. (e.g. Gardner 2007). As far as artefacts are concerned, then, such a functional reading forces them into an instrumentalist role, where they are always already *for* something (*for* eating, cooking, constructing, etc.) (see organisation of the contributions in Aldhouse-Green and Webster 2002 and Allason-Jones 2011). Because such categories are pretty universal placeholders, both practice (the 'how' question) and objects are denied much explanatory value. Instead, an additional explanatory level is invoked over and above everyday practices, be it a habitus *à la* Bourdieu, status, power, or some other *deus ex machina* acting as prime causal mover.

Traditionally, then, objects can be causally involved in history, but only insofar as they slot into human schemes of purpose (instrumentalist) or meaning (representational). Once we widen the spectrum of mechanisms for how material culture works, however, causality changes and the question of 'how' (i.e. practice) is granted explanatory value. The point is neatly made by an example of ethnography of hospital practices (Mol 2002). In a general practitioner's consulting room, the disease of atherosclerosis manifests itself as 'pain when walking a certain distance'. Under a microscope, diagnosis of the same disease relies on '×% blockage of the arteries'. These different definitions are not wholly due to a different *habitus* of 'general practitioners' versus 'surgeons' for instance – some sort of external causal force. Instead, they are shaped by the practices of the settings: the possibility to talk to and touch the patient in a consulting room; the presence of a microscope to visualise the interior of the arteries in the laboratory. These differences in practice themselves have explanatory power: they explain discrepancies and negotiations, for instance in coming up with a diagnosis and deciding on the best treatment. The question 'what did objects do in the Roman world' is therefore no mere trivial addition to existing narratives; it can fundamentally change the dynamics, causality, and agency in historical explanation.

Representation refined: artefact biographies and networks

This book aims to convince the reader of the need to expand and diversify our interpretation of material culture, but also hopes to provide some tools for realising this theoretical move. Just as we are looking for a *more complete* theoretical model of how material culture works – adding to but not precluding instrumentalism and representation – we are not jettisoning the tried-and-tested analytical tools of archaeology. The fact that typologies long outlived the usefulness of the culture-historical paradigm shows how tools can be deconstructed and repurposed as interpretative models change (Van Oyen 2015 on types and material agency). It is clear that we can no longer do without contextual analyses and, for production, *chaîne opératoire* approaches to study the actual practices in which artefacts were produced and used, even if we are asking questions other than 'what did objects represent?'

All the while, the conceptual advancements of the material turn have been linked loosely to a set of new tools that hold great promise for archaeology. A first series of tools helps refine what is meant by representation and how to analyse it. In direct analogy with the human life course from birth to death (and even afterlife), artefact biographies follow objects as they move from production, through distribution and use, to discard (and after). The emphasis is typically on how an object can be redefined and given different meanings as it passes through the subsequent stages in its biography. A single pot can go from being a functional container for cooking to something with emotional value accompanying the dead as grave good; it may later turn into waste, or be recycled as useful building material. The onus is on contextual analysis to reveal the relations and regimes of value into which an object enters at any given stage of its biography. In practice, this means that the biographical approach to material culture tends to pay off particularly when working with single, specific, highly visible objects. Analytically, artefact biographies create conceptual space for an approach starting from material culture. Interpretively, however, they tend to revert to representational narratives, due to their close analogy with human biographies. The different phases in an artefact's biography are triggered, shaped, and given meaning strictly by human agents, with little regard for the material or relational qualities of the object and its preceding 'life course'.

While artefact biographies focus on how objects are redefined in time, networks have become a generic term for tracing the movement of objects in space. Hahn and Weiss (2013b, 4, 7) for instance prefer the metaphor of 'network' for their conceptualisation of material culture, in order to escape the linear connotations of 'biography'. Both such metaphorical and more formal (e.g. contributions in Knappett 2013) versions of networks trace similarities in material culture through space. These similarities can be typological: if artefacts of similar type are found in places x and y, these places become connected in a network. But the similarities at the basis of networks can be of a different nature as well: connections can be predicated upon the use of similar raw materials, for instance. Networks in archaeology thus have a tendency to break up material culture into a series of attributes, in analogy with the social networks by which they are inspired, which analyse different attributes of social actors (e.g. 'class', 'gender', etc.) (Knox, Savage and Harvey 2006). As a corollary, the interpretive framework that comes with this tends to be similarly 'broken up':

networks may well show the spread of a certain pottery shape, but they do not necessarily prove that this was underpinned by the adoption of a particular eating practice. If networks are interpreted as the crystallisation of exchange relations, for instance, different parties in the exchange can attribute different meanings to any traded object. Objects, knowledge and practice cannot be assumed to travel through space as one (cf. Versluys 2014).

While these approaches offer a healthy corrective to the culture-historical equation between material culture and culture, they have the unfortunate 'representational' outcome of dissociating the object world from the world of meaning. As a result, objects can be recipients of meaning attributed to them by humans, but cannot themselves add to the creation of meaning. As they travel through space, objects are redefined according to the contexts they find themselves in. By focusing on redefinition between contexts, both biographies and networks threaten to negate the importance of the analytical similarities on which they were based in the first place. The question of what ties one stage of an artefact's biography to the next, or what connects one node in a network to another, is pushed to the background in favour of local meaning-making and differing regimes of value. For example, in the case of Italian Dressel 1 wine amphorae in late Iron Age Britain and Gaul, the economic explanation of Italian over-production and westward trading networks has little bearing on local interpretations of amphorae in the different value systems that governed the Gallic 'potlatch' (Cunliffe 1988, cf. Poux 2004 for a more comprehensive account).

Biographies and networks work best when focusing on single objects. But they can often run into problems when dealing with a mass of objects, such as a particular type of pottery or brooch. In contrast to the 'odd one out', objects *en masse* reveal the limits of representational readings. When trying to decipher the meaning of e.g. *terra sigillata* pottery or dragonesque brooches in general, the analyst is forced into a representational shortcut not unlike the abolished 'pots equal people' model, although now with various 'identity options' other than ethnicity to account for similarity. The interpretation of objects *en masse* in particular seems to benefit from shifting the research question from 'what do objects mean?' to 'what do objects do?'

Beyond representation: trajectories, entanglement, and globalisation

The previous section discussed tools to refine our understanding of objects as signifiers. In this section we turn our attention to different approaches that have the potential to address the gaps brought about by the dominance of representational treatments of material culture in Roman archaeology. In particular, we suggest the notions of trajectory and entanglement as non-representational ways of tracing objects in time and space.

Trajectories are particularly suited to dealing with objects *en masse*, following the question 'what do objects do'. Although anchored in time, trajectories lack the linear connotations of biographies, necessitating a beginning and an end. By shifting emphasis from the attribution of meaning to possibilities for action, trajectories introduce a forward-looking parameter and reappraise the links between contexts that got lost in artefact biographies. As a result, the objects themselves actually have a role to play in deciding on the direction and the shape of their trajectories (Van Oyen 2016a, 131–2).

Consider *terra sigillata* tablewares, Roman archaeology's most emblematic kind of pottery. *Terra sigillata* pots were highly standardised, both in shape and technology. This standardisation made any two pots comparable – think about the proverb not to compare apples and orange. Apples and oranges cannot be compared, because they belong to different categories; but someone can compare any two apples as to how red they are, or what size they are. Similarly, someone could compare any two standardised *sigillata* pots as to which was the shiniest or the best, etc. This created a possibility of competition between potters and workshop groups. Competition, in turn, spurred a particular model of distribution and exchange. Standardisation also made it easy to stack *sigillata* pots, which greatly facilitated transport in bulk over long distances. As a result, these pots travelled far, but in sets, so that they were rarely the odd one out in consumption and were not particularly suited to working representationally. As sets, *sigillata* pots could be made to fit the parameters of different contexts: in one setting only plates might be needed, in another context decorated bowls may have been selected for. *Sigillata* pots thus could easily and widely be integrated in a variety of practices, not because they represented a desired 'Roman-ness' or even 'luxury' (cf. Wallace-Hadrill 2008), but because of their *material* ability to cater for different parameters. At the same time, their strict standardisation made reproduction difficult and created a fairly centralised production landscape. This argument has been developed in detail elsewhere (Van Oyen 2015; 2016a), but the key point is that the way in which these pots were defined in one context set possibilities for what they could do in the next. While context is still of the utmost importance, a consideration of trajectories helps appreciate how an object's agency and meaning do not necessarily start from a blank slate each time it enters a new context.

Rethinking *terra sigillata*'s production, distribution, and consumption through the lens of trajectory is no mere theoretical fancy, but fundamentally affects historical interpretation. In particular, it frees explanation from the *deus ex machina* that needed to be added to objects in representational accounts. Traditionally competition is invoked as such an external causal force triggering standardisation: as different production sites competed, there was pressure to make the production process more efficient through standardisation (e.g. Picon 2002). Following a trajectory based on the question of 'what possibilities for action did *terra sigillata* allow' rather than 'what did these pots mean', instead, shows that competition is only enabled in relation to a material environment already characterised by a certain degree of standardisation (Van Oyen 2016a, 57). For competition to take place, things have to be made comparable first. Here we have an example of how the specificity of material culture (*terra sigillata*'s standardisation) can itself become a historical explanation, rather like the example of atherosclerosis, without the need for an explanatory *deus ex machina*.

A parallel move to that from artefact biographies to trajectories in relation to things' movement in time exists for the spatial dimension as well. Concepts like entanglement, object-scapes (Pitts, Versluys, this volume), and ecology (Woolf, this volume) invoke metaphors that allow objects to be placed at the centre of inquiry while emphasising their spatial mobility (e.g. Foster 2006; Hodder 2012). Like trajectories, they shift attention away from the identity and uniqueness of individual objects towards greater emphasis on the relations between objects, people and other objects (Hahn and Weiss 2013a). The notion of entanglement, coined by Thomas (1991) and redefined and popularised by Hodder (2011; 2012), draws attention to the mutual dependencies between humans and things, which tend to increase with time and give things a hold over people that exceeds their immediate local context. For instance, the use of grinding stones in the Neolithic created new entanglements by intensifying plant use and increasing nutrient retrieval; by modifying food preparation and making bread into a dietary norm; and by triggering a reliance on heavy stones that reduced mobility (Hodder 2012, 196–9). For the purposes of this volume, entanglement, object-scapes, and similar concepts may help to overcome the problems posed by dealing with objects *en masse*, as well as approaching the issue of what objects did without immediate recourse to exclusively representational analysis or interpretation.

Methodologically, the implications of these kinds of approaches are considerable, not least given the wide geographical and temporal parameters for the circulation of objects in the Roman world, as well as the sheer quantities involved. For this reason, the concept of globalisation could act as one possible overarching framework for object trajectories and entanglements (Versluys 2014; Pitts and Versluys 2015a). For useful application to the Roman world, globalisation can be defined as a condition in which marked increases in connectivity (evident in the inter-regional flow of people, things and ideas) enable the existence of trans-regional consciousness and shared culture. In the first instance, this perspective helps to overcome arbitrary and entrenched boundaries (e.g. between periods; between provinces) that have prevented researchers from effectively studying a broader range of trajectories and circulations of material culture in the Roman world (cf. Jennings 2011 for similar application to other ancient world scenarios). In this way, globalisation breaks with the methodological nationalism that implicitly informs the writing of much 'provincial' Roman archaeology (Pitts and Versluys 2015b, 7–8). Secondly, and crucially for this volume, globalisation fosters an alternative kind of history in which the movement of objects is allowed to take centre stage. Unlike concepts such as imperialism, globalisation does not assume the *a priori* importance of particular structures (e.g. the Roman state), mechanisms (e.g. the *annona*) or cultural processes (e.g. Romanisation) that condition or structure the interpretation of material culture. In this sense, some of the perceived problems of globalisation prove to be real assets, namely the uncertainty over where agency lies, and its paradoxical character as both process and outcome (e.g. Morley 2015). By encouraging an analytical emphasis on tracing objects, people, and ideas in motion, globalisation offers a framework that is well-equipped to address the pleas from material culture studies to answer questions of 'what do objects do?' rather than 'what do objects represent?'.

This volume

The aims of this volume are twofold: first, to refine representational readings of objects in Roman archaeology (Part 1); and secondly, to explore what objects *did* in the Roman world and how this changes historical narratives (Parts 2 and 3). Granting conceptual precedence to questions other than representation in dealing with material culture can avoid cutting loose historical explanations from the objects themselves and from the practices in which they participated. Moreover, by drawing attention to the qualities of objects, such approaches can illuminate the historically specific patterns of human-thing relations that shaped the Roman period. For example, we have already suggested that some objects in the Roman world were exceptionally standardised and that, as a result, they acted in a certain way, creating particular possibilities such as long-distance trade or widespread consumption with low representational capacity. Instead of relying on external forces, explanation then becomes part of the description. And like the description, explanation is cumulative in nature: both change depending on the start and end point, length, and level of detail of the analysis.

This volume aims to put new questions on the agenda, not to provide firm answers. While we should be wary of devising a catch-all model, a first question to be addressed in this volume is how to imagine the interaction between the different ways in which objects can work. The trajectory of *terra sigillata* sketched briefly above, for instance, precisely relies on and tries to account for the apparently flexible representational functioning of these pots. Distribution analyses have neatly shown different *terra sigillata* consumption profiles (for example, for military, urban and rural sites) (e.g Willis 2011), with different preferences in shapes, decoration, etc. A representational approach asks what these different preferences signify (e.g. do they represent distinct consumer identities?), while a non-representational approach is interested in why these different preferences could exist and could be catered for in the first place (e.g. pointing to standardisation as making these pots into flexible signifiers). The object's specificities – in this case the pots' standardisation – at once shaped the possibilities for action and the roles it itself could take up in that playing field. A similar question about the relation between the different ways in which objects can work is whether the new model of explanation set forth above works with single objects – the odd ones outs – as well as with general artefact categories. Perhaps a representational model is better suited to the former?

Secondly, how are archaeological tools and methods shuffled by a non-representational approach to things? Archaeological mainstays like 'context' and 'practice' have featured prominently in this theoretical discussion. These are clearly still key concepts in our toolbox, but the way they slot into interpretation has been adjusted. Whereas practice – the 'how' question – used to merely describe contextual variation, it now has gained explanatory value. Following the concepts of trajectory and entanglement, practice steers humans and things into a directionality that shapes history, and the very description of which conversely explains historical process. By moulding practice (which in turn fuels trajectories and entanglements), the material and stylistic specificities of artefacts can (in part) transcend the defining power of context. Things can shape history beyond their here and now.

But the final and most important question to be explored by the contributions in this volume is whether the question of 'what did objects do in the Roman world' can lead to new historical insights. The brief example of *sigillata*'s standardisation and the phenomenon of competition suggests it can, but the onus is on the chapters in this volume to show that an object-centred approach produces a better understanding of the Roman world rather than merely adding texture to existing narratives.

The rest of this book is structured along three main sections, each followed by a shorter discussion chapter. In Part 1, *Representation Reconsidered* (discussant: Martin Millett), Hella Eckardt, Rob Collins and Martin Pitts address traditional concerns in Roman finds studies such as identity, supply and demand, and consumer choice, in light of the problems identified in this introductory chapter. Here, the contributors make it clear that it is neither possible nor desirable to get rid of representation in Roman archaeology, while at the same time pointing towards either a) more critical uses of representational logic in archaeological approaches, or b) new ways of thinking about material culture that incorporate both representational and non-representational dynamics. Thematically following the chapter by Pitts on standardised pottery, Part 2, *Standardisation* (discussant: Robin Osborne) confronts the issues of object categorisation, typologies and standardisation. Standardisation is arguably one of the most salient features of the material world in the Roman period. But did standardised objects lead to standardised human-thing relations, particular economic landscapes, or even standard time? Using examples drawn from multiple object classes, Jiménez introduces the concept of 'standard time' to provide new insights into the apparent stylistic synchronisation of the material world in particular periods of Roman history. Jeroen Poblome *et al.* address the relationship between artefact typologies and the big-picture cultural and economic constructs of *koine* and oligopoly in the Eastern Roman empire, whereas Elizabeth Murphy considers the constitution of material standards at the micro-level in pottery production at Sagalassos. Lastly, Part 3, *Matter* (discussant: Miguel John Versluys), sets out a blueprint of what going 'beyond representation' really entails for Roman archaeology. From the seemingly mundane world of concrete (Astrid Van Oyen) to the lure of dice and gambling (Ellen Swift) and the exotic (or familiar) use of

Aegyptiaca in Roman Italy (Eva Mol), this section demonstrates the fundamental capacity of objects to guide and influence human behaviour in the Roman world, with a specific emphasis on their material qualities. The volume is completed by two concluding discussions, which respectively contextualise the implications of the collected chapters with regard to the practice of theory in Roman archaeology (Andrew Gardner) and the contribution of material culture to Roman social history (Greg Woolf).

Part 1

Representation reconsidered

Chapter 2

Writing power. The material culture of literacy as representation and practice

Hella Eckardt[*]

While estimates of literacy rates vary widely, and cannot be established using current evidence, much recent work has concentrated on the role of literacy within Roman society (Bagnall 2011; Bowman and Woolf 1994; Corbier 2006; Cooley 2002; Harris 1989; Humphrey 1991; Pearce 2004; Tomlin 2011; Woolf 2000; 2009). Special attention has been paid to the relationship between literacy and power, in terms of 'power over texts and power exercised by means of their use' as well as by viewing writing as an enabling technology (Bowman and Woolf 1994, 6; cf. Pearce 2004, 44). Writing is also an embodied, physical practice associated with a particular range of objects. This is well illustrated by a 9th century source describing how 'three fingers write, two eyes see, one tongue speaks, the whole body toils' (Parkes 2008, 66). Literacy thus relates to the 'big' socio-cultural questions in Roman history, and to the question of the contribution of material culture studies to such debates.

This chapter examines one particular category of writing implement as a case study of contextualised and theoretically-informed finds analysis. Inkwells are cylindrical bronze containers with a central filling hole at the top, which can be secured by a small lid with a sliding lock mechanism. In terms of their cultural significance, inkwells stand for a process of writing that is otherwise dominated by organic materials that only survive under exceptional circumstances; these consist of papyrus or wooden leaf tablets and reed pens. Metal inkwells are rare enough to make an empire-wide survey possible: they have never been studied as a group but are published as individual finds even in older reports. I have compiled a substantial corpus of ca. 450 bronze inkwells gathered from dispersed publications. My current research project is concerned with understanding the practical use and symbolic significance of these objects, and how both relate to the people who wrote with them.

---

[*]Department of Archaeology, University of Reading.

In both a forthcoming book and this chapter I explore the relationship between the material culture of literacy and ancient identities. There are well-known debates about the usefulness of the term 'identity', with some emphasising the sameness of a group and the power of identity politics, and others focusing on the fluid and constructed nature of identities (Brubaker and Cooper 2000; also Meskell 2001). With regards to Roman archaeology, Pitts (2007) argued that studies of identity have often become a continuation of the 'Romanisation' debate, focusing too heavily on cultural identity. However, as for other periods (e.g. Casella and Fowler 2004; Insoll 2007; Díaz-Andreu et al. 2005) Roman archaeologists are now producing nuanced studies that account for the multiple identities (e.g. in terms of ethnicity, gender, age, sexuality, class or caste, ideology and religion) of groups and individuals (e.g. Ferris 2012; Gardner 2007; 2011a; Hill 2001; Hodos 2010; Mattingly 2004; 2011; Eckardt 2014, 4–7).

The idea that the 'consumption'and display of objects somehow directly reflects or expresses nebulously defined identities has been critiqued (e.g. Hicks 2010; Van Oyen 2013). It is clear that as archaeologists we have to pay close attention to the social and habitual practices of past agents within the structures and rules of a given society (e.g. Gardner 2004; Robb 2010) and to the relationships between people and between people and things (Latour 2005; Hodder 2012). Another key concept is the idea of material agency (e.g. Robb 2010, 504–5). Agency in this context is understood as the capacity to make a difference, where the intrinsic qualities of objects 'condition how they can be made or acquired, used and exchanged, controlled and disposed of' (Robb 2010, 497; cf. Gosden 2005; Versluys 2014, 14–18). In other words, we need to ask what pathways for action an object opens or closes. Objects are not mere passive reflections of people and societies but their use can challenge, change, and shape both. There seems to be an issue, however, over the methodology and practical application of these concepts to archaeological case studies (Fewster 2014). All too often, there is a regrettable absence of detailed engagement with the data; instead, single examples are used to stand for the wider argument.

In this chapter I present two case studies, dealing respectively with practice and representation. The first approaches the use of writing inkwells based loosely on a practice-theory framework and considers how inkwells may have shaped the habitual practices of those who used them. In the second case study I show that some aspects of the material culture of literacy can be studied through a representational reading of inkwells in funerary contexts, as long as these readings are nuanced. Depictions of writing equipment and of the act of writing can be viewed as performance, but it is important to take regional, chronological and gender differences into account. I contrast the ideological messages of tombstones depicting writing equipment with burial practices, focusing in particular on female graves. I do not argue simply that inkwells stand for 'elites' or women – but that they represent a particular skill, which had complex relationships to status, gender and other aspects of identity, and which played an important role in social practice. Overall, the chapter aims to understand what inkwells 'did' in Roman society, offering two brief case studies based on initial results of an ongoing research project.

The practice of writing

Writing is a technology and the relationship between the cognitive activity of writing and its various tools is so habitual that it is often ignored. Haas' (1996) research on writing practice shows that writing technologies affect thinking processes in subtle but measurable ways and the same is likely to be true for the Roman period. A good ancient example of the interplay of artefact design and the written 'product' is the observation by Quintilian (10.3.32) that the width of a wax tablet may affect the length of a student's composition (Small 1997, 141–5). In general, technical 'know-how', understanding the modes of operation of any given object and technology, is a powerful form of cultural knowledge. Even the production of the ink itself required a range of ingredients and specific knowledge, as did the operation of the often intricate inkwell lids and of course the act of writing with a reed pen and ink. Previous research on the practice of writing has involved analysis of handwriting styles and posture (Austin 2010, section 9.1; Parássoglou 1979) and recent work examines wear on pens and how this relates to writing practices (Swift 2014, 203–5; 2017).

For this study I examine aspects of published inkwells that have not previously been studied, in particular size and volume. The size of an inkwell has obvious implications for the amounts of ink that could be used, and may give an insight into the practice of writing. Height and diameter measurements are not available for all recorded bronze inkwells, but here we can examine a distinctive inkwell type dated to the first century AD. Inkwells of Type Biebrich, named after the site in Germany where a well-preserved example was found, are characterised by being cast, and often possessing very elaborate lids; the type often occurs as a double inkwell (see Fig. 2.1; Božič 2001, a–b; cf. Fünfschilling 2012, 191). I currently have 48 examples in my database, of which 18 have both height and diameter measurements. The inkwells range in height from 34–53 mm and in diameter from 26–43 mm. There is normally no information on wall thickness, but it is possible to describe all these inkwells as of roughly cylindrical shape and calculate an *estimated* average volume of ca. 43 ml. There is a considerable range in sizes, with the largest inkwell possessing a volume four times greater than the smallest vessel.

How do these metal inkwells compare to glass and *sigillata* inkwells? Glass inkwells occur from the mid first to the early second century AD (Cool and Price 1995, 116–7) and are therefore roughly contemporary with Biebrich inkwells. Calculating volumes for glass inkwells is very much complicated by their usual fragmentary state. Moreover, the very function of this vessel form is still debated as they possibly contained valuable unguents rather than ink (Isings 1980, 288).

The use of *sigillata* inkwells (Ritterling 13) peaks in the first century AD, again making them roughly contemporary to inkwells of Type Biebrich. It has been noted that *sigillata* inkwells are larger than metal ones, perhaps indicating that the increased volume of ink was required by heavy users such as archivists and professional scribes (Božič and Feugère 2004, 36). Another suggestion is that *sigillata* 'inkwells' contained wax rather than ink (Fünfschilling 2012, 194) but it is difficult to envisage how wax would be removed from them. Willis (2005, 97) states that *sigillata* inkwells measure around 70 mm in height and 80–95 mm in diameter, although there are examples of up to 110 mm in diameter (G. Monteil, pers. comm.). A number of complete examples with measurements were considered (e.g. Genin 2007, pl. 45, no. 12; Brulet, Vilvorder and Delage 2010, 65, 187, 197; Fünfschilling 2012, pl. 9.254). *Sigillata* inkwells are not cylindrical, but if we treat them as such for the sake of argument, we arrive at an estimated average volume of ca. 330 ml. *Sigillata* inkwells are therefore indeed hugely larger than metal inkwells of Type Biebrich. More work is needed to explore how the size of metal inkwells may change over time, and what variation there is amongst the ceramic material.

In terms of overall practice, it is possible to make a number of suggestions based on a better understanding of inkwell volumes. Even 30 ml represents a considerable amount of ink, given that modern calligraphers typically use bottles of between 30–60 ml (e.g. Winsor and Newton, Parker, Waterman). Such a bottle of ink lasts a modern calligrapher a considerable amount of time, possibly a month writing five days a week (Cherrell Avery, pers. comm.). Ink also dried up, and of course inkwells would not normally be filled to the brim to avoid spillage and to facilitate dipping pens. This supports the suggestion that the larger inkwells were for group or professional use, although it is difficult to imagine how multiple scribes used a shared inkwell, which ideally is placed close to their side. Perhaps these large *sigillata* inkwells were for the storage of ink, which was then decanted into metal or organic containers?

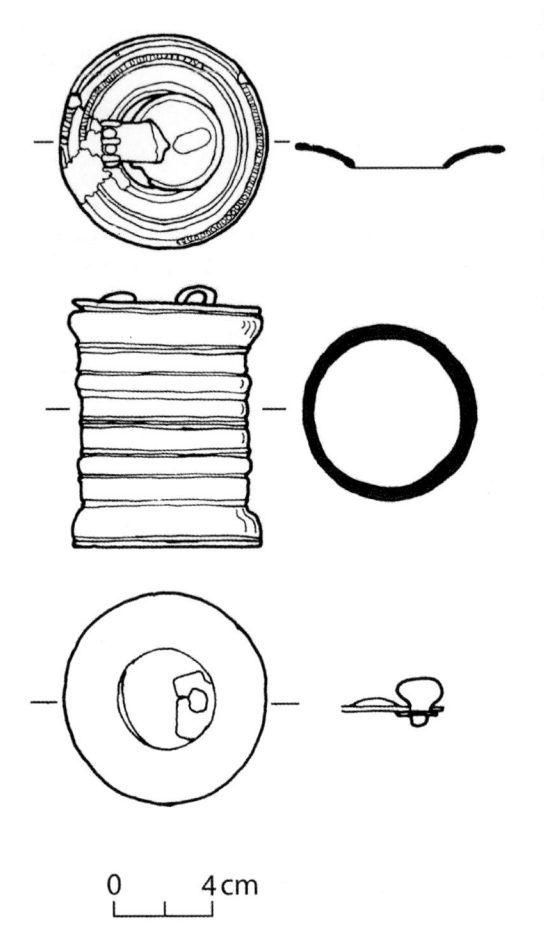

Figure 2.1 Inkwell of Type Biebrich (after Bechert 1974, fig. 84.13).

Literacy as performance and practice: writing equipment in funerary contexts

Writing equipment, including inkwells, is frequently shown on tombstones and other funerary monuments, as well as on Campanian wall-paintings. The *theca calamaria*, the portable leather writing set that usually contained inkwells as well as pens and *styli*, is an important element in the self-representation of educated individuals, and these images are frequently reproduced to illustrate ancient writing practices. The question of *why* they were created is more rarely asked.

Bronze inkwells are depicted on Campanian wall paintings with other writing equipment such as *styli*, writing tablets, scrolls and wax spatula as well as coins (Meyer 2009). These so-called still-lifes of writing equipment are usually interpreted as references to *negotium*, 'the sober, and, especially legal and financial, business of the family' (Meyer 2009, 569). Meyer further argues that this aspect of writing is almost exclusively associated with men. By contrast, she interprets the figures of women holding a wax tablet in one hand and a stylus raised to the lips in contemplative fashion in the other hand as idealised and symbolic images of leisure and literary pursuits (*otium*). Meyer (2009, 589) argues that 'The so-called female portraits instead have the pose and attributes of Muses, but if they attempt to depict 'real' women, they at best convey female aspirations to unreal qualities. Men could aspire to the literary life, but their companions – Muses or women portrayed as Muses – could only aspire to inspire it'. Is this an accurate assessment of female literacy?

Tombstones deliberately communicate aspects of identity, regardless of whether they are set up by (as occurs frequently in the Roman period) or for the deceased. The specific context is an opportunity to commemorate in visual form specific enacted identities (cf. Hales 2010). This self-fashioning of identities can be interpreted by archaeologists in terms of gender, status, and regionality. A striking feature of the tombstones depicting writing equipment and/or the act of writing is the overwhelming association with men in the many different parts of the empire where such images occur, notably Rome/Italy, Noricum and Phrygia but also Germany and Gaul (e.g. Diez 1953; Pfuhl and Möbius 1979, 542–4, no. 579 and no. 793; Schaltenbrandt Obrecht 2012, 32–3). There is only really one, often invoked but nevertheless unique, exception to this rule. This is a tombstone from Rome that depicts a butcher's wife, who is seated in a high-backed chair and writing what are assumed to be the business accounts onto wax tablets (Zimmer 1982, 94–5, no. 2).

How does this compare to what we know about female literacy from other sources? Literacy levels amongst women are generally thought to have been below those of men and higher in the city of Rome and amongst provincial elite (Harris 1989, 259–72; cf. Laes and Strubbe 2014, 99). Such elite women could achieve very high levels of education, although such women's perception in the male sources was complex (Hemelrijk 2004; Cribiore 2001, 74–101). Thus, on the one hand there was an emphasis on the ideals of 'educated motherhood' but on the other there was considerable prejudice against educated women, often accusing them of sexual licentiousness, ostentation and excessive masculinity (Hemelrijk 2004, 59–96). The education of girls may have ended earlier than that of boys, due to their younger age at marriage, but there is some evidence that women were trained for professions that involved literacy, such as teachers and scribes (Cribiore 2001, 78–83; Rawson

2003, 166–7; Haines-Eitzen 1998, 634–40; Treggiari 1976, 77–8). The survival of letters written by women in Vindolanda and Egypt has also changed perception of female literacy levels (Bagnall and Cribiore 2006; Bowman 2003).

What contribution can the study of graves containing inkwells and other writing equipment make to our understanding of female literacy? In particular, is there a possibility that the grave goods tell a different story than the ideological representations on tombstones and other visual media? A forthcoming book-length study of this material explores how the practices of reading and writing relate to the life course and how writing equipment shaped the ways the relationship between literacy, age and gender was expressed in graves (Eckardt forthcoming).

A preliminary survey of inkwells from graves suggests that women are proportionally much better represented than was thought from the literary sources and the tombstone evidence (see Fig. 2.2). My catalogue contains 125 graves with writing equipment, of which 45 were assigned to either men or women by the excavators. These graves come from across the Roman empire, and are dated from the first to fourth century AD, with concentrations in Italy, Switzerland, and Germany for the earlier and in Hungary for the later graves; 26 are thought to be male while 16 are thought to be female; there are also three burials of two or more individuals. There is of course a danger of circular arguments if grave goods are used to assign gender, as is often the case with older excavations. However, there are cases in which writing equipment was found in osteologically sexed female graves. One such example is known from Vindonissa (Switzerland), where Grave 98-1 is that of a woman aged ca. 18–25 buried with a three-year-old child. Amongst the finds were two scalpels,

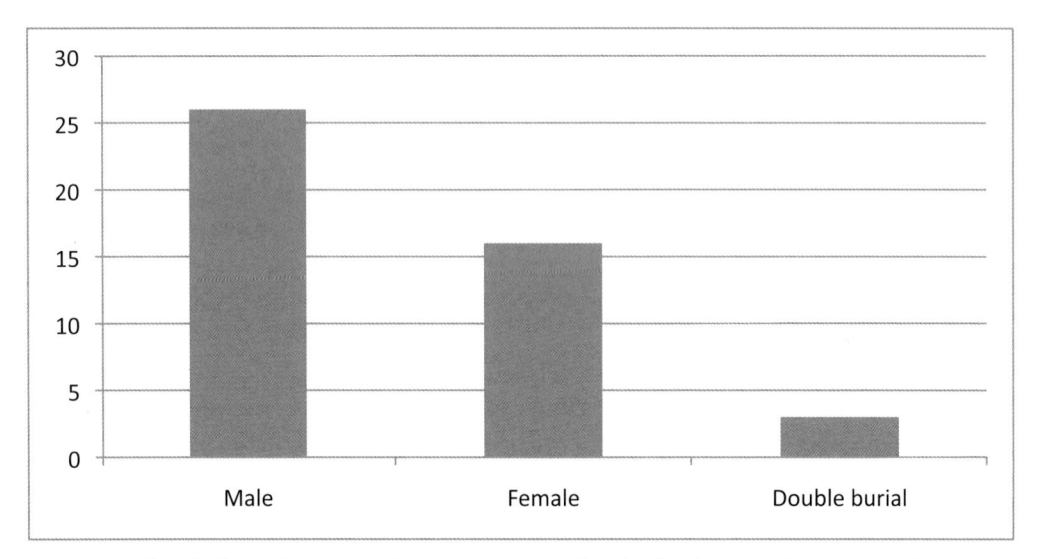

Figure 2.2 Inkwells from the graves of men and women (total 48), where gender was ascribed on the basis of grave goods or osteological sexing.

tweezers and an inkwell, leading to the suggestion that this is the burial of a female doctor (Hintermann 2000, 125–6; Hintermann 2012, 96, fig. XI.6; cf. Božič 2001a). Also found were glass and ceramic vessels, pig bones, and plentiful botanical remains as well as two coins dating the assemblage to the mid first century AD. Female doctors in the Roman world may have specialised in treating women's diseases and childbirth, but also included surgeons and general physicians (Jackson 1988, 86–8; Künzl 2002, 92–9; Künzl and Engelmann 1997). Soranus (Gyn.1.3–4) sees literacy as an important skill for a good midwife, but that may not always have been the reality (Flemming 2007, 261).

Age is another important factor. There is little point in calculating overall proportions as an empire-wide survey by its very nature will only yield biased and incomplete data, but it is worth noting that Bilkei (1980) in his survey of Pannonian material records that three out of 70 inkwells come from children's graves and in Switzerland of 21 graves with writing equipment two were those of children (Schaltenbrandt Obrecht 2012, 42–6). My forthcoming study of the burial data shows a significant number of children buried with inkwells, and this may include one case of a girl or young woman. This is an exceptionally rich, early first century AD grave found to the north of Rome, which contained two inkwells of Type Biebrich and an ivory writing tablet (Platz-Horster 1978, 184–95) as well as a set of miniature silver vessels, lamps, silver mirrors, crystal and alabaster cosmetic vessels and palettes, gold jewellery, beads and cameos, crystal, shell and amber objects, glass gaming pieces; these rich grave goods were originally probably placed into an ivory and another, larger wooden box. The grave was published as that of a young girl on the basis of the size of the ring, the presence of the miniature vessels and the amuletic objects but it is impossible to determine the exact age or sex of the remains, as no osteological data were published. Obviously future, more detailed, work will be carried out on inkwells from funerary contexts to further explore the relationship between their deposition, their use, and the people who were buried with them.

Conclusion

I have argued that good artefact analysis can be about both representation and practice. In some cases, in particular 'ideological' contexts such as tombstones and wall paintings, writing equipment is clearly used to indicate aspects of identity. These seem to relate to status: the erection of tombstones itself is not universal and in many cases the individuals depicted are junior officers, urban officials such as aediles and censors or professionals such as teachers and doctors. Such ancient self-identification can of course be contrasted with the views of others; thus from the perspective of elites in Rome any profession that involved tools and paid work was frowned upon (Purcell 2001). Provincial Roman burial assemblages have also been described as having an emblematic character; they are about fixing the deceased's identity in certain ways and act as an expression of *savoir-faire*, about knowing the etiquette of consumption (Pearce 2015, 21). But that is only really the beginning of the answer to the question. It can be argued that inkwells in graves acted as symbolic representations of a skill, social practice, and important form of cultural knowledge. There are also significant regional differences; these relate both to the depiction of inkwells and to their typologies, although that would not necessarily have been obvious to people in the past.

An interesting variation between funerary representation and burial practice concerns the relationship between gender and writing equipment. Writing equipment appears to be proportionally better represented in female graves than it is on funerary and domestic monuments, perhaps suggesting a tension between the more ideologically charged public monuments and private practice. Of course, it has to be acknowledged that the sample of graves with inkwells is very small and it is therefore difficult to draw broader conclusions. Despite the limitations of the evidence, the case study demonstrates the potential tension between the representational role of inkwells in burials and that in paintings or tombstones. While the former might come closer to ancient practice, both are about skills of cultural distinction (cf. Pearce 2015).

The initial analysis of the practical properties of inkwells has raised more questions than it has answered, which must be a good thing. Close examination shows that inkwell use was not straightforward: ink had to be obtained and mixed with water, inkwells vary hugely in shape, decoration and size and not all appear to have been portable. There may be standardised sizes at certain times, even across different materials, but this needs to be explored in more detail. One of the features only really appreciated when handling ancient inkwells is how small some examples are, and that many forms have what can only be described as 'fiddly' closing mechanisms. These physical features would have resulted in differences in practice, with for example professional scribes preferring some forms over others.

My two case studies may appear to deal with practice and representation respectively, with the first about the 'skill of writing' remaining rather distinct from the second about 'the skill of cultural distinction'. However, both case studies show that thinking about how people do things through artefacts is important if we hope to address big questions about Roman archaeology. One such question is literacy, a practice central to Roman power but also to economies, social customs, and professional know-how. Adopting a range of approaches must be the way forward, as is detailed and close engagement with the data, even if, as in this case, with preliminary data.

Acknowledgements
I would like to thank the organisers for a stimulating workshop, and Owen Humphreys for comments on an earlier draft. Gwladys Monteil and Joanna Bird kindly provided information on *sigillata* inkwells and Victoria Keitel helped with volume calculations. Cherrel Avery provided fascinating information from her practice as a calligrapher.

Chapter 3

Soldiers in life and death. Material culture, the military, and mortality

*Rob Collins**

In recent years, the excavation of new, so-called 'soldier burials' has revitalised interest in the topic of late Roman funerary practice. Fundamental to the identification of soldiers is the inclusion of grave goods that are thought to be linked to the Roman army and can be loosely labelled as military equipment: crossbow brooches; belt sets and accessories; and occasionally weapons. The frequency of this burial rite is lower in Britain than in mainland Europe, and while there is a general correlation between the burial practice and northeastern Gaul and the Rhine *limes* there is no strong frontier association for the practice in Britain. This discrepancy indicates that the practice requires further scrutiny. Of particular relevance to this volume, the objects in question may be considered doubly representational, specifically in the sense that crossbow brooches and belts are linked to the Roman army, and more generally in the presumption that grave goods should be directly associated with the identities of the deceased. Outright rejection of the representational role of military equipment is unhelpful, but uncritical acceptance that such objects identify soldiers is clearly problematic. To what extent can the practice be seen as truly indicative of the status and occupation of the deceased as Roman soldiers or officers?

Traditionally, the Roman army can be identified in the archaeological record by the distinctive morphology of its architectural installations – towers, fortlets, camps, forts and fortresses etc. – and other highly visible material culture, including tombstones, building inscriptions, bronze diplomas, and arms and armour. Figural tombstones provide a good example of the representation of soldiers, employing both textual identification and visual cues (Fig. 3.1). Unfortunately, for most of the Roman West, the practice of inscription is extremely limited after the end of the third century AD. Soldiers are still depicted in other media, for example on mosaics as at Piazza Armerina or in statuary and sculpture as on the Arch of Constantine as well

---

*School of History, Classics and Archaeology, Newcastle University.

Figure 3.1 A 3D scan of the tombstone of Flavinus, found in Hexham Abbey (RIB 1172). The iconography and text share Flavinus' identity as a signifer (standard-bearer) of a Roman cavalry unit. © NU Digital Heritage, Newcastle University.

as in precious metal like the *missiorum Theodosianus*. Military bases continue to provide valuable information, but a particularly prominent source of information for late Roman military material culture are the furnished inhumations of the fourth century AD and after. Inhumation was a widespread burial practice throughout the Roman empire, but the inclusion of grave goods provides another layer of data. Not only do these graves provide useful examples of military equipment for traditional artefact research, they also serve as 'evidence' for a range of models pertinent to the understanding of the late Roman West – principally the incorporation of barbarians, 'decline and fall', and the expansion of Christianity. Artefacts are fundamental to the interpretation of this burial rite and its archaeological interpretation, and by extension the big picture of the late Roman West. As such, the 'soldier burials' of Britain provide a suitable case study to investigate how artefacts can provide answers to big historical questions.

While it is unnecessary to enter into detailed typological description of the specific classes of artefacts considered in this paper, namely crossbow brooches and belt sets, it may benefit readers unfamiliar with these objects to provide a brief introduction. The crossbow brooch is a distinct form named for its visual similarity to a crossbow (see 514AC in Fig. 3.2); the shape and decoration of its principle elements on the head, bow, and foot are used to define its type and sub-types. Discoveries of crossbow brooches

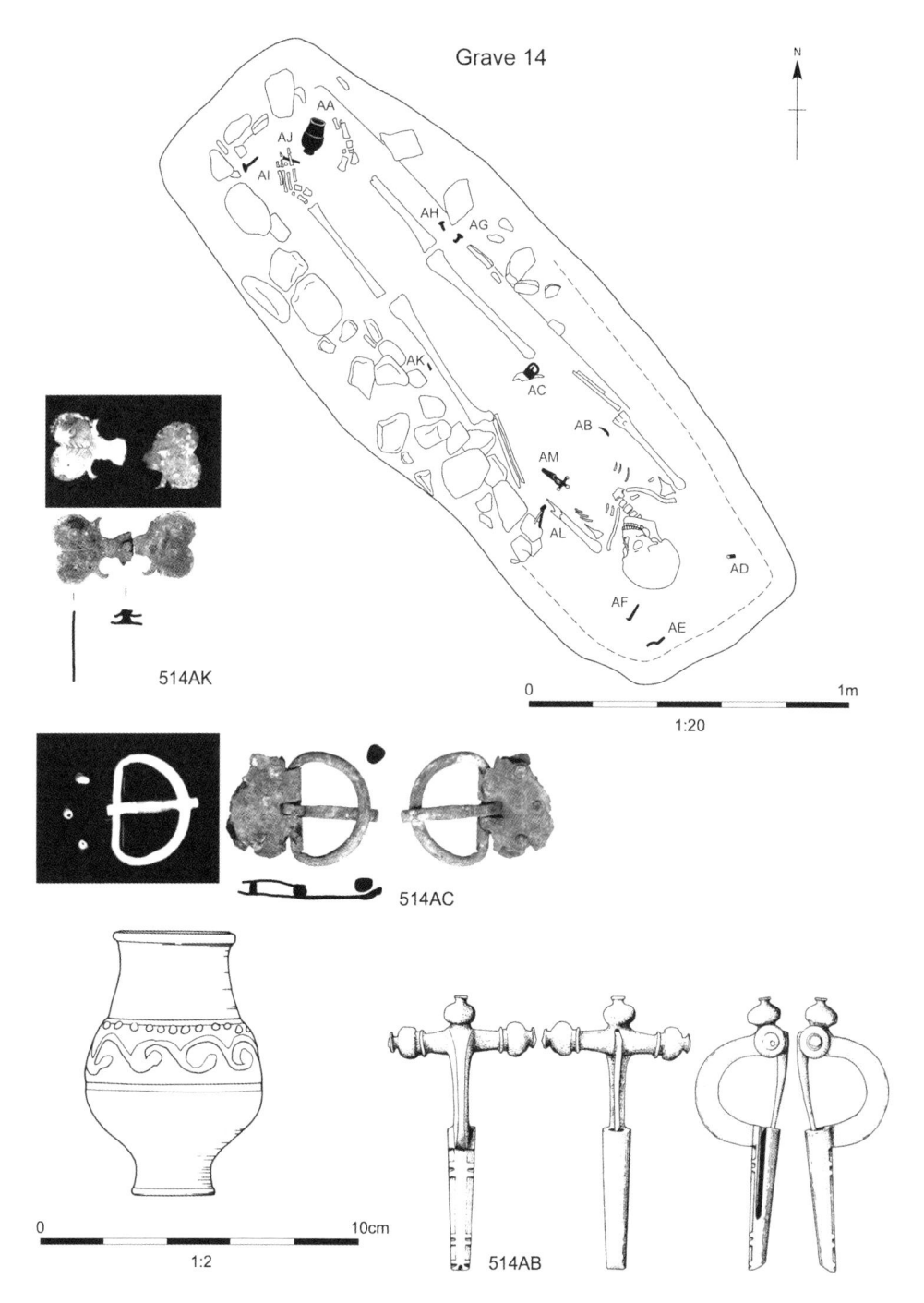

3. Soldiers in life and death. Material culture, the military, and mortality 33

Figure 3.2 Grave 7 from Scorton, Catterick. An example of a soldier burial from fourth century Britain. © NAA and Sarah Lambert-Gates (University of Reading).

found *in situ* in graves confirm its depiction in art historical evidence, with the brooch used to fasten a cloak at the shoulder of its bearer. Belt sets are more complicated, consisting of a number of distinct components brought together for functional and decorative purposes in the form of the military belt – *cingulum*. In its most simple form, the leather belt consists only of a buckle, itself composed of a frame and pin (or tongue) and sometimes also a hinged plate that the frame and pin are attached to. The leather belt may also have a metal object fixed to the end opposite the buckle, known as a strap end. Other fittings can include mounts of various shapes (e.g. rectangular, propeller) and functions (e.g. suspension hooks or rings). A relatively simple belt can be seen in Fig. 3.2 which survives as a buckle (314AC, with frame, pin, and plate) and heart-shaped strap end (314AK); the belt set from Dorchester-on-Thames is a fine example of an elaborate belt with multiple components.

Two theoretical concepts have framed my understanding of the problems surrounding the representational role of artefacts in relation to 'soldier burials'. The first concept is that of entanglement, or haecceities – 'entities that consist of the bundled concretion of specific intersecting 'lines' of becoming' (following Fowler 2013, 24–6; note also Barad 2007; Hodder 2012 is more specific in his definition). Applying this concept to 'soldier burials', the individual objects, their use within a grave, the archaeological recovery of the grave, the identification and interpretation of the objects and grave, and their inclusion into a research framework has created an entanglement of numerous discrete strands. These strands must be disentangled to create a new approach to the problem.

The second concept relates directly to the representational role of specific objects. Accepting that representational roles exist, how do we then allow for change or inconsistency in representation? Arguably, representation is accounted for in Latour's (1999) concept of a reference, in which the chain of knowledge related to a particular entity forms the reference. Within society, circulating references reproduce a fixed representational function while accommodating localised variation (Fowler 2013, 30–5). In this fashion, a crossbow brooch can be understood as having a clear association with the Roman state or military, while the significance of particular forms, materials, or usage may impart different meanings to different people.

Migrant, local elite, or ancestor?

For the purposes of this paper, I define soldier burials as furnished inhumations containing objects associated with the army or warfare that allow the buried individual to be identified as a soldier or warrior. This definition is intentionally broad in order to critically consider the notion of a soldier burial and the roles of associated artefacts. It also accepts that the link between funerary assemblages and aspects of identity can seldom be proven outright (cf. Eckardt, this volume). While the specific type of object(s) and the chronology of practice vary across space and time, the ritual can be broadly said to manifest initially in furnished inhumations bearing crossbow brooches and/or belt equipment, as these objects were explicitly linked in ancient depictions and in modern scholarship with the Roman army (Swift 2000); graves may also include other objects, for example, weaponry or vessels made of metal, glass or pottery (Fig. 3.2). While traditionally perceived as a new burial rite that emerged outside the Roman tradition, the practice of furnishing graves with military equipment should be set within a longer and more geographically extensive tradition of furnished burial during the late Iron Age and Roman period (Haselgrove 1982).

The 'soldier burials' under consideration here are distinguished through a combination of artefacts linked to the Roman state and military, set within a period in which the Roman state is traditionally understood to be in decline. The inclusion of weaponry, however, adds further complications. The appearance of weapon-bearing graves of men alongside the furnished burials of women initially clustered in northern Gaul in the mid-fourth to early fifth century AD (Theuws 2009), and the subsequent development of sizeable row-grave cemeteries (including furnished and unfurnished inhumations) in the fifth–seventh centuries AD saw the distribution of this practice corresponding to the Roman frontier zones along the rivers Rhine and Danube (Brather 2005, 162–8). Graves bearing weapons and military dress accessories were first studied in the post-War era as a group in northern Gaul and the Rhineland, where coins from some graves clearly dated the practice to ca. AD 350–450, and the individuals buried were accepted as soldiers in the late Roman army. Initially these 'soldier burials' were thought to represent German *laeti* (Werner 1950), and subsequently and more widely as *foederati* serving in the army (Böhner 1963; Böhme 1974). The distinction between *laeti* – barbarian colonists settled inside the empire – and *foederati* – barbarians under treaty with the Romans outside the borders of the empire – is minor, but has significance for understanding the origins of the practice.

In summary, it was argued that location *inside* the Roman empire *west* of the Rhine and the presence of equipment identified the individuals as soldiers in the Roman army, but the practice of furnished inhumation had Germanic origins, supported by historic evidence for the settlement of Franks and Alamanni as reported in the *Notitia Dignitatum* and other textual sources. The fact that a similar burial custom could also be found *outside* the Roman empire *east* of the Rhine further validated the interpretation of barbarians serving in the Roman army who had returned 'home'. The rite continued after the collapse of the Roman West in the fifth century AD, and served as a foundation for similar Frankish customs in the sixth and seventh centuries. While the men were generally interpreted as soldiers, it is also important to note the presence of furnished female burials in the same cemeteries, many of which contained tutulus brooches and other 'non-Roman' objects that reinforced ideas of barbarian origins. The discovery of furnished Anglo-Saxon graves dating to the fifth–seventh centuries AD in England further underscored the link between grave goods and Germanic origins, with the ethnic ascription of furnished graves supporting traditional historical narratives of the formation of the early medieval kingdoms.

Early in the debate, De Laet, Dhondt and Nenquin (1952) provided a detailed argument that the late Roman graves of northern Gaul and the Rhineland all shared a common material culture, and that Germanic *foederati* were archaeologically indistinguishable from Gallo-Romans. Shortly after, Hawkes and Dunning (1961) reinstated the association of the graves with men of barbarian origin, on the basis of evidence from the cemetery at Furfooz and the distribution of this material across the frontiers into *barbaricum*. Thus, inhumation with accompanying grave goods in the fourth-seventh centuries AD became intimately bound to notions of ethnicity. While the practice was understood as having barbarian or Germanic origins, it was accepted that the crossbow brooches and belt equipment were 'Roman', distinguishing the cultural origin of some grave goods from the ethnicity of the individual buried. Despite acute criticisms of such ethnic interpretations, furnished inhumations are still often accepted as archaeologically indicative of barbarian groups, either working for the Roman state or having some other relationship with it.

The ethnic reading of furnished inhumations has been critiqued by a number of scholars. Halsall (1992) demonstrated that many aspects of the ritual had no precedents in the traditional Germanic territories east of the Rhine, questioned the supposed Germanic origins of some of the objects included in the graves (e.g. tutulus brooches), and pointed out the uneven distribution of the graves. For Halsall, the graves are indicative of competition among local elites in the absence of effective Roman imperial control, with the burial ritual making statements of prestige and power through the use of symbols – brooches and belt sets, weapons – normally reserved for officials of the empire (Halsall 2000). In this model, the representational roles of these objects were embraced and exploited in the burial ritual for local, presumably familial benefit. Theuws (2009) concurred with Halsall's critiques, but offered a different interpretation, advocating a case for the burial practices as rhetorical communication of the political and ideological agendas of the burying group. Read as ritualised rhetoric, Theuws (1999; 2009) interpreted the furnished burials, particularly the 'weapon' burials of the late fourth-early fifth century AD, as a new ritual in which the burying community was making claims to ownership and control of land, perhaps even creating an ancestor, through display of symbolically loaded material culture. The inclusion of brooches and belts in some of these burials, Theuws (2009, 311–2) hypothesised, may be due to the presence of veterans in groups claiming the lands, or possibly the assistance of imperial authorities. Regardless of the interpretation that one may favour, both Halsall and Theuws highlight the continuing representational significance of crossbow brooches and belt equipment.

Disentangling soldier burials

From this overview, it should be clear that late Roman furnished inhumations are examples *par excellence* of an entanglement (Fowler 2013; Barad 2007; Hodder 2012 is more specific in his definition) of many different representational and ideological models constructed and employed by historians and archaeologists of the past 200 years. Furnished burial practices in the later Roman empire are inextricably bound to a number of key issues in interpretations of the late Roman West, with a long historiography of study that extends across numerous languages and international scholarly traditions. Over time, the archaeological data has accrued a number of added meanings, with each interpretation contributing to an entangled interpretive web, which transforms the way that scholars perceive the data (cf. Pitts, this volume, on the web of representational interpretations and labels attached to pottery). Firstly, the fact that the vast majority of the 'soldier burials' have been excavated in northern Gaul and the Rhineland has artificially privileged particular associations between the archaeological data and related socio-political explanatory models from those regions. Second, the model blends the binary opposites of 'Roman' and 'barbarian' burial practice, the roles of artefacts as signifiers of personal identity, and textual evidence for barbarian migrations. Even when the evidence for barbarian migration or ethnic identification is challenged, as with Halsall and Theuws, there is still a blending of the concepts of identity, burial practice and the role of Roman political hegemony; the difference is the degree to which particular types of objects are understood as having different kinds of representational roles. What is not contested, however, is the representational association of crossbow brooches and belt equipment with the imperial state or military.

At the same time, the models discussed above have not been applied to equivalent graves from late Roman Britain. There is no historical evidence attesting to widespread barbarian migration or settlement in the later fourth century AD, so the barbarisation of the population of Britain can be more easily dismissed. In addition, the occurrence of the graves is much more limited in quantity and geographical range; furnished late Roman burials bearing artefacts identified as military equipment constitute a firm minority of graves excavated to date. How should these graves be interpreted?

'Soldier burials' in late Roman Britain

Graves furnished with military equipment in late Roman Britain are limited in number and distinctly clustered. The largest group is found in the cemetery at Lankhills outside Winchester, consisting of 23 burials with military equipment out of a total of 783 graves, from two excavation campaigns (Clarke 1979; Booth *et al.* 2010). Scorton, north of Catterick, has a small cemetery of six soldier graves from a total of 15 (Eckardt *et al.* 2015). While the Eastern cemetery of Roman London had a total of 851 burials investigated, only one of these can be identified as a soldier burial (Barber and Bowsher 2000). From a small group of eight burials at Kingsholm Drive, Gloucester, another single grave was identified (Brown 1975). A single burial was also located against the external wall of a second century AD mausoleum at Shorden Brae outside the Roman town of Corbridge (Gillam and Daniels 1961), and there are two notable burials at the site of Dyke Hills at Dorchester on Thames (Kirk and Leeds 1954; Booth 2014).

Table 3.1 The number of soldier burials, as determined through grave goods, indicated in terms of real numbers and as a percentage of the total burials per cemetery.

Site	No. of soldier burials	% of cemetery
Dyke Hills, Dorchester on Thames	2	Unknown
Kingsholm, Gloucester	1	12.5
Eastern Cemetery, London	1	0.1
Shorden Brae, Corbridge	1	Unknown
Scorton, Catterick	6	40
Lankhills, Winchester	23	2.9

Table 3.1 reveals the rarity of fourth to fifth century AD burials furnished with military equipment, with only 34 individuals that could qualify as possible soldiers. While Lankhills provides the largest number of burials with crossbow brooches and belt sets, these only constitute 2.9% of the total number of burials (inhumation and cremation). The one burial from the Eastern cemetery in London represents 0.1% of the burials investigated in that cemetery. For Shorden Brae and Dyke Hills, however, it is difficult to determine how these individual burials compare to the larger cemeteries as neither site has received full excavation. In contrast, the cemetery at Scorton provides a significant group, with a very high proportion of graves containing military equipment (40%), and its separation from nearby cemeteries at Catterick (Eckardt et al. 2015).

More detailed examination of a sample of the total burials reveals the variability within this group (Table 3.2). While most of the burials were inhumations, there are examples of cremations, for example grave 895 from Lankhills with a fragmentary crossbow brooch and a probable belt buckle plate as pyre goods (Booth et al. 2010, 238). Burials containing weapons are extremely rare. Only the two graves from Dyke Hills are comparable to the rite in northern Gaul and the Rhineland (Booth 2014, 260–2). It is possible that knives may be an important signal for a British variation of this rite, with the knife acting as a substitute for other weaponry. The Kingsholm, Gloucester burial and three of the six burials from the more recent excavation campaign at Lankhills included knives. Not all knives are the same, and some distinction can be made in regards to the knives from Lankhills (Cool 2010, 276–7). However, it is likely that only some knife-forms may be understood as weapons, and it is noteworthy that most graves containing military equipment do not contain knives.

The most important feature of the British graves seems to be the presence of crossbow brooches and belts. Table 3.2 has only one example of a burial with a crossbow brooch without any associated belt equipment, from Shorden Brae, Corbridge, but other examples are known from Britain, such as a burial from the fort of Binchester excavated in 2016 (D. Petts, pers. comm.). All other burials containing brooches also feature belt equipment. It is worth noting that there are seven graves containing belt equipment in Table 3.2 but lacking a crossbow brooch.

Table 3.2 A selection of soldier burials by site, separating the contents of the grave. An asterisk (*) indicates a cremation; all other graves are inhumations. The date of burial has been given as a TPQ based on the chronology of artefact typologies, unless a C14 date is also available.

Site	Grave	Crossbow brooch type	Belt: Buckle	Belt: Strap end	Belt: Other	Weapon	Other objects	Date of burial	Reference
Dyke Hills	1		1	1	20	sword (prob)		360+	Kirk & Leeds 1954
	A		1		3	axe		390+ (artefacts) 240–430 (cal ¹⁴C)	Booth 2014
Gloucester			2	2		knife		400+	Brown 1975
East Cemetery, London	538	6	1	1	3		2 × glass vessels	390+	Barber & Bowsher 2000
Shorden Brae		6						390+	Gillam & Daniels 1961
Scorton	1	3/4	1					350+	Eckardt et al 2015
	5	3/4	1				2 × ceramic vessels; purse hoard; 'styli'	360+	Eckardt et al 2015
	6		1					330+	Eckardt et al 2015
	7	3/4	1				glass vessel; 2 × ceramic vessels; jaw bone	360+	Eckardt et al 2015
	12		1				bracelet; purse hoard	340+	Eckardt et al 2015
	14	2	1	1			ceramic vessel	340+	Eckardt et al 2015
Lankhills	745	3/4	1	2	1		ceramic vessel	350+	Booth et al 2010
	1075	3/4		1			2 × ceramic sherds	330+	Booth et al 2010

(Continued)

Table 3.2 (Continued)

Site	Grave	Crossbow brooch type	Belt: Buckle	Belt: Strap end	Belt: Other	Weapon	Other objects	Date of burial	Reference
Lankhills	1175		1			knife	coin; 4 × ceramic sherds	388–395 (coin) 237–400 (cal ^{14}C)	Booth et al 2010
	1846	3/4	1	1			2 × spurs	350+ (artefacts) 255–414 (cal ^{14}C)	Booth et al 2010
	1921		2			knife	8 × ceramic sherds; hobnails	350+	Booth et al 2010
	1925	3/4	1					330+	Booth et al 2010
	3030	3/4	1		1	knife	4 × ceramic sherds	330+	Booth et al 2010
	895*	3/4	1				glass vessel base, iron object; hobnails	330+	Booth et al 2010

For those graves featuring belt equipment, three simple groupings can be distinguished, based on the collation of belt components. The most likely component of a belt to be encountered is a buckle (complete or evidenced only by a frame and/or plate), seen in nine burials; less frequently another element is the only evidence, for example the strap end from grave 1075 at Lankhills. The next most common occurrence is a buckle and strap end, although there may be one or two other simple components like a suspension ring. The belts that are most exceptional in terms of rarity and quality are those bearing five or more elements, for example those from the Eastern cemetery, London and Dyke Hills. The Dyke Hills belt from grave 1 has at least 20 surviving components, consisting of a buckle, strap end, and a number of stiffeners and suspension loops (Kirk and Leeds 1954). The belt from grave 538 at the Eastern cemetery, London has only five components, but these consist of large, 'chunky', chip-carved pieces of the buckle, strap end, and three end plates/mounts (Barber and Bowsham 2000, 206–8). These two examples contrast with the majority of other belts, which have fewer surviving elements. The most important point, however, is that simple belts with only a buckle or a buckle and strap end are the most likely to be encountered. This further underscores the presumed high status of the individuals buried at Dyke Hills and London's Eastern cemetery.

The typologies of the brooches and belt equipment are also worthy of attention, at least in brief, following the crossbow brooch typology of Pröttel (1988) and modified by Swift (2000). Within those graves containing crossbow brooches, nine are of type 3/4, one of type 2, and two of type 6. Type 3/4 crossbow brooches are the most widespread and frequent, and probably are representative of the crossbow brooch at its peak usage dating roughly to AD 340–420 (Swift 2000). Type 2 tends to be an earlier form dating to the first half of the fourth century, and type 6 dates roughly to AD 390–430. It is no surprise that the majority of crossbow brooches can be assigned to type 3/4, and those associated with belts tend to be associated with simpler belts consisting of 1–4 surviving components. The type 6 crossbows are found in the burial with no associated belt at Shorden Brae and from the burial with the impressive chip-carved belt from the Eastern cemetery, London. Type 6 crossbows are known to be associated with the highest echelons of imperial society through art historical evidence such as the Stilicho diptych, and therefore should not be presumed to be exclusively military in their association. This ambiguity perhaps explains why the Shorden Brae burial lacked a belt and why the burial from the Eastern cemetery had such an elaborate belt despite being broadly contemporary.

While the potential insight gained through typological analysis and association can be useful, a number of concerns must also be addressed. In the first instance, although a broad typology and chronology is accepted for crossbow brooches, it has been widely accepted that a looser typology has to be employed in Britain, to reflect variation through local production (Swift 2000, 211; Cool 2010, 279; Collins 2015, 474). Furthermore, the broad types of crossbow brooches can be associated with independent dating information such as coins from graves and stratified deposits, but less dating evidence is available for examples in Britain. In addition, there is good evidence to suggest that crossbow brooches were curated and enjoyed a long use-life, as observed at Lankhills and Scorton (Cool 2010, 284; Eckardt *et al.* 2015, 7).

Accepting arguments for the localised production of crossbow brooches in Britain and their long lives raises further questions about the production and distribution of brooches. Was there any mechanism of control over who could produce crossbow brooches? If not, were locally made brooches still deemed 'official', or even visually distinguished by their wearers and viewers? Once produced, how were the brooches distributed, through imperial channels and officials, or were they available to a wider public? These concerns and questions regarding crossbow brooches equally apply to belt equipment.

The strong association of crossbow brooches and belt equipment with adult males is beyond question, as demonstrated at Lankhills and Scorton (Cool 2010, 283; Eckardt *et al.* 2015, 7), but are these men soldiers? And if so, what type of soldiers? In principle, the late Roman army was separated into three tiers: the *limitanei* permanently garrisoned in the frontiers, the *comitatenses* that formed the regional field armies, and the *palatine* that served in the armies attached to the emperors. In practice, these three arms were not kept separate, as offensive and defensive operations would see the *comitatenses* and the *palatine* armies work alongside the *limitanei*. However, there were practices that distinguished these branches, for example, recruitment and supply. Supply is a particularly important issue here, since the production of equipment like brooches and belt elements will have come from different workshops. There is reasonable evidence for local production of belt equipment along Hadrian's Wall, in the form of a casting template of a strap end for making moulds at Stanwix fort, and an unfinished strap end from the fort at South Shields (Coulston 2010). The army was led by a professional officer class, and perhaps brooches (if not belts) were restricted to certain groups within the army. As noted above, the type 6 crossbow brooch was associated with the upper echelons of imperial society, who may not have been soldiers.

Certainly, it seems probable that these brooches were worn by soldiers, or their officers, but the brooches may not have been the exclusive preserve of soldiers. Roman Winchester was not known as a military base, which raises the question: who were these men wearing crossbow brooches and belts? Were they soldiers detached from their home base on another duty, veterans, or another group not officially linked to the army? In this regard, typological variation in buckles may be quite significant. Scholarship in Britain has tended to focus on the zoomorphic forms studied by Hawkes and Dunning (1961), but this preoccupation may be obscuring associations that can be made between particular buckle forms and belt equipment and different types of soldiers or state civilian officials. Scorton, outside of the Roman fort and town at Catterick, may provide a clearer case for soldiers/officers bearing military metalwork, though Eckardt *et al.* (2015, 27) wisely note that it may not be possible to distinguish between military and civilian administrative personnel in imperial service. However, it may be significant that none of the buckles from Scorton are zoomorphic forms, in contrast to examples from Lankhills and Dyke Hills.

Isotopic evidence has been able to reveal another interesting facet regarding the origins of some of the individuals under consideration. The individual in the recently recovered weapon burial at Dyke Hills is likely to have originated in continental Europe outside the Roman empire (Booth 2014, 268). Analysis of the individual in the Kingsholm burial at Gloucester suggests migration from southeastern Europe or southern Russia, which fits with the geographic associations of the artefacts from the grave (Evans *et al.* 2012). At Scorton, isotopic analysis revealed that a central European origin was likely for the individuals buried in graves 1, 5, 6 and 7, and non-local (though possibly still British) origin for the individuals in graves 12 and 14 (Eckardt *et al.* 2015, 24). All the men buried with military equipment at Scorton appear to be non-local, based on comparison of the isotopic signatures from individuals at Scorton with individuals and livestock from other cemeteries associated with the Catterick fort and town.

It remains the case that the diverse geographic and likely cultural origins of these individuals are linked by the objects with which they were buried, and by the burial rituals observed. The male buried in grave 12 at Scorton was not locally raised, but he was also isotopically distinct from the other men buried in the cemetery, indicating a different geographic origin; despite this, his burial was still consistent with the other men, including a buckle and other objects (Eckardt *et al.* 2015, 26). At Lankhills, men buried with both imported and 'hybrid' crossbow brooches of probable British manufacture were demonstrated to have foreign isotope profiles (Cool 2010, 283). These examples further indicate the significance of crossbow brooches and belts, such that 'status in the sense of a professional identity and as expressed through objects which are almost like insignia of office was more important than geographical origin or ethnicity' (Eckardt *et al.* 2015, 26). This suggests that brooches and belts in the fourth and fifth century AD were material markers of the phenomenon of occupational identity, which has been attributed to the Roman army elsewhere (Collins 2006; 2012). This does not change the representational nature of crossbow brooches and belt equipment, but shifts its significance away from geographic or ethnic associations to one of occupation.

Concluding discussion

In contrast to the continental evidence, the distribution of later fourth and early fifth century graves with military equipment in Britain does not correspond with the militarised frontier zones. While the burials at Shorden Brae, Corbridge and Scorton, Catterick, fall within the northern frontier zone, it is worth noting that Corbridge was not a fort and Catterick was home to both a fort and sizeable extra-mural urban settlement. Roman Winchester and Gloucester were both cities, and Dorchester-on-Thames was a smaller civilian centre. London, of course, was the capital of the diocese of Britannia. The fact that the burials are associated with urban settlements does not preclude the possibility that the deceased were soldiers, but rather contextualises the connected environment in which these prospective soldiers lived.

The furnished 'soldier burials' from the south contrast with a dearth of funerary evidence from the northern frontier zone. Four inhumation graves found outside the southwest gate of the fort at South Shields, located at the eastern end of Hadrian's Wall, contained only human bone. There was no evidence for accompanying grave furniture or goods, though the burials could be confidently dated to the fifth century AD based on the *terminus post quem* of the stratigraphic sequence and C14 samples (Snape 1994, 143–4). More recent excavations outside the Hadrian's Wall fort of Birdoswald and at the coastal fort at Maryport have revealed a further ten graves that appear to date to the late fourth century AD or later. Analysis is still in progress, but what is significant is that these were characterised by stone cists or simple earth-cut graves without grave goods, with the exception of one grave with a bead necklace at Maryport. This small sample may prove to be the normal burial rite in the Wall corridor, making it difficult to identify any of the deceased as soldiers, even if this is likely. The discovery of a new furnished cemetery in this area would dramatically change the current picture, but on existing evidence it is important to stress the contrast between this small handful of late Roman burials from the Wall and the 'soldiers' buried further south.

How can this contrast within Britain, and the contrast between Britain and northern Gaul and the Rhine *limes* be explained? Theuws' model, that the graves indicate new claims to land, does not readily apply to Britain; there is no evidence for Britain suffering from the same settlement abandonment and shrinkage in the later third and fourth century as northern Gaul. Halsall's model, that the graves signal increased local competition in an environment of reduced imperial control, may have more validity. But the difference in the distribution of military burials suggests a different sense of local competition. In Britain, 'soldier burials' can be generally associated with urban settlements, though this is not necessarily the case in northern Gaul or across the Rhine in *barbaricum*. Furthermore, there is little association of the funerary ritual with military bases in Britain, even though these sites were still occupied.

If the burials can be accepted as representing soldiers or civil military officials (still unproven, if likely), then it must be concluded on present evidence that there is an important difference in the way that these identities were expressed in the mortuary ritual in southern Britain. Following Halsall's argument, it may be the case that the ritual was being used to emphasise military identity in a locality where it was under pressure from other elite roles and identities. In northern Britain, where soldiers were more common, there was likely to be less competition between military elites and civilian power structures. Alternatively, the presence of soldiers may have been so commonplace that it was unnecessary to emphasise aspects of occupational identity in the mortuary sphere through inclusion of military equipment.

Perhaps at present, 'soldier burials' are too limited in number in Britain to draw firm conclusions, although artefacts are clearly crucial to solving the dilemma. Further work is required on artefact typologies and chronologies, and the associations between individual types, particularly for belt equipment from Britain. In this regard, Britain is particularly well-served by data from the Portable Antiquities Scheme, which should help to further distinguish between the broad patterns of typological distribution and examples associated specifically with mortuary activity.

A more fundamental question for further research concerns the utility of representational readings of objects. Accepting a simplistic representational reading is a potentially damaging first step; a representational role has already been broadly applied to nearly all crossbow brooches and belt equipment. The more pressing challenge is to not allow a representational reading to mask significant patterning and nuances within the data. At one level, crossbow brooches and belt equipment were explicitly and conscientiously used in a representational fashion by the Romans themselves. However, for a more analytical approach, it is necessary to push beyond the simple acceptance of these representational readings, and to give much closer scrutiny to the diversity of form and the archaeological contexts of the objects in question.

One suggestion for advancing analysis is to accept the representational role of particular types of material culture in societies as a circulating reference, as defined above. The crossbow brooch and military belt would be widely recognisable as symbols of the military and by extension of military privilege in late Roman society. However, the way in which the military was situated within any particular region or locality would have varied. Therefore, while symbols of military authority must have had universal recognition, the reception and use of such symbols was open to variation. Framing particular objects as circulating references not only embraces their representational role, but prompts archaeologists and historians to explore the complexity and nuances of how representational artefacts functioned in the past and in contemporary research.

Acknowledgements

I would like to thank my colleagues at Newcastle University, James Gerrard and Chris Fowler, for discussion which helped me to formulate thoughts in this chapter. Observations and discussion at the *Rethinking Artefacts in Roman Archaeology* seminar helped to frame the chapter. Thanks to Hella Eckardt (Reading University) and Greg Speed (NAA) for permission to reproduce the image of grave 14 from Scorton.

Chapter 4

Gallo-Belgic wares. Objects in motion in the early Roman northwest

Martin Pitts[*]

A far-reaching material impact of Roman expansion in northwest Europe was the spread of *standardised* pottery vessels, supplementing a hodgepodge of handmade and wheelthrown wares from different local traditions. This phenomenon is routinely addressed in big picture scholarship focusing on a single category of pottery, the standardised fineware *par excellence, terra sigillata* (e.g. Millett 1990, 123–6; Woolf 1998, 185–205; Wallace-Hadrill 2008, 407–21; cf. Van Oyen 2016a). Despite the frequency of claims made about the social dispersal of *terra sigillata*, its early distribution was often concentrated around Roman military supply routes and newly founded urban centres. Many societies in the new province of Gallia Belgica (as well as large parts of southern Britain and adjacent areas) were more likely to encounter standardised vessels in the guise of so-called Gallo-Belgic wares. This reality is attested in the substantial quantities of Gallo-Belgic wares in indigenous settlements and cemeteries in northern Gaul and southern Britain, from ca. 25 BC to the late first century AD. The aim of this chapter is to explore the proliferation of Gallo-Belgic finewares as a phenomenon – their occurrences and combinations in different kinds of cultural context, their participation in social practices, and the degree of any relationship between the style of vessels and their itineraries (Hahn and Weiss 2013b). In other words, what did Gallo-Belgic wares *do* in the early Roman West?

Introducing Gallo-Belgic wares

'Gallo-Belgic wares' is an awkward umbrella term used to describe a broad repertoire of mostly fineware pottery produced in Gallia Belgica and adjoining regions, ca. 25 BC to AD 85. The most common Gallo-Belgic fabrics are orange-red *terra rubra*, fired in oxidising conditions approaching those of the production of *terra sigillata*, which it

---

[*] Department of Classics and Ancient History, University of Exeter.

imitates in appearance, and black *terra nigra*, fired in a reducing atmosphere favoured in the production of pre-Roman black-gloss wares (Wightman 1985, 144) (see Fig. 4.1 for some common examples). Despite impressions of the apparent separation between 'Romanising' *terra rubra* and 'native' *terra nigra*, this division is largely arbitrary: there is great similarity and overlap in the shapes of vessels produced in red and black, their distribution and chronologies are largely complementary, and vessels in both fabrics are routinely deposited together in settlement and funerary contexts. While many Gallo-Belgic vessels may be seen to derive directly from *terra sigillata* forms, a roughly equivalent number of types have a more diagnostic north-western European genealogy, or indeed, are innovations of the period and the fusion of styles broadly associated with temperate and Mediterranean Europe.

Gallo-Belgic wares are typically viewed as 'second-class' finewares compared to *sigillata*, both in terms of their perceived importance to archaeologists and their perceived significance to ancient users – a view that is doubly problematic. Like *sigillata*, Gallo-Belgic wares were produced in a series of highly standardised shapes at multiple production centres and kilns, with manufacturing foci located near urban

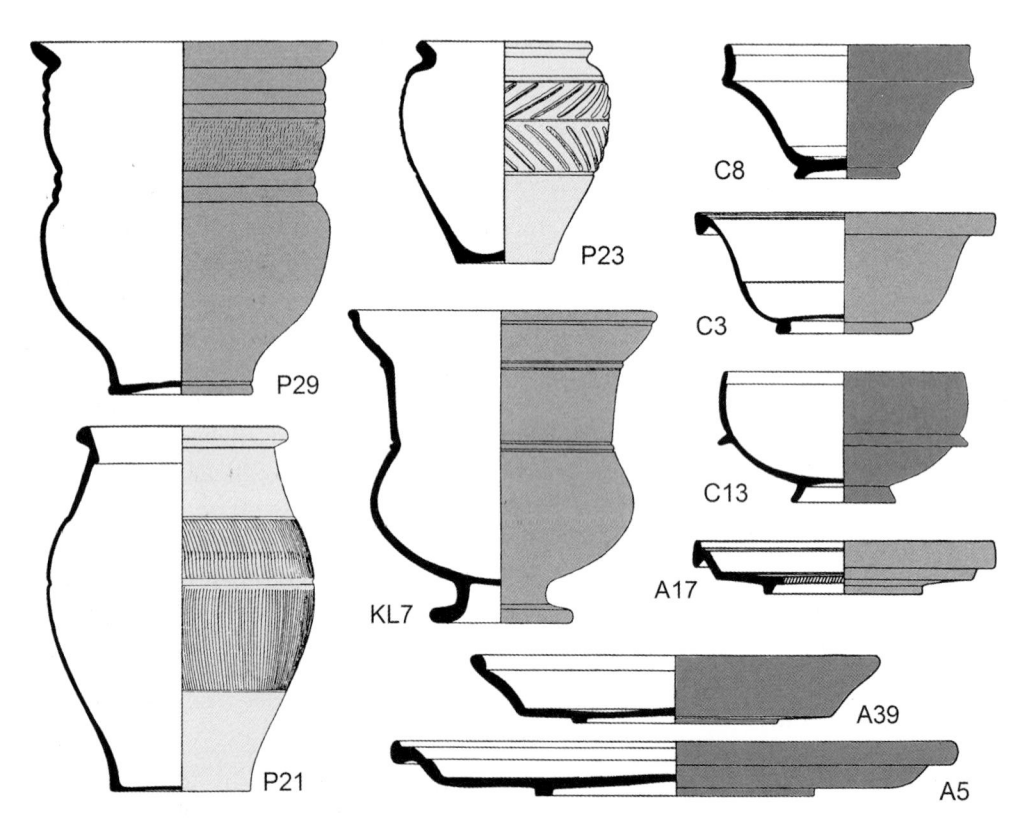

Figure 4.1 A selection of Gallo-Belgic pottery types from Britain. Codes are from the Deru (1996) type-series.

centres such as Reims, Tongeren, Trier, Metz, Cologne and Nijmegen (Deru 1996, 263–317). While long-held wisdom links the origins of Gallo-Belgic production with the requirements of military supply (e.g. Wightman 1985, 144), by the early-mid first century AD Gallo-Belgic wares merely supplemented more extensive supplies of *terra sigillata* for many military communities (Pitts 2014). In contrast, the impact of Gallo-Belgic wares was arguably greater among civilian communities in northern Gaul and southern Britain, for whom it frequently outstrips quantities of *sigillata* by a considerable margin. For example, while the ceramic assemblages from the Augustan-Neronian graves at the cemeteries of Feulen, Luxembourg (Schendzielorz 2006) and Wederath-Belginum, Rhineland-Pfalz (Haffner 1971; 1974; 1978; Cordie-Hackenberg and Haffner 1991; 1997) are composed of 40–60% Gallo-Belgic wares, the same assemblages feature less than 3% of *sigillata*. Towards the end of the first century, a tendency for increasing civilian supplies of *terra sigillata* to be viewed differently from Gallo-Belgic wares can be seen at cemeteries such as Septfontaines-Dëckt (Luxembourg), where *sigillata* is more frequently included separately on the pyre rather than in the grave (Polfer 2000).

The civilian predilection for Gallo-Belgic wares – whether by accident of supply, deliberate marketing, or cultural selection – ought to make them a priority for study owing to their potential to shed new light on material change among indigenous societies. Such potential is nevertheless constrained by the largely representational ways in which Gallo-Belgic wares have been treated so far, with some examples outlined in the next section. In the first place, their marginalisation from the study of *terra sigillata* reinforces a view of history in which the perceived products of the 'core' metropolitan civilisation are valued more than those of the 'periphery'. Secondly, at an interpretive level, Gallo-Belgic wares are poorly served by prevailing thinking that has tended to view them as 'proxies', typically for certain kinds of economic activity (e.g. the imperial economy) or differentiated cultural practices (evidence for Romanisation).

Representation and beyond: what did Gallo-Belgic wares do?

A good example of the partiality of representational thinking concerns the interpretation of Gallo-Belgic wares at the site of Sheepen, Camulodunum, the oppidum and royal centre of the Catuvellaunian dynasty, and major stronghold of resistance to the Claudian conquest of southern Britain in AD 43. Writing on the extensive 1930s excavations at the site, Hawkes and Hull (1947, 49–50) surmised the following about the impact of (mainly Gallo-Belgic) pottery imports on the pre-conquest community:

> The sheer material superiority of the imported pottery must have made for greater refinement, and in addition, there is its clear-cut specialization of form. This is of course no mere typological parade: it implies specialization of use, connected mainly with food and drink. The wine imported in the amphorae we have found may have been primarily for

the rich who would drink it from the appropriate Arretine cups, but the wider popularity of Gallo-Belgic cups, less costly but still specialized for wine as no doubt were beakers for beer, proves a more general diffusion of civilized manners. Such a diffusion is still better attested by the abundance of platters, off which men had never been accustomed to eat in Britain before.

Despite recognising the social roles of Gallo-Belgic wares in eating and drinking, for Hawkes and Hull the appearance of this pottery reified Romanisation as a civilising process – the diffusion of manners from centre to periphery. Cups and platters were something new, and are therefore assumed to have participated in practices diffused from the distant continent – in this example Gallo-Belgic wares stood for the trope of the *diffusion of civilised manners*.

By the time the next major excavations at Camulodunum were published in the 1980s, the social and intellectual climate of British archaeology had changed. Despite the rigour of their excavations, the diffusionist perspective of Hawkes and Hull had been discredited, and economic perspectives came to take precedence over cultural concerns. Niblett's (1985, 25) interpretation of the site, which essentially considers the same artefactual evidence as Hawkes and Hull, reaches a very different conclusion:

> One of the most interesting aspects of the contents of the pits, however, is the light they throw on the life of the inhabitants of Sheepen. Samian, fine glass, Gallo-Belgic wares, and amphoras were abundant… These argue for a fairly high standard of living, certainly much higher than that apparent from the small huts found along the line of the filled-in Sheepen dyke in the 1930s. It was argued then that the inhabitants of Sheepen were downtrodden and enslaved native *corvées* forced to work supplying the new *colonia* (Tacitus, *Annales*, xiv, 31; Hawkes and Hull 1947, 38). Although such an element presumably existed in the Sheepen population, the impression given by the 1970 excavation is rather one of independent craftsmen successfully exploiting the opportunities provided by the new market.
>
> Where the craftsmen originate is a matter for speculation but it is interesting to note that fragments of 135 amphoras from the 1970 excavations indicate the use of Italian and provincial wine, fish sauce, and nearly 1400 litres of olive oil. The large number of such vessels compared with what is normally found on native sites gives a picture of a cuisine that was much more Roman than British and may well imply the presence of immigrants from abroad.

While Niblett's account maintains the logic that new pottery vessels represented the spread of civilised Roman eating habits, here the presence of Gallo-Belgic wares stood alongside other imported wares to represent *entrepreneurial immigrants*, a far cry from the uncouth 'natives' identified by Hawkes and Hull. But as with that of Hawkes and Hull (1947), this interpretation seems to be more reliant on the interpretive packaging of seemingly like artefact classes (the imports) together, rather than scrutinising them more closely as independent evidence.

More recent studies that compared contemporary patterns of pottery supply and deposition at the Sheepen site at Camulodunum with those of the fortress and *colonia*

4. Gallo-Belgic wares. Objects in motion in the early Roman northwest

(ca. AD 44–61) highlight the fragility of both the 1940s and 1980s interpretations of Gallo-Belgic wares (Bidwell 1999, 488–93; Pitts and Perring 2006; Pitts 2010a; 2010b; Perring and Pitts 2013, 232–8). These studies show that after conquest, the pre-existing communities at Camulodunum and its environs continued to use 'suites' of Gallo-Belgic wares in traditional forms of social display evident in funerary contexts and feasting assemblages, often alongside increasingly prevalent *terra sigillata* vessels. In contrast, the veteran colony established at Colchester in AD 49 (Colonia Claudia Victricensis) eschewed most Gallo-Belgic vessels completely, receiving only a trickle compared to its huge supply of *sigillata*. Being primarily interested in what artefacts might reveal about social and cultural identities, I interpreted these patterns in terms of cultural differences between the local community and the incoming colonists. While this effectively re-stated the position of Hawkes and Hull (1947), it emphasised the agency of Sheepen's community to distance themselves from the Roman colonists through their selection and use of Gallo-Belgic wares, rather than assuming that all imported wares represented a linear diffusion of civilised values from the continent. Gallo-Belgic wares had now come to represent *indigenous cultural practices*.

While I stand by my previous interpretations of the pottery from Colchester, I concede that the conclusions I drew are partial in certain key respects. This is in large part because I was interested in what the pottery might reveal about the elaboration of group identities, perhaps at the expense of a more thorough understanding of pottery as material culture. But this problem is by no means confined to the recent spate of identity studies in Roman archaeology. Indeed, commenting on the same patterns, Fulford (2009, 255) preferred to place the distribution of Gallo-Belgic wares in a wider economic context – as 'a competitive, entrepreneurial mode of distribution and consumption' running 'alongside a system driven and paid for by the state', a valid – if similarly partial – interpretation using representational logic. In this case, Gallo-Belgic wares became proxies for *non-state economic networks*.

So far, this introduction to the archaeology of Gallo-Belgic wares in British contexts has emphasised the pitfalls of representational modes of interpretation. The Gallo-Belgic assemblage from just one site has variously stood for the diffusion of civilised manners (Hawkes and Hull), entrepreneurial immigrants (Niblett), indigenous cultural practices (Pitts and Perring), non-state modes of distribution (Fulford), as well as offerings by religious pilgrims (Willis 2007, 121–2). It is clear that the overwhelming urge to 'people the past' and to use objects to stand for social categories (or more recently, social practices and identities) has obscured more nuanced ways of interpreting the evidence. As I demonstrate below, taking a less overtly representational approach to the same class of artefacts not only reveals richer patterning, but also provides a valuable new perspective on the same historical scenario at early Roman Colchester.

In contrast to the approaches discussed above, a rather different perspective on Gallo-Belgic wares is provided by the prehistorian Chris Gosden in his article 'What do objects want?' (Gosden 2005, 205–7). The starting point for Gosden is not to pursue abstract notions of the Roman economy or identity formation, and nor is it to uncover the definitive meaning of Gallo-Belgic pottery. Instead, Gosden focuses on the material properties of Gallo-Belgic ware, most notably its eclectic stylistic genealogy (drawing from traditions across the Mediterranean and Gaul), its genealogical impacts in influencing local pottery (in Britain), and its effect on human users. In terms of archaeological material culture, 'genealogy' refers to specific material traits in an object or group of objects that can be seen to derive directly from similar traits in an identified group of chronologically preceding objects. For Gosden (2005, 206–7), Gallo-Belgic ware is not simply a passive indicator of culture or society, but rather a historical agent in its own right:

> The ability of different materials, shapes and finishes to impose themselves on people shows the true promiscuity of pottery which acted as a nexus for influences coming from many parts of the object world...

Gosden's discussion of Gallo-Belgic pottery is regrettably brief and does not provide archaeological examples to develop his approach further. Nevertheless, it does provide elements of a blueprint for the non-representational analysis of Gallo-Belgic wares – a focus on pottery's material properties, notions of stylistic genealogy and lineage in standardised pottery repertoires, and the capacity of mobile objects to influence the adoption of similar stylistic traits in more local repertoires (cf. Biddulph 2013 on memes in the reproduction and imitation of *terra sigillata*). With these broad concepts in mind, the following sections aim to explore what Gallo-Belgic wares *did* in early Roman northwest Europe, starting with regional variations in the make-up of assemblages in terms of vessel shape, and considering the localised impacts of vessel genealogy.

The rest of this chapter is based on the analysis of Gallo-Belgic assemblages drawn from across the breadth of northwest Europe, from the interior of Britain to the Rhine and Moselle. This is essentially the same dataset as that of a recent study that contextualised the early fineware assemblages of the first Roman cities in Britain (Pitts 2014), in which most continental data was drawn from Deru's (1996) corpus (see Fig. 4.2). To ensure a more holistic comparison of assemblages across the wider region, the pottery vessels are re-classified here in terms of the Deru (1996) type-series as opposed to the Anglo-centric *Camulodunum* series (Hawkes and Hull 1947), which enables the comparison of extra sites, such as Tongeren and Liberchies. This area corresponds with the core region in which Gallo-Belgic wares circulated before ca. AD 70, and as such provides vital information on Gallo-Belgic wares as a broader canon of style (cf. Gosden 2005). Only by comparing a representative sample of locations in which Gallo-Belgic wares circulated is it possible to properly appreciate its local *and* global impact.

Trajectories and object-scapes

To gain an impression of the pan-regional and local trajectories of Gallo-Belgic wares, I use the concept of object-scapes to refer to repertoires of objects at hand in given localities in particular historical moments (Versluys, this volume; Pitts and Versluys forthcoming). In analytical terms, the concept can help to characterise recurrent combinations and selections of objects en masse at a variety of scales, from micro/local to macro/global. Analogous to the notion of 'relational constellations' (Van Oyen 2016b), thinking in terms of object-scapes can help place the relationality of material culture at the centre of analysis (e.g. through object-object relations at different analytical scales), without recourse to representational logic.

To get an impression of what Gallo-Belgic ware object-scapes looked like in early Roman northwest Europe, Fig. 4.3 considers them in terms of the proportions of six major fineware shapes (beakers, butt-beakers and their derivatives, bowls, cups, dishes and platters) at over 20 archaeological sites. It is worth bearing in mind at the outset that this broad-brush analysis simplifies complex chronological and stylistic variation, and glosses over vital information on depositional context. Nevertheless, it gives a basic picture of the geography of Gallo-Belgic wares that may be further contextualised.

The most obvious pattern in Fig. 4.3 is the apparent similarity of assemblages from civilian sites in Britain (upper-tier) and Gallia Belgica (middle-tier). The majority of these assemblages are dominated by platters (e.g. A5, Fig. 4.1) and butt-beakers (e.g. P21, Fig. 4.1). Looking closer, the similarities in supply may be broken down into regional groupings (i.e. southern Britain, eastern Britain, western Belgica, and eastern Belgica), as well as along axes of connectivity (the Somme–Amiens and southern Britain, and the Moselle–Rhine–Thames – eastern Belgica and eastern Britain). At this point, there are a number of routine presumptions that might be invoked in interpreting such patterns. In economic terms, the supply of what might be described as the primary market (Belgica) looks very similar to that of the secondary market (Britain), suggesting blanket supply or even uniformity of demand. Likewise, the smaller regional variations may be explained by the peculiarities of local production and minor variations in regional shipments.

In contrast to the patterns just discussed, the Gallo-Belgic ware assemblages from this seemingly eclectic group of sites in the lower-tier of Fig. 4.3 could not be more different. This creates problems for a model of blanket supply that might be proposed from looking at the civilian centres alone. The sites in the lower-tier received very different combinations of Gallo-Belgic vessels in quantitative terms. Unlike those from civilian centres across the Channel and to the south, the assemblages from Tongeren and Liberchies are more heavily dominated by butt-beakers, whereas those from Nijmegen (the Hatert cemetery) and Cologne feature an emphasis on different beakers and bowls, each case suggesting a local predilection for particular vessels. In contrast, the Gallo-Belgic assemblages from known military (Exeter), colonial

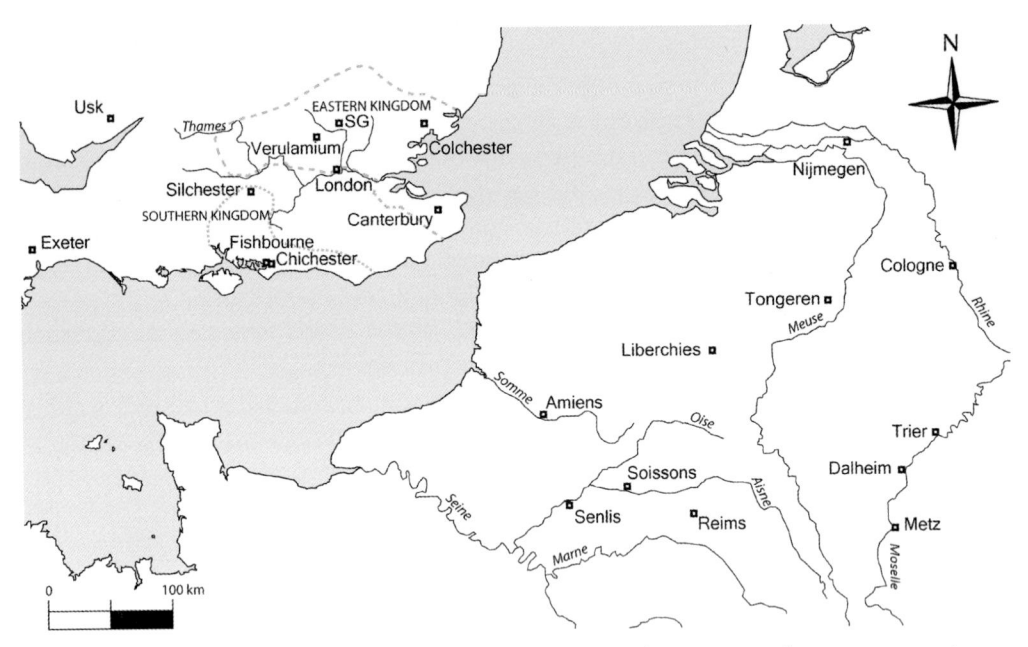

Figure 4.2 Map showing the location of selected cities and sites. Drawn by A. Montesanti.

(Colonia Victricensis) and suspected colonial (London) centres in Britain share a similar dominance of dishes, and a virtual absence of butt-beakers. But the exception that really proves the rule is the idiosyncratic assemblage from Usk, which eschews both military and civilian templates of supply for Britain, displaying closest affinity to Cologne (in this sample). This last pattern is surely the result of the historically attested movement of Legion XX from Neuss (a military base just north of Cologne) to Usk, and adds a new dimension to the interpretation of the big picture, with object-scapes from the Rhine being transplanted to south Wales.

So far, a description of Gallo-Belgic ware object-scapes in terms of vessel shape in Fig. 4.3 can be summarised as follows: rough homogeneity across the majority of civilian Belgica and southern Britain, with more distinctive combinations of vessels in northeast Belgica and in association with military foci in Britain and the Rhine. What can this crude overview of proportions of basic shapes contribute in historical terms? Returning to the example of Colchester and its various interpretations, the wider context provided by Fig. 4.3 suggests that the contrasting supply and deposition of Gallo-Belgic wares at Sheepen (Camulodunum) compared with Colonia Claudia Victricensis were not simply a 'native' reaction to Roman colonial domination. Instead, the assemblage at Sheepen fits a typical profile of civilian object-scapes on either side of the Channel, whereas the material from Colonia Victricensis closely follows the pattern of object-scapes from military sites in Britain (Exeter) and those of likely official origin (London) (Perring 2011; Pitts 2014; *contra* Wallace 2014).

However, the main headline from the general picture is that consistently different yet replicated configurations of Gallo-Belgic ware object-scapes mattered, possibly contributing to what Greg Woolf described as 'styles of consumption' (Woolf 1998, 176). This is acutely illustrated by the transplanting of combinations of Gallo-Belgic vessels from the Rhine to Usk in south Wales – probably carried by soldiers over great distance rather than maintained in later provisions – and more generally in the distinctive regional character of assemblages around northeast Belgica, the Rhine, and for military and colonial communities in Britain.

For communities in Gallia Belgica, particularly those close to major Gallo-Belgic ware production, for example, at Reims and Trier, it may be safe to assume that the combinations of different vessel shapes effectively *represented* local demand. However, the apparent similarity in configurations of Gallo-Belgic object-scapes in southern Britain is less easy to explain. One option is that the British communities effectively saw themselves as part of the same cultural milieu as those in Belgica, as attested by various strands of evidence – written sources, funerary practice, coinage, tribal names etc. It is possible that the similarity of Gallo-Belgic ware object-scapes might *represent* degrees of (fossilised) shared cultural practice, involving the use of finewares in the spheres of domestic consumption and funerary practice. At face value, the case for the patterns belying some form of cultural choice is also reinforced by the massive impact of Gallo-Belgic style on local pottery production, a point not lost on Gosden (2005).

Another way of explaining the apparent homogeneity in Gallo-Belgic ware object-scapes in civilian Britain and Belgica might be to cast such patterns in terms of the over-supply of the civilian market in Belgica, and the relative disinterest of military communities in Britain in Gallo-Belgic wares (in contrast to *terra sigillata*). This sort of economic explanation is frequently encountered in Roman pottery studies and shifts the agency and choice to a different social group – the military, who are often implicitly seen as exerting more agency than indigenous communities due to their representational connections (real *and* imagined) with Rome. Leaving aside these overtones of centre-periphery logic, it is possible that the combinations of Gallo-Belgic vessels on civilian sites in southern Britain did have limited cultural significance, as surplus (and therefore much cheaper) products that would have been effectively dumped on uncaring recipients. In this scenario, combinations of vessels that might have had particular cultural significance in Belgica would have been completely lost on British users, who may have instead associated Gallo-Belgic wares with the general changes attendant on Roman annexation (in line with Niblett 1985).

To address these competing hypotheses to explain similar configurations of Gallo-Belgic ware object-scapes in civilian Britain and Belgica, it is necessary to take a closer look at the assemblages in question, returning to the theme of what the objects did. As has been pointed out, in order to visualise patterns across such a wide area, the data in Fig. 4.3 are summarised in a way that masks a great deal of the variation in the style and appearance of the pottery. Taking up some of the themes discussed in Gosden's (2005) consideration of Gallo-Belgic wares, the following sections return to the topic of object genealogies, focusing on the itineraries of styles of vessels of broadly Gallic genealogy (butt-beakers and their derivatives), as well as those deriving from Mediterranean inspiration (especially platters).

Figure 4.3 The relative proportions of Gallo-Belgic tablewares at selected sites in NW Europe. Top tier: sites in Britannia with pre-conquest origins; middle tier: civilian centres in Gallia Belgica; bottom tier: military/colonial sites in Britain and sites in NE Belgica.

'Rooted' styles and cultural innovation in a globalising context

A strong pattern in Fig. 4.3 is the overwhelming civilian popularity of butt-beakers and related forms like the grätenbecher and girth-beaker (P21, P23 and P29 respectively in Fig. 4.1). While I have characterised the butt-beaker as a Gallic design, its genealogy of influences is complex. Hawkes and Hull (1947, 237) describe the general vessel form as a 'late La Tène and early Provincial adaptation of pre-Imperial Mediterranean prototypes.' One source of likely genealogical inspiration for this design are the tall jar vessels of the La Tène D1a (later second century BC) that occur in cemeteries such as Wederath (e.g. Haffner 1971, grave 300). However, other influences are possible. It is notable that some of the earliest dated occurrences of butt-beakers, such as in the princely graves at Goeblange-Nospelt (Luxembourg, ca. 30–15 BC) (Metzler and Gaing 2009) are contextually associated with Italian thin-walled ware ACO beakers, a vessel which bears a striking typological resemblance to some early butt-beakers in terms of shape, size and decoration. While the ACO beaker, a.k.a. Conspectus R12, was produced in *sigillata* and non-slipped forms in northern Italy as well as enjoying short-lived

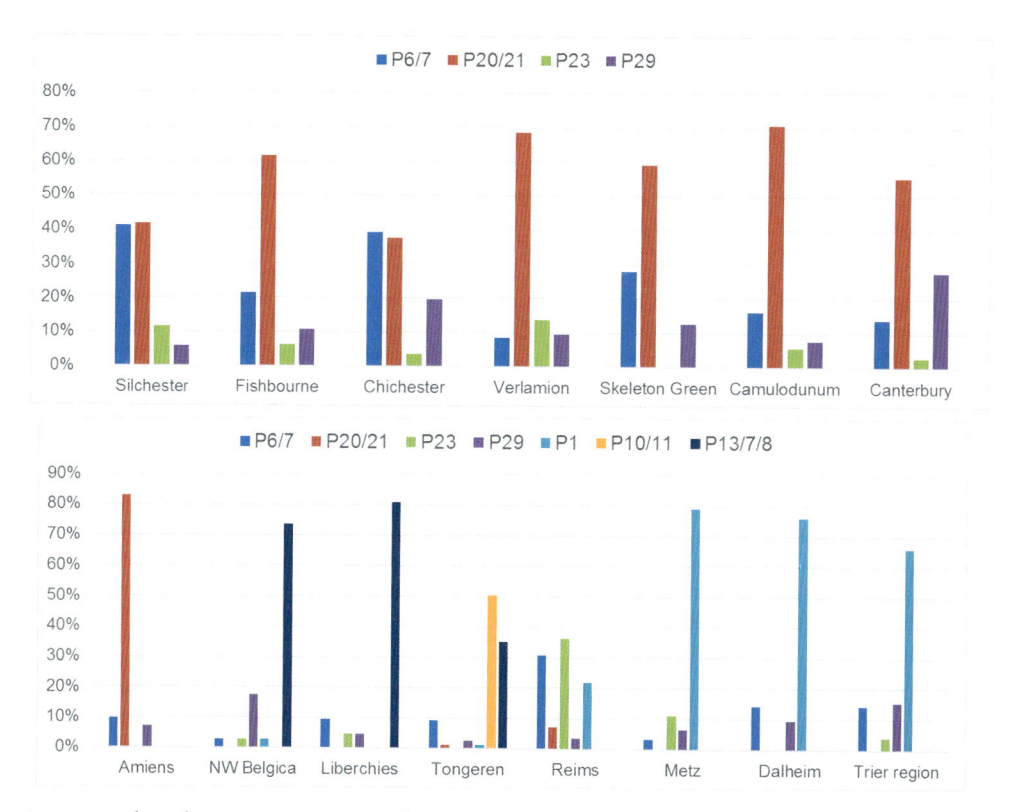

Figure 4.4 The relative proportions of the most common butt-beaker (and related beaker) types at civilian sites in Britannia and Gallia Belgica, using the Deru (1996) type-series.

production at Lyon (Ettlinger *et al.* 1990, 182), it had limited distribution and longevity in northwest Europe, and is more typically associated with early military sites. There are also no long-lasting direct equivalents of the butt-beaker in the repertoires of either Italian or Gallic *sigillata*. Therefore, while Gallic and Italian influence may have been factors in the initial genesis of the butt-beaker, the phenomenon it became was an unquestionable *innovation* of northwest Europe.

What did the butt-beaker and its related forms *do* in early Roman Europe? Fig. 4.4 breaks down the Gallo-Belgic butt-beaker category according to its most common circulating types, according to Deru's type-series (1996). It is worth pointing that Fig. 4.4 concentrates almost exclusively on civilian sites, owing to the relative scarcity of butt-beakers in military contexts in this sample – a significant finding in its own right. The patterning within Fig. 4.4, however, hints at a much more complex story. While the supply of British sites in the upper-tier appears largely homogenous (as with Gallo-Belgic vessels in general from Fig. 4.3), Gallia Belgica is characterised by pronounced regional differences in combinations of butt-beaker types.

To attempt to make sense of Fig. 4.4, I begin by focusing on the itineraries of individual butt-beaker types. It is clear that while the butt-beaker was in some sense a universal form, styles and types of butt-beaker varied widely across the Roman northwest. While some forms, such as the P6/7 (Cam 112), P23 (Cam 114) and P29 (Cam 82/4) occurred in modest quantities at most sites, others have more pronounced regional distributions. For example, the P1 butt-beaker completely dominates assemblages in the territory of the Treveri (Metz, Dalheim and Trier), but does not appear at any of the other centres in particular quantity (apart from Reims, located immediately to the west). The same appears to hold for the P10/11 and P13/17/18 with Tongeren and northern Belgica, and the P20/21 with southern Britain and Amiens.

Why did some butt-beakers dominate particular object-scapes but fail to travel longer-distances, while other Gallo-Belgic vessels achieved much more widespread distribution? Why did other butt-beakers achieve more universal distributions in the civilian sphere without dominating in any single region? Standard representational logic might account for these patterns in terms of market economics or the expression of regional identities. However, as this book stresses, viewing artefacts only in terms of their capacity to stand for social categories or economic processes is intrinsically partial. Instead, focusing on the stylistic and typological properties of the vessels in question reveals more promising lines of inquiry.

An important observation seems to be that the butt-beakers with more pronounced regional distributions also look very different from one another. There is no obvious direct genealogical connection between the P1, P10/13 and P21 types (Fig. 4.5). At the same time, all of these regionally distinct types share clearer similarities with the seemingly universal P6/7 (i.e. in terms of characteristics such as pronounced rim, bands of decoration and vessel profile). In other words, the regionally-specific butt-beaker types appear to be localised innovations that only make sense through their

4. Gallo-Belgic wares. Objects in motion in the early Roman northwest

collective reference to a shared universal style maintained by circulating objects with which they share a mutual *dependency* (cf. Collins, this volume, on material culture as circulating references). While further quantitative research is needed to verify this interpretation, it provides a more holistic explanation than simply considering the patterns in terms of local identities and niche markets, which do not do justice to the global picture. Indeed, it is difficult to envisage individual butt-beaker types as isolated local developments *without* the existence of a shared cultural milieu.

Closer inspection of the British material in Fig. 4.4 emphatically refutes the idea that Britain was an uncaring 'secondary market' for Gallo-Belgic wares. The most notable feature of the British Gallo-Belgic butt-beaker assemblage is the dominance of type P21 (Cam 113), which is only paralleled in quantity in this sample at Amiens (crucially in a different fabric). Both Hawkes and Hull (1947, 238) and Niblett (1985, 23)

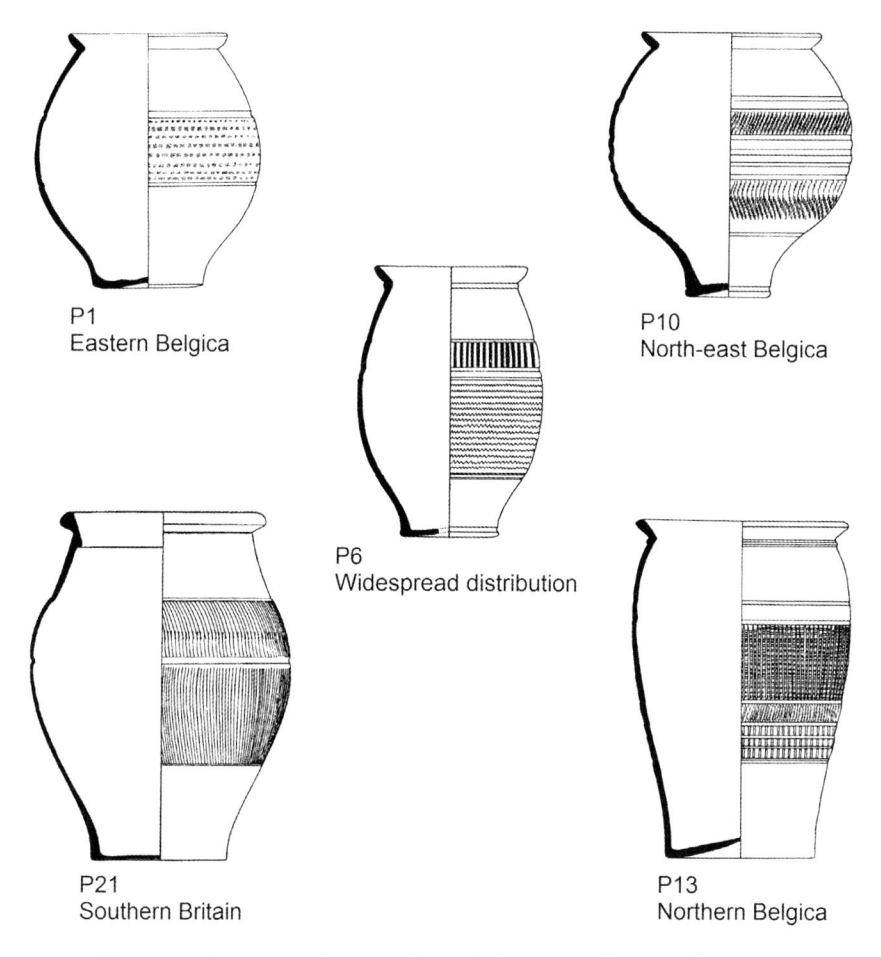

Figure 4.5 Common Gallo-Belgic butt-beaker types from northwest Europe.

firmly believed that the Cam 113 beakers found at Camulodunum were not imports, but instead products of local manufacture close to the site. This case is supported by the sheer quantity of vessels at the Sheepen site – over 2,750 individuals, if the figures of Hawkes and Hull are to be believed, the most common fineware vessel at the site by some margin. Although this view has been questioned by Timby (2000, 205), citing the lack of identified kilns in Britain and the similarities with the assemblage at Amiens, the virtual absence of Cam 113 vessels across Gallia Belgica in fabrics and quantities akin to those routinely found in Britain is inexplicable if they were of Gallic manufacture. The Cam 113/P21, being typologically similar to the P6/7 (Cam 112), must be interpreted as an innovation that took place within Britain that directly referenced a larger repertoire of circulating objects.

Returning to the bigger picture, the situation at Camulodunum and in southern Britain begins to make more sense. The Gallo-Belgic butt-beaker was an enigmatic design borne of the unique fusion of styles rooted in potting traditions from northern Italy to southern Britain. Not only did it dominate fineware assemblages at civilian centres spanning a wide area that crossed multiple tribal and indeed provincial boundaries, it also spawned major local innovations that often corresponded to the territories of powerful political entities, such as the Treveri (P1), the Tungri/Batavi (P11 and P13), and Catuvellauni (P21). The impact of this new style of object was such that while the same communities would happily rely on imports of other standardised Gallo-Belgic wares, they were compelled to create their own distinctive forms of butt-beakers – even if the technical expertise to do so was lacking amongst local potters. Both Hawkes and Hull (1947) and Timby (2000) agree that the high *quality* of Cam 113 (P21) vessels at Camulodunum was such that they must have been produced by migrant potters from the continent. If this was the case, it underscores the importance of the butt-beaker within a shared northwest European cultural milieu that was independent from military and colonial communities associated with the Roman state.

The social distribution and subsequent local innovation in butt-beaker design is highly reminiscent of the recent discussion by Van Oyen (2016a; 2016b) of the 'rootedness' of Trier Rhenish wares (third century AD). Through their colour, shapes and inscriptions on the vessels, Rhenish wares were created as a local category distinct from the more homogenous and universal *terra sigillata*, despite sharing many of the same technical characteristics in production. A definition of rootedness as denoting 'local entanglement as explicit and fundamental to the definition of a thing and its possibilities' (Van Oyen 2016a, 112) fits both the innovative off-shoots of Gallo-Belgic butt-beakers and Rhenish ware motto beakers very well – accepting that both phenomena likewise depended on the existence of a more homogenous, universal canon of style. It is perhaps no coincidence that both phenomena took place in the same region, and involving beakers ostensibly for alcohol consumption. Indeed, despite the gap of over a century, the general designs of both kinds of vessel are similar and a genealogical connection seems likely. The connection, however

Standardisation, universality and cultural imagination

The previous section, addressing the trajectories and local innovations of a vessel with broadly 'Gallic' genealogy, stressed the likely existence of a shared cultural milieu underpinned by a universal canon of styles of evocative objects (cf. Poblome, this volume, on *koine* and pottery productions in the Roman East). In contrast, this section examines Gallo-Belgic vessels with a more obvious *Mediterranean* genealogy. The other most numerous class of Gallo-Belgic wares favoured at civilian sites in southern Britain and Gallia Belgica was the platter – of which some of the more common forms are illustrated in Fig. 4.1 (A5, A17, and A39). Unlike the butt-beaker, most of the platter forms in the Gallo-Belgic repertoire can be seen as imitations or derivations of equivalent forms in Italian-style and south Gaulish *terra sigillata*. Whereas the butt-beaker was evidently more 'rooted' in northwest European styles

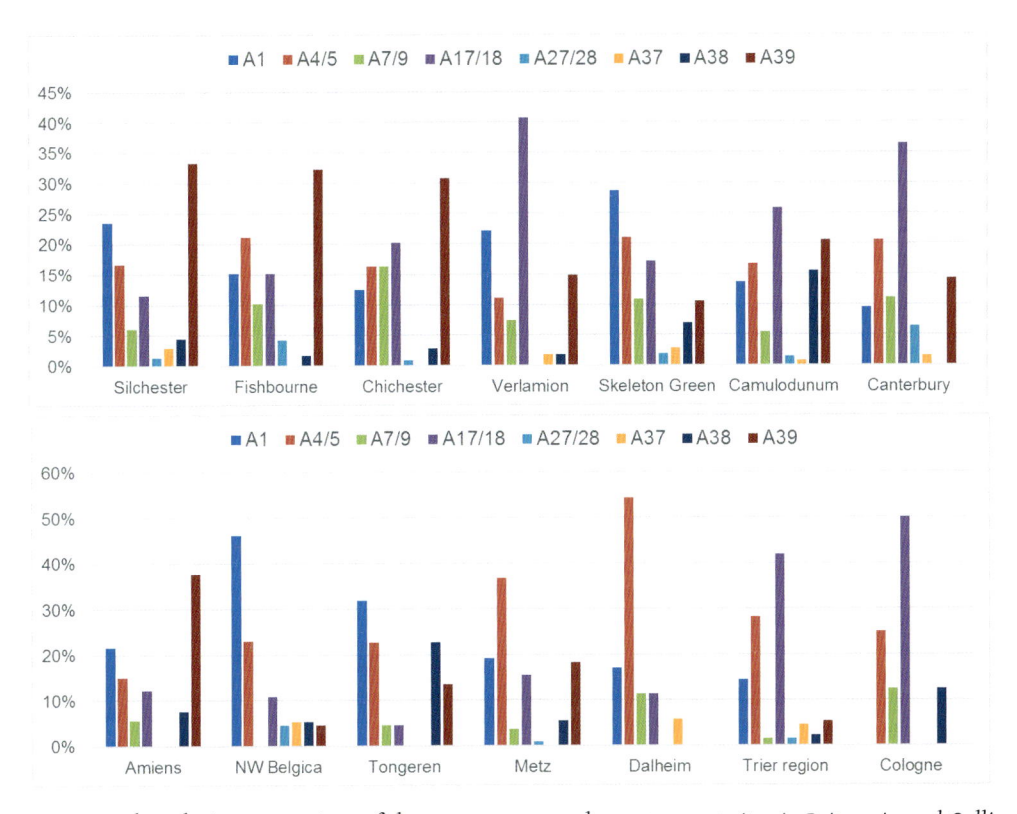

Figure 4.6 The relative proportions of the most common platter types at sites in Britannia and Gallia Belgica, using the Deru (1996) type-series.

of pottery production as well as spheres of practice such as communal drinking and funerary display, the platter is often taken to represent the arrival of new cuisine and new individualised habits of consumption (Hawkes and Hull 1947, 49–50; Cool 2006, 164–8).

Fig. 4.6 outlines the proportions of the most common circulating Gallo-Belgic platter types at civilian centres in southern Britain and Gallia Belgica. In contrast to the eclectic butt-beaker itineraries in Fig. 4.4, the picture is overwhelmingly uniform. Most platter types achieved wide circulation in the sample of sites considered, and most centres received similar quantities of each type. While closer inspection reveals many of the same regional groupings apparent from Fig. 4.3, such as the similarity of Amiens and central southern Britain, and parts of south-east Belgica with south-east Britain, these are not very pronounced, and are likely to be affected by chronological variations in the *floruit* of the different sites and their pottery supplies.

Given the striking variation in the global object-scape of Gallo-Belgic butt-beakers (Fig. 4.4), the uniformity among local configurations of Gallo-Belgic platters (Fig. 4.6) is initially puzzling. The absence of equivalently rooted local innovations suggests that the platter, as a general stylistic object category, lacked the same special qualities of the butt-beaker. This is not to downplay the importance of the platter – indeed, it rivalled the butt-beaker in terms of raw numbers of vessels, and was subject to greater stylistic variation with over 50 different types in the Deru (1996) type-series. Unlike the butt-beaker, which was effectively a design unique to the Gallo-Belgic repertoire, the platter closely referenced vessels from a firmly established global object-scape in *terra sigillata*. The same can be said for other popular Gallo-Belgic forms, notably cups, which likewise have a broadly universal distribution of types across northwest Europe. The uniform and universal itineraries of Gallo-Belgic vessels with Mediterranean genealogy must have mattered – not due to some oversight in production which required them to be dumped wholesale on an unsuspecting 'secondary market' – but rather for their capacity to evoke and complement competing suites of *terra sigillata*.

A combination of rooted (butt-beakers) and universal (platters and cups) styles of vessel ensured that the Gallo-Belgic repertoire was ultimately successful in both cultural and economic terms. In the first place, this was achieved by appealing to the traditional aspects of local practice, involving large and elaborately decorated drinking vessels. Likewise, the standardised vessels of Mediterranean genealogy in the Gallo-Belgic repertoire must have helped bridge the huge cultural gulf apparent with the more exotic and expensive styles of consumption and object-scapes associated with Roman military and colonial communities. These universal shapes would go on to form a major element of provincial pottery assemblages well into the second century AD. This is not, however, either the end of the story or a simple case of the old wine of Romanisation in new skins. Despite the popularity of Mediterranean-derived Gallo-Belgic platter and cup forms in the mid-first century AD, both lacked the same local 'rootedness' of butt-beakers. In the longer-term, platters and cups were gradually eclipsed by dishes and beakers in northwest European fineware object-scapes, yet the rooted butt-beaker and its derivatives arguably had much longer lineages. The story of changing pottery assemblages in the Roman northwest seems less one of progressive Romanisation, but rather an eclectic fusion of influences that gradually gave way to regional styles as the Roman world ceased expanding.

Conclusion: interpreting pottery beyond markets and identities

Rather than casting consumption patterns of Gallo-Belgic wares as (variously) local reactions to colonial domination, expressions of local identity, or the products of non-state controlled entrepreneurs, I have attempted to sketch a different account of Gallo-Belgic pottery by investigating aspects of their configurations in local object-scapes, genealogical origins, and stylistic innovations. While this attempt at an object-centred discussion by no means avoids the representational logic that has dogged artefactual interpretation in Roman archaeology, I hope that it has opened up some fresh avenues for approaching pottery and artefacts in the Roman northwest. At the very least, there is good reason to think that paying closer attention to *what objects did* can result in better interpretations that put archaeological data first instead of subordinating them to prevailing assumptions from the outset. If anything, this is the major lesson from the countless failed attempts to find direct archaeological correlates of historical phenomena such as named ethnic groups (cf. Collins, this volume). Rather than the complexity of the archaeological record making such tasks impossible or undesirable, it follows that objects are better understood independently from historical phenomena first, from their production and genealogies to their itinerant pathways and relational associations within broader object-scapes. Indeed, continuing to subordinate the study of material culture to research that treats artefacts representationally risks a kind of methodological circularity in which the framing of questions constrains rather than nurtures the possibilities for new findings.

Taking a more object-centred approach to the study of Gallo-Belgic wares in particular highlights the flaws of previous interpretations that attempted to cast them as a unified category, either with a single universal meaning (old-fashioned blanket Romanisation), or indeed meanings that are contingent entirely upon *local* context (to caricature nativist and post-colonial approaches). A major implication of asking *what standardised objects did* entails looking at particular types across a sample of the full extent of their distribution, including multiple modern nations, ancient tribal territories, and provincial divides. Such an approach has significant implications for new interpretations at both global *and* local levels. This example underlines the inherent flaws of the prevailing tendency in (Roman) archaeology to think in terms of 'containers' (Versluys 2015, 143), from individual provinces to regions demarked by modern national boundaries, and even single sites. A connected empire mattered not just for the machinations of a centralised taxation system or the long-distance exchange of commodities like olive oil, but at a more fundamental level of shared cultural imaginations that are most evident in a richly varied global object-scape. To do proper justice to this mélange of innovating styles and objects at a historical level means engaging more closely with ideas of globalisation – both in terms of big-picture cross-cultural analogy (Hodos *et al.* 2017) and methodological perspectives for coming to grips with objects in motion (Versluys 2014; Pitts and Versluys 2015a, cf. Foster 2006).

Lastly, I return to address a common interpretive challenge in the study of Roman artefacts, especially pottery – the apparent paradox that a distribution pattern must either be explained in terms of local (cultural) choice or the manifestation of a bigger (economic) market systems (see also Poblome, this volume). This is an especially familiar debate in the study of commodities exchanged over long-distances in amphorae, as well as mass-produced finewares like *terra sigillata*. As the examples in this chapter demonstrate, supply versus choice is an entirely false dichotomy. Indeed, Roman archaeology is poorly served by the arbitrary separation of the study of cultural and economic phenomena, as if one does not matter at all to the other. Mass-produced and standardised objects in motion require both cultural demand and economic imperative to achieve pan-regional distribution – the two are intrinsically connected, as an object-centric approach makes abundantly clear. In the case of Gallo-Belgic wares, neither the replication of configurations of vessels from the Rhineland at Usk (south Wales) nor the general popularity of Gallo-Belgic forms in Britain's first civilian communities (for example) would have been possible without underlying cultural demand and economic logic. Likewise, the relative failure of Gallo-Belgic wares (especially butt-beakers) to 'compete' with *terra sigillata* in many Roman military and colonial communities can be attributed to an intersection of economic and cultural rationale. In such contexts, the 'rootedness' of butt-beakers hand-in-hand with perceptions of inferior pottery favoured by recently conquered provincials may well have made Gallo-Belgic wares less 'profitable'.

Acknowledgements
This chapter represents a preliminary attempt to think through the core issues for a larger project, 'Mass consumption in the early Roman northwest', supported by study leave from the College of Humanities, University of Exeter (2015–6). I thank Xavier Deru and Rien Polak for their helpful suggestions on earlier presented versions of this research at the AHRC-funded 'Big Data on the Roman table' network in Leicester (2015) and Exeter (2016). I am greatly indebted to the comments from Astrid Van Oyen, which have significantly helped to clarify and sharpen the argument. Any errors or omissions remain my own.

Chapter 5

Discussion. Reflections on the representational use of artefact evidence

Martin Millett[*]

The seminar on which this volume is based, and the chapters in this section of the volume provide considerable food for thought. I apologise if the following text is too self-referential, but my own engagement with Roman artefacts goes back a long way, to a period when I was first captivated by the archaeology of Roman Britain, and reflecting on my past work seems to serve a purpose in drawing out some points for discussion in the present context. In common with many others, my interest was stimulated first by excavating objects, and this curiosity developed into a desire to study and understand what I was finding. Only later did my work on finds and their excavated contexts lead me to wish to better understand the society that produced and used the objects, with the eventual product being an urge to make sense of Roman Britain and the Roman empire more widely. Hence, I return to the subject of artefacts now from the 'bottom-up' perspective of one whose archaeological career has always sought to engage with material evidence.

In the context of my own academic biography, it is worth noting that I focused originally on pottery, in part because no-one else in my local archaeological society in the early 1970s wanted to study it, instead preferring coins or small finds. But my interest was also increasingly caught because pottery as a finds class appealed to the then fashionable desire to have decent amounts of material to quantify in order to make apparently soundly-based statements that could be supported by numerical analysis. The first serious work I did used automatic seriation to establish the chronology of a pottery industry in an area where there was insufficient stratigraphic evidence to provide a time frame (Millett and Graham 1986, 63–93). Having sorted out the dating, I became interested in tracing the distribution of the pots produced by that local industry across southern Britain, hence thinking about the relationship of the industry to trade and the broader economy (Millett 1979b). I use this autobiographical

---
[*] Faculty of Classics, University of Cambridge.

example to make the point that although in the schema explored by the editors of this volume, my work at that time was partly using artefacts in a representational mode, this was the product of a progression in thinking based on the problems posed by first site, then material. I came to be influenced by approaches promoted at that time by progressive archaeologists like Ian Hodder, and by the development of computer-based methods of study. Using pots to say things about society seemed like a good idea at the time, especially when contrasted with the more conventional dry typological approaches that had treated such objects simply as materials for dating (Hodder 1979; Millett 1979a; Spriggs and Miller 1979). As this work progressed I gradually came to question the automatic association of pottery with 'the economy' and thought I could detect ways in which it represented social choices. Thus, for instance, lying at the margins of the distribution of both Oxfordshire and New Forest finewares, those living at the site at Neatham seem to have carefully selected particular products from each industry, to produce a complementary assemblage (Millett and Graham 1986, 90).

My career with finds then took a turn – which immediately afterwards appeared as a blind alley – but in retrospect I find to be of greater interest. As I worked on ceramic distributions across southern England, and as I was engaged in excavation, it became increasingly clear that variations in the composition of pottery assemblages (and incidentally, 'the assemblage' was then not that often the unit of study) were not simply a function of chronological differences, but reflected other factors. Hence, I came to argue, statistical analysis of variation between contemporaneous assemblages might provide a route for exploring social, economic and other variations within Romano-British society – provided one could control chronological variation (Millett 1979a). For my doctoral thesis, I thus examined all the known deposits supposedly associated with the Boudiccan destruction of AD 60/61 (Millett 1983a; 1987a). Partly as a result of the limitations of the computing methods available at the time, and partly because of a limiting empirical methodology, the exercise proved rather more barren than I had hoped and my career moved in other directions. It will be clear that this approach was also largely based on using pottery representationally, but perhaps in quite subtle ways, and significantly for me, seeking to access social information.

As my academic work has developed I have returned time and again to seek to use artefacts from both excavations and surveys in meaningful ways to try to tackle some big issues, like the relationship between survey data and ancient populations levels (Millett 1991), and in doing this I guess I am generally guilty of the 'sin' of using the material to represent other things without being sufficiently reflexive. In doing this I have at times moved away from pottery (e.g. Millett 2015), but I continually face the problem that it is more difficult to make general statements about patterns in the past with small data sets than with larger ones. My undergraduate training in the analysis of coinage clearly shows the influence of Richard Reece, who has done so much to encourage thinking about coin assemblages (e.g. Reece 1987). His influence can also be traced in some of the ways I have sought to approach other artefacts, including pottery, but most recently brooches and other small finds (Millett 2015). The tension between the study of finds individually or as groups/assemblages raises a series of questions to which I return below.

Now, my reason for opening this discussion in this autobiographical manner is not wholly self-indulgent: I hope that this brief contribution may help contextualise the fashion for thinking about artefacts as representational, even though I accept the editors' critique of this trend. It is also worth highlighting that in reading the papers here I am reminded of some of the issues that I came across in my work on pottery, and the perspective that this brings may be helpful in current debates. Not least is the fact that the archaeological study of any artefacts for anything other than a simple descriptive catalogue is an extremely challenging business. Aside from the inherent complexity of the material – especially when studied contextually – there is also a major leap involved in linking the data with the sorts of big issues about past societies that most of us aspire to address. In the short space available to me here I would like to reflect on a few of these complexities stimulated by points in the papers in the section.

Naming and identifying

One of the concerns I frequently return to in thinking about archaeological material is the false security created by the familiarity of Roman material culture. This issue is one that I contemplated again in reading Hella Eckardt's contribution to the volume. At a very superficial level, this is manifested by our *apparent* ease in identifying and hence labelling the objects we study, for instance cooking pots or drinking vessels. A lack of awareness that this is a potentially problematic area can weaken our arguments, as can ignoring the much more varied real-life uses of objects made for one purpose but used for another. I am reminded here of an odd group of burials from Roman Gaul in which some of those interred wore upturned *mortaria* as hats (Schneider 1965; de Boüard 1966). Such occasional aberrant (?) uses can be identified as such because they stand out from the general pattern of use that can be seen from significantly sized samples of material. The careful contextual study of large samples may equally reveal unexpected and widespread patterns of changed use – such as Jerry Evans' demonstration that many *mortaria* in northern England were apparently used for cooking on an open fire (Evans 2016, 518). Naturally, any recurrent pattern of alternate use will call into question the use of artefact evidence in a representational manner – for instance linking the distribution of *mortaria* to the adoption of Roman-style cuisine. The identification of such patterns of use is much more difficult for less widely distributed types, like the inkwells discussed by Eckardt – especially in the absence of obvious evidence of use.

So I am cautious about questions like 'when is an object an ink-well?' or 'how far can objects of very specific design-function be used to identify specialised knowledge in the ancient world?' This seems to me to be a problem that is especially difficult when studying thinly spread distributions of scarce objects – like metal inkwells, whose inherent qualities may have made them desirable for a variety of reasons quite distinct from showing knowledge of the technology of writing, unless there are contextual reasons for believing that they were widely used for their designed function (always assuming that they *were* all made as ink-wells). In a similar way, when one deals with more common object types – like the belt sets and crossbow brooches discussed by Rob Collins, I worry that in the absence of contextual information at the margins of a distribution, the specificities of meanings conveyed by objects may have been both more mutable and more subject to ambiguity of understanding. In the specific case of the late Roman world discussed by Rob Collins the distinction between the military and civilian officials was arguably far less distinct than might be assumed. In this context objects like the crossbow brooch may have become more generalised symbols of power or authority, so it is very easy to see how their use may have spread beyond just those representing the Roman state. Although such objects thus arguably represent social power, it is not easy to relate them to very specific historical manifestations of it – like the army. Equally, their scarcity leaves them prone to becoming special objects, used for instance as heirlooms, representative of the ancestor rather than the office.

Aggregating evidence

Against this background, it is interesting to note how both Rob Collins and Hella Eckardt turn to the funerary evidence in seeking to understand their material. There is no doubt that the very deliberate construction of funerary assemblages provides an accessible way into appreciating the use of objects in the Roman past, even allowing for the fact that their layout and content are not as straightforwardly representational as has traditionally been assumed. In these circumstances, it is possible to gain valuable contextual information but this is evidence that it is rather difficult to generalise from. This leads to the paradox that there may be excellent evidence for a single case, but little clarity about how this relates to others. In the context of contemporary trends in archaeology this may be a good outcome, but for me it leaves a certain level of dissatisfaction because of my wish to think about bigger issues – the *lack* of representativeness of the individual example seems a problem for me.

This seems to be recognised as a problem by other scholars too, hence the trend towards broader contextual work in finds studies over the last few years – a period during which there has been something of a renaissance in the sub-discipline (e.g. Hingley and Willis 2007; Eckardt 2014). Such work has commonly adopted two complementary approaches, both of which seek to overcome the issues of low-density distributions and often low grade contextual data: first, the classification of finds into broad 'functional' categories as initially suggested by Nina Crummy (1983, 5–6) – so, inkwells as 'objects used for or associated with written communication', crossbow brooches as 'items of personal adornment or dress'), and second, looking at occurrence

5. Discussion. Reflections on the representational use of artefact evidence

by site type (town, fort, villa etc.). These methods have certainly led to exciting new information, and the utility of this kind of comparative analysis of aggregated data is well illustrated in Martin Pitts' paper in this section, which discusses how certain ceramic types have different patterns of deposition in various regions and on certain types of site.

Despite the success of such studies I have some concerns about them, both at a theoretical level and because of the way in which methods are sometimes applied. At the theoretical level, I am worried by the unproblematised use of simple exclusive categories for classifying both finds and sites. In thinking about the categories used for objects, it is obvious to anyone who has attempted to apply Nina Crummy's categories that attribution is problematic in at least two ways. First, do we categorise by supposed designed-use, or can we use broader contextual information about actual function? Second, many objects have multiple functions even in designed-use. So, in the case of the late Roman soldier's belt buckle from a grave, the object might legitimately be categorised as a 'personal adornment or dress', or an item of 'military equipment' (using Crummy's categories), whilst its context shows that it was also a grave-good – and if it has an image of a deity on it, it also has a religious aspect. Given that most analyses of objects using this classificatory system label objects as representing single functions, they are evidently over-simplifying the evidence. This is not to say that Crummy's approach is wrong – it is immensely better than previous systems that classified finds in publications by material (the 'Objects of Iron', etc.). It does however suggest that more sophisticated – multivariate – approaches to artefact classification might be more useful. Similarly, the system used for the classification of sites is also an over simplification, both in terms of categorisation and scale. There is immense value in distinguishing site types, as Eckardt's study of lamps (2002) or Pitts' work on pottery (2014) both demonstrate, but there are enormous pitfalls if we are not very careful. Richborough starts out as a fort, but develops into a town (? small town) with a port, before resuming a parallel function as fort – but its finds will almost invariably be dealt with as coming from a military site. Furthermore, it is interesting how such studies tend to privilege the more Roman site types (towns, forts, etc.) whilst categories like 'rural settlement' are left undifferentiated, thus effectively undervaluing the lives of perhaps 90% of the population. Such categorisations also tend towards positing materials as representative of certain site-types, without allowing sufficiently for individual human agency.

These types of analysis raise the further problem of smaller-scale variation. The process of aggregating data to provide assemblages for study is clearly useful in allowing us to make more robust statements. So, the careful analysis by Martin Pitts allows reasonably strong statements to be made about the kinds of sites and communities that used different types of pots in the early years after the Roman conquest of Britain (Pitts 2014). But this evidence is not without its problems – to take two examples, evidence of absence and contextual variation. Aggregation of data works well where there are finds, but the evaluation of absence is problematic, and gaps are prone to be overlooked. For instance, in the introduction to his chapter in this volume Pitts suggests that over much of southern England *terra sigillata* was initially generally related to areas of military supply, whilst away from these, people were 'far more likely to encounter standardised vessels in the guise of so-called Gallo-Belgic wares'. I am happy to support this as a general statement based on the aggregated data, but this fails to acknowledge large gaps in the distribution which may or may not be significant. My own work long ago on sites in northeast Hampshire in the environs of Silchester (Millett 1983b; 1986; Millett and Russell 1984) showed that Gallo-Belgic wares were largely absent from most rural sites (as was early *terra sigillata*) implying some mechanism that led to its rejection prior to the mid-late first century AD when forms of this style began to be produced in local fabrics, albeit platters and bowls, not beakers. I do not have an explanation for this absence, although it does seem real, but I think it makes a more general point – aggregating data allows for sound (statistical) generalisations but tends to suppress patterns of absence. This is important because very interesting information often lies in the patterning of deviations from any norm as much as in the norm itself – and more generally in archaeology, as elsewhere, statistical generalisations, although robust, suppress information about (potentially interesting) variation between samples.

    This brings me to another point raised by Pitts' paper, returning to my own D.Phil. thesis work and concerning intra-site variations. It is interesting to see how Pitts' work on Gallo-Belgic wares has picked out some of the same variations between the Colchester assemblages (at Sheepen and the *colonia*) as emerged in my own work. But I had also noted some other subtle variations for instance between the Balkerne Lane sites just outside the *colonia* and those within (Millett 1983a). This highlights the fact that identifying intra-site patterns depends to some extent on the size and definition of the sub-groups studied – and it also brings into question any simple categorisation into 'civilian', 'military', and 'official'. This is further underlined by the pattern I noted at Verulamium where there are significant variations between contemporaneous assemblages. Within the settlement, *terra sigillata* was in regular use although Gallo-Belgic wares were comparatively rare, but by contrast Gallo-Belgic vessels were common in the King Harry Lane cemetery whilst *terra sigillata* was generally excluded from the graves (Millett 1993, 270–5). We might debate the significance of these variations, but their occurrence underlines the problem of using aggregated data. I think it may be time to start further work exploring intra-site patterning for two reasons. First, to see how finds analysis might contribute more to the understanding of settlements. Second, because unless we better understand the extent of normal variations from regional patterns of distribution we will not be able to evaluate whether patterning can be linked to factors like the character of the population rather than being a result of stochastic processes.

    Finally, and returning to gaps in distribution patterns, I note Pitts' comments about the supply of Gallo-Belgic wares in civilian areas. This raises for me another issue that I have wondered about on a number of occasions. I think that many of our

5. Discussion. Reflections on the representational use of artefact evidence

presumptions about archaeological distributions in Roman provinces like Britain are unduly influenced by modern western experience where whatever we require is readily available if we have the resources to obtain it. In much of the Roman world, this was perhaps not the situation, and objects were probably available less frequently and less evenly: a situation that brings to mind my experience of East Berlin in the 1970s where commodities were available in very unpredictable ways. I suggest that we need to be ready to rethink some of our assumptions and conclusions in terms of the very imperfect market. To take a final example, returning again to *mortaria*, I would draw attention to a small but well-excavated site at Thorpe Thewles in the Tees Valley of northern England. Here the Roman pottery assemblage was very small, but largely dominated by *mortaria* – suggesting to me that their presence was perhaps partly a product of periodic availability, or a glut in supply, without denying the agency of those who chose to acquire them (Millett 1987b). Whatever the explanation, this surely implies that we cannot think of the region as one where the pattern of distribution is subject to any neat categorisations, and this underlines an important general point. The investigation of material culture patterning in the Roman world remains a fascinating challenge. In addressing this challenge, we need to be aware of the sorts of complexity touched upon here as revealed by earlier research, but we should equally aspire to think about the problems and materials in new ways, like those explored by Van Oyen and Pitts in the introduction to this volume. Only by thinking creatively in different ways will the subject continue to flourish.

Part 2

Standardisation

Chapter 6

Standard time. Typologies in Roman antiquity

Alicia Jiménez[*]

Standard time is a recent invention. Until the mid-nineteenth century, the valid standard of time was the local time of each city or town. Back then clocks reflected solar time, which varies depending on the position of a given point on the globe. Communication among communities was sufficiently restricted and the time required to travel between locations with different times long enough for the need for calibration of local times not to arise. Railway transportation created a new scenario, in which a difference of four minutes between local times could mean missing a train passing through only once a day. Increased interdependence among communities made the synchronisation of clocks to a single standard necessary for the first time (Zerubavel 1982, 6–7).

In this chapter I propose to use the metaphor of the creation of a shared, standard time around the globe as a consequence of an unprecedented increase in connectivity and integration in the nineteenth century to investigate the apparent 'synchronisation' after the Roman conquest of certain types of objects produced *en masse* and architectural styles from the eastern to the western ends of the Mediterranean. Why and how did the appearance of certain kinds of things become so similar in different provinces of the Roman empire? I will make a few comments on how the concepts of style and type can illuminate processes of standardisation. Then I will briefly compare different examples of mass produced objects (such as coins, statues, and pottery) and ask some questions about our interpretation of practices attached to standard objects and the creation of categories through repeated imitation.

I would like to highlight two ideas from this overview. First, conquest and increased connectivity, which has often been linked with cultural *koines*, may in fact lead to a range of very different results, from convergence and standardisation to the assertion of identity and increased heterogeneity. The latter can be observed in a few early Roman provinces and Italy during the late Republic and is a phenomenon that needs to be distinguished from the later 'provincialisation' of Roman material culture in the

[*] Department of Classical Studies, Duke University.

early empire. And second, studying the rhythms of change and continuity, the 'tempos of change' to use Andrew Bevan's expression, seems to be particularly relevant (Bevan 2014, 412). An important wave of standardisation occurred in different provinces and types of materials around the same time, during the second half of the first century BC or the first decades of the first century AD, in a process of 'synchronisation' over vast territories that reached some sort of 'cultural standard time' at the beginning of the principate coinciding with the phenomena described as the 'consumer revolution' (Woolf 1998, 174) and the 'Roman cultural revolution' (Wallace-Hadrill 2008). Even during this particularly important episode in the homogenisation of Roman material culture, it is necessary to contrast different types of archaeological materials and the various regional practices attached to the same objects in order to get a better insight into the creation of categories in the Roman past and in present archaeological interpretations.

Style-typologies

Archaelogical analysis of Roman colonialism leans heavily on typologies and similarities, on catalogues of things that look almost the same, even if variation inside a single type is acknowledged. And yet, despite the long-standing tradition of typological studies, analyses of the meaning of style in art history (Elsner 2003), style variation (Wiessner 1989; Sackett 1990), and the forces that shape the 'evolution' of artefacts (Lake 1998; Kirsh 2010; Shennan 2008; Hodder 2012, 138–57), the role of standardisation in the transmission of culture is still relatively ill-defined from a theoretical point of view in archaeological research. How is the standard created? What does 'ubiquity' mean in cultural terms? What happens when a society is flooded with a type of object easily recognisable?

The concept of style received attention in the pioneer work of James R. Sackett and Polly Wiessner in the 1980s. Style is, according to Wiessner (1989, 57), 'one of several means of communication through which people negotiate their personal and social identity vis-à-vis others.' The mechanism underlying stylistic development and stylistic change is for Wiessner social and its social identification takes place via comparison with others. Sackett (1990), on the other hand, stressed the unconscious characteristics of style that result from passive enculturation in social groups (isochrestic style), acknowledging that style can be also actively used to send intentional messages of social identity (iconological style). The discussion back then revolved around the possibility of distinguishing ethnic groups in the material record, but it is valuable for our purposes here in that at the very least it shows that the traditional distinction between function and style (the attributes that allow an artifact to perform its intended task versus the non-functional traits of the artifact) is flawed, since style has a series of important social functions and is part of what an object is used for as well. It also stresses that stylistic universes go beyond individual classes of objects and crosscut different categories, a key question to understand the

6. Standard time. Typologies in Roman antiquity

repetition of shapes and their recreation in different materials within the Roman empire: representations of statues and candelabra adorned wall paintings; bronze candelabra imitated the shape of marble columns; ceramic container forms were inspired by the shapes of metal vessels; while bronze lamps were very similar to pottery lamps; a characteristic honorific type of female representation (the so-called Large Herculaeum Woman) can be traced in marble and limestone statues, statuettes and over-sized full round figures, reliefs and sarcophagi (Wallace-Hadrill 2008, 367, 376, 381; Trimble 2011, 93). But standardisation often led to an over-stylisation of a particular shape in the same type of object. In their travels from the east to the west, the shapes of bronze lamps were simplified in the productions that used them as a model in Italy, which were in turn simplified when these lamp forms reached the provinces (Wallace-Hadrill 2008, 381–6). When Ebusan coins travelled eastwards to Pompeii and started to be imitated by the inhabitants of the town after a period in which originals circulated in the settlement, the same phenomenon of simplification of forms took place: the 'naturalistic' detailed representation of Bes in the coins from ancient Ibiza gave way to a synthetic schematic depiction of the god in the coins that imitated them in the heart of Italy (for possible explanations see Stannard 2013).

When people resort to self-conscious sets of aesthetic choices, those choices are to be understood as a response to objects of the same type or as 'comments' on another class of objects when a thing imitates the design of a similar artefact made from another material, in the case of skeuomorphs. The imitation of the shape of metal containers or even basketry in Minoan ceramics during the Middle Bronze Age (Knappett 2002, 109–10) is a disclosure of the change in the characteristic raw material of a particular type of artefact, as much as a visual representation of the genealogy of the object. Things themselves, the palimpsest of past and new forms, create the grounds for our understanding of them, establishing links with a perceived, suggested, claimed or real source, as Chris Gosden (2005, 207) has pointed out. The object is the model, not a pre-existing platonic ideal of how things are. But it is precisely the reference to a *precedent* that supposedly looks the same which allows change to happen. In the late 1990s, Alfred Gell (1998, 218) showed how stylistic shifts occur by the least difference principle, through variations that still allow us to see links between objects. Change of this kind is 'invisible' to the eye, it occurs thanks to apparent similitude, relying on memory and stereotype: since rarely in antiquity individuals would have had access to the necessary information to oversee the expansion in space and time of a complete series of the same type of object.

Ironically, that is precisely what we archaeologists do. However, we are far better equipped to highlight changes in types – noticeable differences in shape, color or properties that were also visible in the past – than to explain the diffusion of a single form without resorting to the movement of things (commerce) or people. The creation of archaeological categories of ancient objects sometimes makes ancient categories of objects as clear as mud or at least more difficult to study, since every given category may have had different genealogies as well as meanings in the past and the present. Well-known examples include what the Romans considered to be 'Samian' ceramic from the Greek island of Samos, which archaeologists today refer to as Campanian black-glaze pottery (produced in Campania, Etruria and in lesser quantities in Sicily and Rome), or the label 'Arretine' used in antiquity for pieces of ceramics which in fact were not only produced in workshops at Arezzo, but also in hundreds of kilns in the surrounding area and as far away as Pisa, Pozzuoli, the Po Valley, Lyon, and La Graufesenque in Gaul. Some of the modern labels we use for this production – such as Italian *terra sigillata* – are therefore inaccurate too. The solution proposed by Wallace-Hadrill (2008, 411) is privileging 'style' over 'origin', which is probably what the ancient Romans did when thinking about that particular class of artifact, and use the term 'Italian-style *terra sigillata*'. Even when an archaeological category seems to map fairly well onto an ancient type, as, for example, in the case of *sigillata*, the potential overlapping still does not clarify how things became categories in Roman antiquity in the first place and the possibilities attached to the object or the things it could do – its 'material agency' (Van Oyen 2015, 63–4, 66). What an object 'is', the category it fits in, influences what it is capable of doing (holding liquids, resist the contact with fire), as much as how it is going to be used (the practices attached to it in a particular context) and perceived.

Types include things that look the same, but in many cases are actually not: types allow variability because what defines the type is not complete resemblance, but the establishment of a series of elements that are easily distinguishable and recognisable. The type is created through the selection of certain characteristics that are crucial in contrast with others that are accessory. The external characteristics that marked a 'typical' Roman city (the intersection of *cardo* and *decumanus, fora* and temples, baths, theatres, amphitheatres, basilicas and *curiae*), made towns around the empire look like each other, even though they did not reproduce the very individual topography and series of unique monuments found at Rome (Zanker 2000, 27–8). Some elements clearly recognised by archaeologists may have been considered of lesser importance in the past and vice versa. Some of these traits allowed distinguishing a group of things inside the type, marking them to signal a better quality, origin, different taste or properties inside their group category. In this sense, as David Wengrow (2010, 13–14) has shown, the anonymity of mass consumption of a particular category simultaneously creates novel systems to differentiate otherwise indistinguishable goods and packaging, sometimes on the basis of shape, raw materials or qualities of the object, including its origin and alleged discovery. That was the case of prestigious 'marks' of value linked to Greek place names, such as the 'Corinthian bronze', an alloy of bronze, silver and gold developed in the eastern Mediterranean in the second millennium, which however, according to Pliny (*Historia Naturalis* 34.6), was discovered through the accidental fusion of bronze with silver and gold during the sack of Corinth by Mummius and collected from that point by Roman elites. Some bronze candelabra were considered to be 'Corinthian' even if they were not made of 'Corinthian bronze' (Wallace-Hadrill 2008, 373–4), which shows how a type may carry certain attributes even when the techniques and materials that are part of its material essence have changed.

Mass-produced objects

While it is not unusual to explain diversity as a consequence of connectivity and the arrival of imported items, Roman expansion poses the question of standardisation, of apparent similarities across well-connected areas, of diversity within perceived homogeneity in material culture (Mattingly 2004, 8–9; van Dommelen and Terrenato 2007, 7).

Wallace-Hadrill has proposed a three-wave pattern comparable to the systole and diastole of the cardiac cycle that maps increased connectivity and movements inward and outward from the perspective of the centre, from the beginning of the Roman expansion in the Mediterranean in the second half of the third century BC to the Roman provincial cultures of the early principate. During the first phase (second–first century BC), comparable to the diastole, imports and looted objects from the eastern Mediterranean flooded Rome. Italian centers produced imitations of imported objects in the second stage (second half of the first century BC–Augustan), transforming them in the process. In the last stage, similar to the systole (early empire), Italian products reached the provinces, which contributed to the diffusion of Italian styles with their own local versions of Roman products, increasing the circulation around the Mediterranean to previously unknown levels (Wallace-Hadrill 2008, 360–1).

It is useful comparing the consequences of the Republican conquests in Rome before the middle of the first century BC as described in Wallace-Hadrill's model with the effects of the conquest in the provinces and analysing the decentralising perspective it produces. The radical transformation of Rome's urban landscape was the consequence not only of the arrival of works of art from the Greek East, but also of slaves and bullion from the newly incorporated territories in the West, which financed the construction of temples and triumphal arches *ex manubiis*. The influence of the arrival of provincial 'exotica' in Rome during the first phase described above can be considered similar from a conceptual point of view to the incorporation of certain Roman imports, mostly from Etruria and Campania (Greco-Italic, Dressel 1 amphorae, Campanian ware, Italian bronze drinking vessels) in the early Republican provinces and even some regions of temperate Europe before the conquest. The key in both contexts, as Greg Woolf (1998, 176) suggested, is 'to draw a distinction between the consumption of Roman goods and Roman styles of consumption' in the provinces, which equally applies to the fairly limited range of imports from the provinces used in the context of particularly Roman practices, such as the triumph, or dining, in Rome.

Understanding the genealogy or trajectory of things, how categories were created in the past, is particularly important in Wallace-Hadrill's (2008) model's second phase, dated to the late Republic and the reign of Augustus, in which the imitation of imports creates new versions of them in Rome – and I claim in the provinces as well. This seems the necessary first step for provincial objects to be conceptualised as a *type* to be imitated in Rome, as Wallace-Hadrill suggests, or for an Italic artifact to be replicated in the provinces. Because repeated imitation contributes to creating the model, the recurrence of motives and shapes can function as a starting point in our investigation of types in the past, especially concerning the stabilisation of traits that would make a category recognisable in opposition to, and in relation with, its own category of things.

The evolution of ceramic types at the end of the first century BC and the beginning of the first century AD illustrates this point. Red glaze Arretine is easily distinguishable from the earlier back glaze Campanian ware that it would displace in the second half of the first century, even if at the very beginning many forms derived from the Campanian ware and were produced in both black and red glaze. Standardisation, as mentioned before, fosters change, in the form of alterations inside the same type – as in the different regional variants of Italic style or Gallic *sigillata* marking differences in origin and chronology – or radical departures from it – as in the black Rhenish ware launched at Lezoux after the middle of the second century AD, which helped in turn to stabilise the standard type of Central Gallic *sigillata* by opposition (Van Oyen 2015, 71; 2016a).

Trajectories reveal not only the creation of new categories concealed within variation, but also important information about synchronisation and the spread of types in different regions. Roman female honorific statues of the late Republic and the early empire relied on 'individual' heads mounted on stereotyped bodies that differed in attributes, but followed a limited series of types with the same poses and garments inspired by models that were popular in Greece in Hellenistic times. In Rome, female honorific statues began to appear only in the late first century BC and seem to have crystallised into standard forms. Pudicitia and Herculaneum women are the most popular types between the late Republic and the second century AD. Pudicitia types are particularly abundant during the late Republic, while the Herculaneum women were set up mostly in Greece and Italy in the Julio-Claudian period, to become a 'dormant' type in the Flavian period and reach their real production peak in the second century AD. The spread of standard classes of female statues in the provinces (particularly in North Africa, Greece, and Asia Minor) suggests that the stereotyped images responded to a general ideal appearance of elite women around the Mediterranean, not only in Rome, and which in fact can only be understood if the statues are studied in their regional and chronological settings, in connection with other female and male honorific statues as Alexandridis (2010) and Trimble (2011) have done.

No doubt certain production techniques contributed as well to the standardisation of forms in some particular categories of objects produced in quite large numbers, as Wallace-Hadrill (2008, 363, 387) has pointed out. The 'lost wax' process allowed Roman sculptors to create copies of an 'original' and modify it by adding details to the wax version. The moulds used to create glass and ceramic containers, as well as the dies employed in the minting of coins, were individually made, but produced a respectable amount of fairly similar replicas, even if not at an industrial level (but see Murphy, this volume). Both moulds and dies had a 'second life' of sorts that prolonged their capacity to produce modified copies. Moulds were discarded when the decoration deteriorated or when they broke. The craftsman could then create a new mould from scratch or fabricate a copy of the first one from a pre-existing piece. Dies were recut or repaired when they were damaged or suffered wear until they were replaced by a new one. The punch or reverse die had a tendency to last less than the anvil or obverse die and was commonly replaced earlier than the obverse die. The process resulted in groups of coins that share the exact same obverse but have 'different' reverses (from a the 'new' reverse die) within a type that remained, however, unchanged (Crawford 1983, 208).

What is different about the early Roman empire is not the interconnectedness of types or the emergence of a particular form that became widespread around the Mediterranean – that happened before and would happen latter – it is the emergence at roughly the same time of several of these categories (Arretine ware, bronze and pottery lamps, statues of women in the guise of Pudicitia, funerary monuments, inscriptions in stone) enmeshed with the new possibilities and constraints created by two hundred years of Roman expansion in the Mediterranean.

It may seem counterintuitive to say that the earliest wave of synchronisation took place around the same time in different provinces independently of the time of first incorporation. That the process of standardisation was not an immediate consequence of Roman conquest is, nevertheless, better observed in provinces that were created well before the cultural revolution described above occurred, such as Hispania. Roughly two hundred years passed between the beginning of the Second Punic war in Iberia and the pacification of the province by Augustus. The first two centuries under Roman control saw changes in this province that can be assimilated to the ones described by Wallace-Hadrill during the diastolic phase in Rome: a limited range of Roman goods (table ware, monumental styles in religious architecture, coins) arrived to the Hispaniae and were transformed to fit local practices (Jiménez 2011). The formative process involving different elements (such as Latin epigraphy, monumental architecture and sculpture) occurred in the Hispaniae, as in some other provinces around the end of the first century BC and the beginning of the first century AD, despite the chronological differences in the dates they were conquered by Rome (Woolf 1995). The confluence may be at least partially explained by the very nature of the Republican provinces and colonialism during the second century and the first half of the first century BC. Republican provinces did not necessarily entail a claim of possession of a given territory, they were mainly conceptualised as the task or sphere of influence assigned to a Roman magistrate or promagistrate (Richardson 1986, 5; 1994, 564–5). In fact, the imposition of direct Roman rule was undertaken in certain territories without waiting for a clear definition, military control or pacification of the *provincia* (Lintott 1981, 60), or even the existence of provincial institutions (Richardson 1994, 568). In this stage, the governor treated the communities within his *provincia* in many respects as self-governing entities, which they were *de facto*, enjoying (or not) certain privileges according to their statuses as states with a treaty (*civitates foederatae*), free states (*civitates liberae*) or states paying *stipendium* – regular taxation – to Rome (*civitates stipendiariae*). These differences among settlements, which belonged to a system of diplomatic relations between states (i.e. Rome and a series of towns outside Italy), existed within and outside the province (Richardson 1994, 592). Likewise, people were divided into two categories: Roman citizens (*cives*) and non-citizens (*peregrini*) 'and remained so whether they were within the area of a *provincia* or not' (Richardson 1994, 591). During the first two centuries of Roman military and political expansion (third and second centuries BC) 'imperium' seems to mean essentially the right to command within the Roman state vested in the magistrates and pro-magistrates. The territorial concept of empire came into existence around the same time as the territorial concept of province, by the late first century BC and the early first century AD, together with some major changes in colonisation patterns, epigraphy, and ceramic production (Richardson 2008, 8). The new territorial conceptualisation of the empire closely linked to an increase in colonisation and a new administrative system of the provinces between Caesar and Augustus was likely the origin of the apparent synchronisation of some aspects of Roman material culture around the turn of the millennium.

The provincial network can be considered at least partially responsible for the dissemination of Italian styles in the provinces (a phenomenon identified by Wallace-Hadrill as the systolic third phase), which came hand in hand with the diffusion of provincial items in Rome (for example olive oil amphorae from the Baetica) and the circulation of provincial items in the very provinces (such as the supply of Gaulish *sigillata* in Britannia). The location of different parts of the production process in the provinces and the addition of different details in the final destination of the product further contributed to standardisation of shapes and types. In the case of stone statues, Trimble has noted that the mass production of the Large Herculaneum Women in the second century AD apparently coincides with the imperial reorganisation of the quarry system and perhaps with the delocalisation of production of sarcophagi, column capitals, and other marble objects that were roughed out in the main eastern quarries, and fine carved in destination workshops that worked on pre-shaped, standardised blocks of stone that had been already outlined (Trimble 2011, 93–4). In parallel, provincial material culture becomes the standard to the point that the production of some imperial coins is centralised outside Rome in *Lugdunum* from 15 BC and for part of the first century AD (Howgego 1994, 8–9), which could be interpreted both as a sign of maximum centralisation (the periphery has become the core) or provincialisation of the network.

Concluding remarks

Synchronicity and standardisation (why, when and in which realms it did and did not happen) are concepts worth exploring. Although these phenomena seem interconnected with imperialism, military conquests and economic integration, they overflowed these processes in the sense that they did not completely overlap in time or were only caused by them.

It is important to note the central role of certain categories in the process of standardisation, since archaeologists have a clear tendency to focus on regular urbanism, modular architecture, mass-produced items (such as coins or ceramics), and artefacts with quite fixed types (such as sculpture). Some objects apparently became 'more similar' than others. A more detailed comparison of categories that were standardised across the empire with categories that were not would probably provide information as interesting as the one obtained by comparing the dynamics of standard types among themselves. Clearly, not all standardisation waves were equal: the processes involved in the replicas of the forum of Augustus in some provincial capitals (such as Corduba, Emerita, and Tarraco in the Hispaniae) were probably mostly related with the creation of new imperial structures (Jiménez 2010), while certain types of female statues may have more to do with social normativity, and the wide dissemination of some products, such as Arretine ware, with patterns of mass-production, consumption and dining. When types of artefacts are compared and analysed together with the social practices attached to them, we get the most complex picture about the role of standardisation in domestic, urban, religious or funerary contexts.

Finally, we should not forget that some of the networks created in this process of synchronisation of imperial territories led in fact not only to the standardisation of certain Roman items outside Rome, but also to the spread of typical provincial material culture in the provinces, such in the case of the presence of amphorae carrying Spanish olive oil to Gallia or Gallic *sigillata* to Britannia. The question of whether the Roman market was truly integrated is directly related to our interpretation of this interprovincial trade, and has been answered in divergent ways by substantivists (underlining the constraints of the ancient economy) and formalists (in favour of explaining the expansion of the economy through a process of integration), despite the fact that economic activities are shaped by social and cultural as well as economic features (Scheidel 2012, 8), that the degree of integration varied widely depending on the type of commodity and that, concerning our inquiry on the standardisation of forms, market integration is not automatically followed by an 'integration' of styles (Harris 2015, 407). Coin populations, for example, varied across the empire, in part as a consequence of decentralized production, in part as a result of non-economic factors determining coin circulation. One of the best documented examples is the closed currency system of Roman Egypt, in which a system based on the billon tetradrachms in use from the Ptolomies until Diocletian served the monetary needs of the area, although the province clearly did not have a closed economy. Similarly, the local-style silver coins of Syria had a distinctive denomination system and a regional pattern of circulation, while the Roman *denarii* and *antoniniani* produced in the same mint in Syria have often been found in the western part of the empire (Howgego 1994, 15).

It is important to acknowledge then not only the existence of a multi-centered economy and its effects on a more or less homogeneous material culture in the provinces, but also, as David Mattingly (2007, 221) has suggested, the coexistence of three broad structures, an imperial economy, provincial economies, and extraprovincial economies, based on contacts with territories beyond direct Roman control, which channeled waves of standardised objects in very different ways (Bowman and Wilson 2009, 16–17; Harris 2015, 411). In that sense, as Martin Pitts (2015) has pointed out, it is less the case that some sites were attracted to imported goods and others to local goods. Increased levels of 'synchronicity' might have had more to do with access to new networks and nodes that set a template for availability shared by the provinces as a consequence of a series of changes discussed in this chapter around the turn of the millenium. A 'Roman standard time' of sorts came to existence right then, when the administration of the provinces and the Italian peninsula was re-invented, the foundation of new colonies reached a new peak and both the provinces and Rome were labeled as part of a territorial empire in the eyes of the Romans.

Chapter 7

Different similarities or similar differences? Thoughts on *koine*, oligopoly and regionalism

Jeroen Poblome, Senem Özden Gerçeker and Maarten Loopmans[*]

Local and global/similar and different

Roman artefact studies tend to explore the tension between specific finds at a given site and their comparison to materials found at different sites and regions. This tension between similarity and difference is not uniquely linked to object types or material categories, functionality of deposits or nature of sites, and is not even specific to the Roman imperial period *an sich*. Moreover, such tensions surface in a variety of thematic debates, on form *vs.* function, globalisation, consumerism, class systems, technology, imperialism, cultural identity, gender, ethnicity, religion, nationalism and regionalism.

Figure 7.1 Coin minted at Sagalassos, during the reign of Valerian I. The reverse publicizes Sagalassos as friend and ally of the Romans as well as the first city of Pisidia. CNG electronic auction 169, 25 July 2007, 108.

---

[*]Departments of Archaeology and Geography, University of Leuven.

This chapter addresses one variety of this tension: how regional differences in artefact assemblages are balanced against the integrative forces of the Roman commonwealth. For instance, the votive and funerary relief *stelai* of Phrygia dated to the later second to early fourth centuries AD are often considered parochial in style and content, reflecting rural Anatolia's society. Their codified and repetitive corpus is considered to result from particular, regional predilections, which are unattested in contemporaneous urban contexts in western Asia Minor, to name but the most obvious contrasting tradition. Nevertheless, Jane Masséglia (2013) pointed out how the typical Phrygian focus on self-display in portrait and text, with an emphasis on personal industry, is actually a translation of social flexibility, successfully mixing Anatolian, Hellenistic and Roman cultural traits. These *stelai* exemplify how the local, while meaningful on its own, simultaneously evolved in reciprocal dialogue with more universal traditions.

At times, such mixing of cultural elements did not work. In discussing the late Hellenistic to early Roman imperial traditions of mould-made ceramic oil lamp making at Pergamon, Ephesos and Knidos, Anita Giuliani (2007) demonstrated how the early first century AD phase of lamp types mixing Hellenistic and Roman morphological traits was short-lived. Notwithstanding pre-existing distribution patterns and exchange mechanisms of these lamps in late Hellenistic times and the general demand for this type of objects serving all sectors of ancient daily life and death, in this case, mixed messages were no commercial success. The Hellenistic stylistic traditions remained separate from Roman Republican lamp repertoires, which hardly circulated in these regions. But even the early Roman imperial imported lamps would not affect local traditions. Only from the second quarter of the first century AD did local potters adopt the designs of Italian oil lamps and abandon the traditional Hellenistic models. This case study shows that the production of mundane objects could evolve in apparent disconnection from contemporary geo-political proceedings.

To be sure, examples of material culture translating active policies of mutual dependency are also available. The imperial Roman mints did not supply the cities and markets in the East with small coinage. Yet, local administrations wishing to fuel their economies with coin were generally granted the privilege by the imperial authorities to do so (Stroobants in press). Both local and imperial authorities had an interest in continuing these practices. The associated iconography makes this clear: messages of imperially-induced ideological unity are combined with local self-propagation in competition with peers (Fig. 7.1). Julie Dalaison (2014) recently presented an overview of how Pontic cities propagated their independence even in a context of firm dependency on Roman central authorities, in a region that had shown formidable resistance to Rome. In this way, all parties involved built on the complexities of inter-related realities, expounding different traditions, histories, claims and aspirations.

Many initiatives were also taken by private parties, which sometimes tried to boost local economic success by tapping into wider phenomena. On the basis of survey evidence from the Cide Archaeological Project, for instance, Philip Bes (2015a) proposed the presence of estates involved in probable vine cultivation in late Roman times. The local provenance of the related amphorae can be presumed based on the particularities of the clay fabric of the transport vessels. Their morphology, on the other hand, was very similar to the amphorae produced on estates related to Herakleia Pontike and Sinope, with documented distribution patterns around Black Sea, the Sea of Marmara and the Aegean Sea. The shape of the late Roman Cide region amphorae resulted from conscious decisions on behalf of estate owners or managers to try and blend into existing exchange patterns, based on regional produce from the coasts of northwestern Asia Minor.

Whether the artefacts under study are stelai, oil lamps, coins, or amphorae, meaning emerges from the tension between patterns of similarity and difference. These patterns seem to work in complementary ways and therefore form an essential part of how the Roman world worked, or at least materialised itself. Rather than enumerating more examples of this same phenomenon, this chapter engages in exploratory modelling. Based on the disciplines of archaeology and geography, we will consider whether the linguistic and socio-cultural concept of *koine* has pertinence to the economic concepts of opportunity cost and oligopoly, and finally whether comprehending the workings of these concepts affects our understanding of regionalism – the level at which many of the discussed tensions seem to play out.

Koine

In a 2011 paper, we argued for the re-introduction of an old term into the study of late Roman pottery tablewares (Poblome and Fırat 2011): that of 'Late Roman D' ware (henceforth LRD), as originally introduced by Frederick O. Waagé in 1948 in relation to material from Antioch-on-the-Orontes. LRD represents a recognisably similar way of designing and producing tableware shapes and fabrics shared by a range of documented production centres in southwestern Asia Minor and western Cyprus. The common language or *koine* of LRD highlights the existence of 'a range of regional production centres involved in the making of a cohesive and consistent range of tableware types and forms' (Poblome and Fırat 2011, 49). Recognising LRD as a *koine* places the ware on the same footing as the other contemporary types of tableware with wide circulation in the late Roman East – African red slip ware (henceforth ARSW) or Late Roman C ware (henceforth LRC), which is important for the general positioning of the ware. Acknowledging the internal cohesion of LRD as a stylistic product range, however, does not resolve issues related to attested fabric differences, their coupling to specific types linked to particular production centres, their archaeometrical provenancing to specific sites and the attribution of specific origins in LRD distribution patterns. We remain convinced that the re-introduction of LRD as a term and its recognition as a *koine* represents an opportunity for research, potentially making typologies more meaningful in their ancient contexts (Poblome and Fırat 2011, 54).

According to the Oxford English Dictionary (oed.com, accessed on 3 February 2016) the ancient Greek word κοινή is the feminine singular derived from κοινός for 'common, ordinary'. *Koine* is defined as:

- Originally the common literary dialect of the Greeks (ἡ κοινὴ διάλεκτος) from the close of classical Attic to the Byzantine era. Now extended to include any language or dialect in regular use over a wide area in which different languages or dialects are, or were, in use locally.
- A set of cultural or other attributes common to various groups.

Building on this definition, the concept of *koine* implies that the commonness of the language or cultural attributes would be impossible to grasp if it were not for the existence of variations or differences at other operational levels. In this way, scale, context and tension between similarity and difference circumscribe each *koine*. Looking into the linguistic context of *koine* helps to understand how similarities and differences co-constitute each other.

As a linguistic phenomenon, *koine* does not exist but comes into being. The Hellenistic *koine* of Greek is traditionally cited as the original language *koine*. The First Athenian Sea League (477–404 BC) constituted the framework in which larger speech communities could emerge: providing the matrix for the mixing of dialects within the league's territories, leading to phonological and morphological compromises and levelling between the dialects allowing the *koine* to settle. In its stable form, a *koine* is the 'result of mixing of linguistic sub-systems such as regional or literary dialects. It usually serves as a *lingua franca* among speakers of the different contributing varieties and is characterised by a mixture of features of these varieties and most often by reduction or simplification in comparison' (Siegel 1985, 363). It was the stabilised form of Greek, the Attic-Ionic *koine*, which was exported throughout the Hellenistic kingdoms leading to its adoption for literary purposes by the likes of Polybios, Plutarch, Flavius Josephus and Lucian (Bubenik 2010).

The problem with LRD is that it never existed *an sich*, in contrast to the *lingua franca* of Hellenistic *koine* Greek. LRD is useful as a meaningful level of classification, in the same way as ranges of pottery sherds are identified as ARSW or LRC tableware. In this sense LRD is a construct, albeit one that works, as it only takes little training to differentiate LRD from ARSW and LRC. As with ARSW and LRC, however, the common denominator of LRD *koine* represents a conglomerate of specific production centres, including Sagalassos; a site near Pednelissos (Jackson *et al.* 2012); and elsewhere in south-western Asia Minor and western Cyprus. *Koine* is not only an artefact of archaeological classification; it was also meaningful in antiquity, as the potters and customers wanted to make and use LRD-type of wares and not ARSW or LRC bowls and dishes. LRD represents a fashion, a taste, a design of particular ranges of products, which is consciously different from other wares and could bind people together, feeding the notion of regionalism.

The concept of *koine* helps explain why a classification that did not exist as such in the past, such as LRD, could nonetheless have been meaningful in antiquity. This paradox can be resolved by further considering the linguistic nature of *koine*, in particular through semiotic phenomenology as developed by Charles Sanders Peirce (1839–1914). According to the latter's theory of signs, the process of semiosis which includes the production of meaning is realised through icons, indices and symbols. An icon is a sign inoculated on the 'thing' it refers to, signifying by resemblance. A Roman floor mosaic with a banquet scene retains some of the visual qualities of actual banquets. An index refers to things by participation, as in smoke being an index of fire, and signifies through cause and effect. Language, on the other hand, does not build on links to things nor stimuli, but on symbols, whose meaning must be learned, with language mediating the construction of meaning (Christidis 2010). That is why different words in different languages can mean the same thing, as these refer to a generalised abstraction of that thing. LRD as a *koine* of tableware does not refer to actual tableware, but to a generalised abstraction of it, which was meaningful to its users. LRD conformed to an underlying set of real objects, dishes and bowls projected to a more general idea of tableware, which was, in the minds of its users, sufficiently cohesive in design of forms, attributes and material qualities to be recognisable as LRD, and as different from ARSW or LRC.

If LRD was meaningful as a *koine* in antiquity, the question arises how to approach the actual tablewares constituting LRD. We take our cue from Sagalassos red slip ware (henceforth SRSW), one of the tablewares under the LRD umbrella. SRSW exists with its typological and chronological specificities (Poblome 1999), own path dependency (van der Enden, Poblome and Bes 2014), local *chaînes opératoires* (Murphy and Poblome 2012; Poblome 2016), embedded in local urban society (Poblome *et al.* 2013) and networked into its own economic framework (Willet and Poblome 2015). Taken together, these elements are what it takes to make SRSW into a 'ware' – the common denominator of ceramic analysis. In this sense, an individual potter's workshop does not represent SRSW, but all SRSW workshops active in a given period do. At the same time, SRSW forms part of a larger commonality, LRD. Individual wares constituting a tableware *koine* can be considered as linguistic sub-systems or dialects, creating 'a recognisable mix of vocabulary, pronunciation and grammar used by a particular group of speakers, who are regionally or socially connected' (Poblome and Fırat 2011, 54). In ceramological terms, Michel Bonifay (2004) proposed the term *faciès géographique* to denote the real wares, within their regional zones of production and, when possible, the actual workshops or potters' quarters.

As a matter of fact, there can be different *faciès géographiques* without there necessarily being a *koine* and their existence also does not entail an inevitable evolution towards a *koine*. Once a *koine* can be identified, however, it does presuppose the existence of different *faciès géographiques*, as well as dialectic relationships between these wares. *Faciès géographiques* and *koine* should be easy to define, based on tangible archaeological criteria and should combine etic and emic qualities. Etic criteria should best be defined based on workable practices of classification suited to the specifics of the artefacts under study; emic criteria ideally result from the analysis of the individual *chaîne opératoire* of each of the constituting wares (Read 2007). In that way, *faciès géographiques* and *koine* can be operationalised methodologically. As a result, both concepts are not synonymous with terms as culture, style, social identity, micro-regional interaction or macro-regional networking (Galanakis 2009), which remain problematic in definition and difficult to operationalise in archaeological terms, especially when trying to reach higher-level synthesis. *Faciès géographiques* and *koine*, in contrast, are not only within reach of archaeological methodologies, these concepts also derive their strength from the potential overlap of etic aspects of classification with emic ones related to past practices of production and use.

The LRD *koine* could in turn form part of other, larger stylistic frameworks of cultural pertinence. This could range from skeuomorphic inspiration from contemporary silver plate (Leader-Newby 2004; Willet 2012) to a globalised sharing of cultural symbols in the late Roman world. Miguel John Versluys (2015) recently demonstrated how the Roman globalised *oikumene* transformed the semantic system of the Hellenistic *koine* through processes of universalisation, in which styles and cultural elements lost part of their original meaning in order to play a role in a larger system; as well as particularisation, reconfiguring meaning in local contexts. When these larger systems share etic and emic analytical potential, these could also be labelled *koine*, but terminology preferably avoids redundancy.

A distinguishing feature of *koine* is that, whichever scale or context it represents, it is never static. *Koine* comes into being, develops and dissipates. Apart from the demonstrable cohesion in the development of form and design of LRD between the fourth and the seventh centuries AD, there might well be a shared origin (Özden 2015). A fill deposit containing various thousands of sherds of mostly tablewares was found sealed by a mortar layer during the 2006–10 excavations of Lot 159 within the western necropolis of the ancient town of Perge, extending from its West Gate (Fig. 7.2). Of the 1845 sherds studied, the majority conformed typologically to SRSW, whilst Cypriot *sigillata*, Eastern *sigillata* D (henceforth ESD) and Cypriot red slip ware (henceforth CRSW) were also represented albeit in markedly smaller quantities, as well as token presence of some other tablewares. Chronologically, most material was datable to the second half of the second and the first half of the third centuries AD, while the stratigraphy ran from the first to the seventh century AD. Macroscopically, the fabric and slip characteristics of the majority of material were comparable to SRSW, albeit containing qualitative variations which proved difficult to systemise macroscopically.

This large group of material contained mostly SRSW types, but also some Cypriot and other types. A small group of sherds had different slip and clay fabric characteristics applied to both SRSW and Cypriot shapes.

XRF-analysis and thin sectioning applied to 22 samples of second/third centuries AD standard SRSW types of both macroscopic groups discriminated between three different compositional groups. Eight samples conformed entirely to all compositional characteristics of SRSW (Degryse and Poblome 2008). Eleven samples, macroscopically classified with the largest group of the material and representing traditional SRSW types, could not be traced to the Sagalassos clay beds, but were made from CaO rich clays of unknown provenance, albeit not from the region of Sagalassos (Figs. 7.2–3). Finally, three standard SRSW types were made from yet other clays, poor in MgO and containing medium-sized metamorphic rocks and minerals. These sherds conformed to the small group, distinguishable macroscopically by a more reddish hue of the fabric and a matt slip (Figs. 7.4–5). The archaeometrical composition of this last group was comparable to the fabric of an as yet unprovenanced pottery production centre in south-west Anatolia (Poblome *et al.* 2001), implying that it produced standard forms known from the SRSW, ESD and CRSW type series between the second and the seventh centuries AD. In its late antique phase the products from this centre have already been classified under the LRD umbrella (Poblome and Fırat 2011).

This evidence suggests at least mid-imperial origins for the phenomenon of the LRD *koine*. As LRD originates only in the course of the fourth century AD, the existence of an ESD *koine* is here suggested. As with LRD, the ESD *koine* highlights the existence of a range of regional production centres involved in the making of a consistent range of tableware types and forms located in the wider regions of southwestern Asia Minor and western Cyprus (Poblome and Fırat 2011, 49). Clearly, further research is required to elucidate the roles of the different production centres in these respective regions.

John Lund (2015) studied pottery circulation to throw light on the people and history of Cyprus – an important region in the *koine* discussed in this chapter – from the third century BC to the third century AD. Both Cyprus' physical geography, with the Troodos mountain range structuring connectivity, and material culture bring the theme of archaeological regionality to the fore. Archaeology is rich in regional studies, be this driven by geographical aspects such as river valleys (Thonemann 2011), settlement patterns (Winther-Jacobsen and Summerer 2015), perceived historical cultural identities (Dörtlük *et al.* 2006), ancient regionality (Thonemann 2013), urban development (Raja 2012), or, as in the recent case of John Lund, the specifics of producing and consuming material culture, and the permeable boundaries this seems to indicate.

Lund concludes that the 'spectrum of ceramic finewares and transport amphorae in Western Rough Cilicia and Western Cyprus was similar in many respects – but

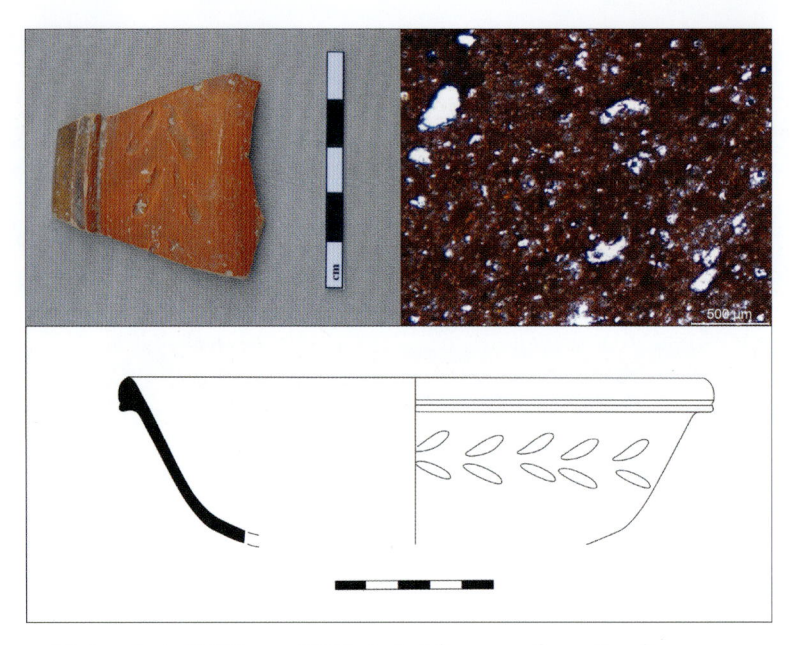

Figure 7.2 Sample 9. SRSW type 1B191, CaO rich group of non-Sagalassos provenance

Figure 7.3 Sample 15. SRSW type 1A150, CaO rich group of non-Sagalassos provenance.

Figure 7.4 Sample 20. SRSW type 1B190, MgO poor group of non-Sagalassos provenance.

Figure 7.5 Sample 28. ESD, Hayes form P40, MgO poor group.

not identical' (Lund 2015, 182). This cohesion between western Cyprus and south-western Asia Minor – our analysis reaches further west and northwest into Asia Minor – is linked to the importance of Nea Paphos as Cypriot metropolis and main port of entry for many goods into Cyprus (Lund 2015, 210), as well as the role of regional connections 'in structuring maritime interaction and market formation' (Leidwanger 2014, 33). Importantly, however, 'the figures from Cyprus indicate ... that pottery was primarily manufactured for local and regional consumption' (Lund 2015, 217), implying that Cyprus participated in general socio-cultural terms in the globalised Roman world, but not in the strict economic sense of fully integrated markets. The importance of the big players on the tableware market, such as ESD, however, was to grow: 'from the 1st century BC onwards, pottery consumers in the Eastern Mediterranean turned increasingly towards imported ceramic finewares with the consequence that local fineware producers were apparently forced out of business' (Lund 2015, 220). In other words, momentum was building for the establishment of *koine*, such as ESD. The picture is again one of similarities and differences at different scales and times, which Lund tries to capture in the concept of archaeological regionality, defined by similarities in the production and exchange of different types of material culture. Of crucial importance is Lund's argumentation against the traditional view that ascribes the apparent uniformity of Hellenistic and Roman culture on Cyprus as resulting from *koine* trends emerging in the Classical period. Instead, he reconstructs different regional compositions of material culture, relating pottery circulation patterning to burial practices and belief systems (Lund 2015, 230–6). The next question is whether we can move beyond archaeological and socio-cultural description in approaching these multi-scalar patterns of similarity and difference.

Opportunity costs and oligopoly

What was the force behind the idea of LRD and its constituting wares? Why did potters not all opt to make ARSW dishes and bowls? Why did customers not all want only LRC? Why was a ware merging LRD, ARSW and LRC never made? How come that in the supposedly globalised Roman world most studied sites are characterised by discrete combinations of types of artefacts, or, the other way around, that distribution patterns of artefacts appear as multi-morphous sets expanding and contracting in time and space with little or no overlap? Social, political, cultural, religious, and even military factors can contribute to answering these questions, but when the distribution of goods is concerned, it makes sense to consider how the documented patterns could result from an economic circumscription of possibilities.

To be sure, eventually human beings and their intentions, relationships, interests, practices and decisions in changing time-space circumstances are behind the similarities and differences discussed in this chapter, but the nature of the archaeological record, especially in the Roman East, rarely allows us to come close to these. The available evidence induces abstraction. In his overview study of the chronological and geographical distribution of tableware in the Roman East based on the ICRATES-database, Philip Bes (2015b, 142–51) elucidated a couple of such mutually dependent abstractions, such as the notion of supply and demand, the nexus urban hub/productive countryside, pulling factors such as big cities, and connectivity.

The ARCHGLASS Project, coordinated by Patrick Degryse (2014), reminds of methodological differences between artefact types. Pottery is ultimately provenancable, if not analytically at least in descriptive terms. Few suppliers of raw glass in Syro-Palestina and Italy would deliver their semi-manufactured goods to the many secondary workshops throughout the Roman commonwealth who finished the objects. Sometimes recycled glass could be added to the mix, making inoculating morphological variety of finished products over compositional recipes a near impossible task. Considering the time-space frameworks involved, it would be hard to presume that each primary production centre would have been in direct contact with every one of its customers running a secondary glass workshop. The indirect nature of the attested exchange implies a range of networks in which information and goods were exchanged, as it were organically tapping into one another. Typical for pre-industrial economies is how these networks did not function as a free market economy nor as a highly centralised and institutionalised, hierarchical economy, but as something in between. Indeed, these networks were socially embedded relying on 'relational trust, reciprocity, extra-legal sanctions, high commitment among parties and interdependence' (Broekaert 2015, 147). In this sense, time, place, commodities, people and information became interconnected and interdependent, raising the possibility of degrees of connectivity/globalisation/market integration characteristic of the Roman economy (Pitts and Versluys 2015b; Morley 2015).

We tried to explore such basic economic market forces in two recent papers (Brughmans and Poblome 2016a; 2016b), based on the ICRATES-database (Bes and Poblome 2008). The papers respond to a need for more formal computational modelling in order to compare existing conceptual models of the Roman economy, and for evaluating their ability to explain patterns observed in archaeological data. Based on the distribution patterns of the four main types of *sigillata* tablewares in the Roman East (Eastern *sigillata* A, B, C and D), we combined exploratory analysis with computational modelling of hypothetical distribution mechanisms, applying agent-based modelling to examine the effects of different degrees of market integration in the Roman empire. The computational model simulated the structure of social networks between traders and thereby the flow of commercial information and goods. The results suggest that a high degree of market integration leads to generally widely distributed wares, while strong differences in the potential for large-scale production of tablewares resulted in variable distribution patterns among wares, similar to those observed in the archaeological record as collected in the ICRATES-database.

As a result, to a certain degree the economic rationale of market-functioning can also help explain the attested similarities and differences in Roman material culture. Can we actually describe that economic rationale? An earlier paper (Poblome 2013), concluded that pottery was both available and affordable in Roman markets, and that in those markets there was money to be earned for artisans. The concept of opportunity costs was introduced in order to translate each of these artisanal efforts as the value of the best alternative – but not chosen – employment of those means. In antiquity, the obvious alternative employment of means was agriculture in its widest sense. The opportunity costs of artisanal production to subsistence production ranged from very low to high depending on the scale of the combined output of the craftsmen. To be clear, we do not envisage opportunity costs to have determined or steered the socio-cultural aspects of material culture, discussed above. On the contrary, economic, social and cultural trends (along with other aspects not explored in this chapter) worked together to co-constitute material culture. But dependent on historical circumstances, the influence of these respective trends on the constitution of material culture need not always have been equal.

Production lines with mostly local distribution presumably represented very low opportunity costs to subsistence. At this level of production, typologies of artefacts could be idiosyncratic and only very loosely forming part of a *koine*. The spectrum of forms was fairly basic, with types possibly re-occurring in different fabrics. Connectivity was presumably low and the action radius town-countryside limited. In linguistic terms, sub-systems of regional dialects were only mixed to a limited degree. The locally produced wares from Boeotia can serve as a case in point. Local production can now be presumed or demonstrated at Thespiai, Koroneia, Tanagra and Askra. Each city's ceramic repertoire presented both individual forms and traits, as well as a number of shared morphological and decorative characteristics (Fig. 7.6). Understanding the shapes and decorative styles is not straightforward, and the fact that we are dealing with surface survey material without much chronological granulation does not help. The nature and direction of associations with other wares, local or imported, cannot be elucidated, but as a whole the material does indicate that such processes played a role in the constitution of the local products. In any case such relationships, when they existed, did not necessarily follow linear paths, and can be traced geographically only in general morphological terms to south Italian and Greek/Aegean sources (Bes and Poblome in press).

If, however, artisanal production output proportionally increased, for instance as represented by SRSW (Willet and Poblome 2015), the opportunity costs rose through the greater loss of output of subsistence goods. To be clear, growth of the artisanal sector was not endless, but mediated by the lowest level of need for subsistence goods of the associated community and the connectivity resulting from the town-countryside nexus. Really big wares such as Eastern *sigillata* A were therefore logically dependent on large urban centres, as suggested by the agent-based modelling exercise, while the scale of output of each ware resulted from rational economic choices and behaviour. The higher the opportunity costs, the more successful distribution of the ware depended on the opportunities inherent in integrated markets, and the more typologies would cohere towards *koine* in order to appeal to more customers on more markets. By following the *koine* style, producers reduced the risk of their wares lacking appeal and not selling. The range of each *koine* is therefore dependent on its sustaining economic factors, such as the distribution of its inherent opportunity costs, connectivity of the associated production communities and the carrying capacity of the urban/rural framework within which opportunity costs were balanced out. In the minds of its producers and users, LRD referred to their notion of tableware, and this was simultaneously socially and culturally meaningful as explained above, as well as economically co-constituted.

In addition to the socio-cultural processes described above, the notion of oligopoly (Poblome 2013) can help explain, from an economic point of view, why typologies of individual wares constituting a *koine* cohere morphologically. Such typologies are mostly associated with production centres that aim at markets beyond their own locality. This is, for instance, the first century BC evolution John Lund sees in the field of tableware production in the eastern Mediterranean. The archaeological record of the Roman empire indicates that for most material categories typically only a few production centres developed an economic policy to integrate these higher opportunity costs, with concomitant large distribution reach. This is not only the case for the limited amount of widely distributed ceramic tablewares produced in the Roman East, but, as we saw, also for glass. Markets of this nature are considered to function within the framework of oligopoly.

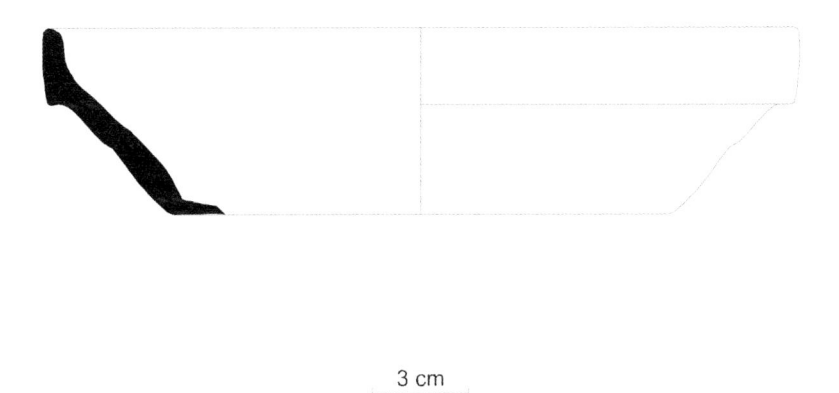

Figure 7.6 Dish with off-set rim typical for Boeotian fabrics with attested production at Koroneia and Thespiai, and morphological parallels in ARSW, Eastern Sigillata *B and Athenian products.*

> Within an oligopoly, the customers are many, preventing them from influencing pricing or the market individually or as a group. The suppliers are few, however, making strategic market behaviour possible, with suppliers needing to take each other's strategic decisions into account. In this case, the policies and products of each supplier are influenced by those of the other suppliers in the same market … In this respect, the degree of competitiveness of oligopolital markets can be situated between so-called perfect global competitive markets and monopolies. By definition, the ancient oligopolital market strove towards stable conditions…with guaranteed sales for the few suppliers in the immediate known environment and satisfied customers with a product of a constant quality level (Poblome 2013, 92).

In this way, culturally defined *koine* and economically circumscribed oligopoly are really flip sides of the same coin. The dialectics between these fields hold the key to the attribution of meaning to patterns of similarity and difference, both in past practices and in present analysis.

Regionalism

This particular coin has three sides, however. The time-space framework in which meaning is constituted for Roman material culture needs to be considered as well. After all, an instituted economy such as the Roman imperial one is always also a political economy and hence involves spatio-temporal strategies of control and power aimed at establishing, maintaining or overturning oligopolistic situations. This discussion revolves not only around the political governance of oligopolistic production and distribution but alsp around the various spatial forms regionalism can take and its relation to socio-cultural expressions. In this final section of the chapter, we discuss political and competitive strategies of regionalisation which could explain the development of a *koine* in an oligopolistic situation, and reflect on the spatial form these could be expressed in.

To begin with, the spatial form of the relation between socio-cultural *faciès géographique* and *koine* will reflect the political organisation which, consciously or not, underpins oligopoly. Space is produced, contested, and transformed through a range of socio-political processes, strategies, and struggles, resulting in an institutionalisation of economic and cultural relations (Elden 2007; Harris and Alatout 2010; Allen 2016). Broadly speaking, the *faciès géographique-koine* nexus could be instituted as either nested hierarchical scales, relating to and fitting into each other like Russian dolls, or as interlocking networks co-determining each other in various directions.

The former interpretation of scale as nested hierarchies of territories, with regions occupying a particular level, implies that those further up the scalar ladder hold power over those further down the hierarchy by being able to constrain the latters' activities (Brenner 2001; Marston *et al.* 2005; Collinge 2006). This is possibly the way in which most Roman emperors approached *res publica*, and imperialism by definition encapsulates such attitudes, but it is difficult to explain the similarity/difference issues of material culture within this framework. The other conceptualisation of power as operating in interlocking networks implies more complex scalarities in which parameters of scope and level are more spatially contingent (Allen 2003; Taylor *et al.* 2010; Agnew 2013). In this interpretation regions are overlapping and porous clusters of variable scope in a spatially discontinuous network (Derudder *et al.* 2003; Derudder and Taylor 2005; Allen and Cochrane 2007; Taylor *et al.* 2013). Clearly, this framework resonates more with how the discussed socio-cultural and economic concepts co-constituted meaning for material culture. In this respect, it is too often taken for granted 'what centralized institutions are capable of bringing about at a distance' (Allen 2004, 22). Territorial scales always have a network dimension to them in the sense that organisation and control are built upon infrastructures, allowing and directing the circulation of humans, things and ideas across space (Collinge 2006; Loopmans 2007; Harris and Alatout 2010). As a result, inequalities exist in the coverage of territories by more or less central powers, or in their particular policies on the ground, which, in the case of the Roman empire, can hardly be described as uniform in time/space/agency.

Importantly, a networked organisation of space is qualitatively different in the sense that it is relational and horizontal, instead of hierarchical and vertical. Relational spaces are spaces of mutuality, of sharing and trading, and hence are capable of stimulating agglomeration economies (Rosenthal and Strange 2004; Combes and Gobillon 2014), which could support connectivity and oligopolistic tendencies even without political control. In economic geography, the clustering of industries has been demonstrated to strengthen the competitive position of the actors involved in a variety of ways, apart from benefiting from local natural advantages such as the availability of natural resources. These advantages deriving from spatial proximity have been classified by Duranton and Puga (2004) as a) sharing of local infrastructure and facilities, input suppliers or workers with similar skills; b) matching between employers and employees (e.g. with specialised skills for specific industries), or buyers and suppliers (e.g. suppliers of specific product types catering for buyers with a specific cultural preference) and c) learning (e.g. about innovative or complex production technologies or business practices). The limits of the archaeological and historical record of the Roman empire do not allow to immediately list how these advantages would have worked in the case of LRD or any other *koine* of Roman material culture for that matter, but a wider comparative exercise amongst and between crafts should represent a promising avenue of research.

Indeed, whereas Classical Economic Geography studies have focused on territorial agglomeration (e.g. in certain cities or regions), more recent theorising about space and distance suggests that such agglomeration advantages do not necessarily rest on direct physical proximity, but rather on network proximity relying on infrastructural accessibility (Fujita and Thisse 2002; Ottaviano 2008; Yu *et al.* 2016). Infrastructures permit the circulation of goods, symbols and ideas in a spatially fragmented way (Graham and Marvin 2001). These infrastructures, which can be material, but also social or institutional (e.g. Simone 2010; Silver 2014), are increasingly regarded as vital mechanisms of clustering, but also of selection and exclusion (Graham and McFarlane 2015), and hence could function as tools to strengthen *koine* and oligopolies on the basis of agglomeration economies and political economic regulation.

In this way, debates in geography on the spatial form of regionalism can be instructive in an archaeological context to map the connection between political economic structure and the culture of everyday life. On the one hand, depending upon the political and economic processes underpinning oligopolistic production and distribution, the spatial distribution of material artefacts expressing a *koine* or *faciès géographique* can take different albeit mostly networked spatial forms. On the other hand, *koine* and oligopoly are potentially connected to spatial agglomeration and its benefits and drawbacks. The spatial distribution of artefacts is hypothesised to be crucially related to the material and social infrastructures through which these artefacts have circulated. Hence, the correlation (or not) of artefact distribution and the material relics of infrastructural networks can point to the specific spatio-temporal institutionalisation of the relation between society, culture, economy, and politics, and to how these co-constituted patterns of similarity and difference in material culture.

Acknowledgments
This research was supported by the Belgian Programme on Interuniversity Poles of Attraction, the Research Fund of the University of Leuven and the Research Foundation Flanders (FWO). We should like to thank the editors for providing structure and inspiration in setting up the workshop and bringing its results to publication. John Lund, Peter Talloen, Tom Brughmans, Rinse Willet, anonymous reviewers and especially the editors provided comments to drafts of this chapter, which very much helped in making the argumentation more inspiring.

Chapter 8

Rethinking standardisation through late antique Sagalassos ceramic production. Tradition, improvisation and fluidity

Elizabeth A. Murphy[*]

Roman red-slipped tablewares – perhaps more than any other ceramic type from the ancient Mediterranean – have been understood as both mass-produced and mass-consumed. A mixture of ubiquity, aesthetics, and the archaeologically intrinsic interest in standardisation has driven and drives our conceptualisation of these glossy red pots (Roberts 1997). These highly-distinctive, well-attributed wares, slotted into refined chronotype schemes, are then subsequently consumed by archaeologists as temporal and cultural signifiers. Yet this unrelenting focus on standardisation in some respects ignores or suppresses variability in the data, particularly as many of these data are derived from the analysis of consumption contexts. Contexts of consumption are very much the success stories of the ancient production world, but in blinkering ourselves to the alternatives – 'failure' included – we risk obscuring the nature of making things in the Roman world. We also tacitly construct a teleology into our reasoning, a 'manifest destiny' from artisan's hand, to consumer's table, to archaeological depot. Knowing the end of the story, we build the data along the way into fine-grained typologies of ITS (Italian *Terra Sigillata*), GTS (Gaulish *Terra Sigillata*), ARS (African Red Slip Ware), SRSW (Sagalassos Red Slip Ware), etc. (Van Oyen 2015 for a more extensive treatment of these processes). Variability, skill (or lack thereof), serendipity, and calamity – everyday functions of an intrinsically messy and unpredictable world – recede into the background. In this recession, we have missed something worth knowing about innovation in material culture.

Considering standardisation and variability (and the forces through which these are constituted) implies a broader interest in how styles, traditions, and material forms are maintained and change. Understanding the drivers for formal

---

[*] Research Center for Anatolian Civilizations, Koç University.

and decorative change in pottery, however, is not straightforward. In the case of late antique ceramics in the eastern Mediterranean, impetus for material culture change has been interpreted from a variety of perspectives – consumer demand associated with changing dining practices and aesthetics (Swift 2007; 2009, 107–14; Hawthorne 1997; Hudson 2006; Vroom 2007, 343); product commissions by landlords (Cockle 1981); or 'imitation' of more widely distributed wares, such as ARS (Hayes 1997, 62–4), or wares crafted from more valuable materials, such as metal plate (Harper 1992, 148). To some degree these are external influences bearing on the production process. Prior to distribution for consumption, however, the products of any workshop were subject to internal selection, culled at the site of manufacture in a process that reflected concerns and standards often specifically related to local community dynamics, traditions, and the lived experience of making. The tablewares manufactured across the eastern Mediterranean present a particular challenge for tracking the works of individual potters, workgroups or workshops, in that they typically lack maker-stamps; but looking more closely at the small-scale social context of production offers some direction.

Between the clay pit and the waste dump there exists a universe of alternative outcomes to sale and consumption, from the minor – vessel collapse on the wheel – to the dramatic – devastating firing explosion in the kiln. These alternatives, and how they are navigated towards an idealised final outcome, necessitate a focus on multiple agencies – human (the potter, the kiln-loader, the clay-digger), but also non-human; how the world of material properties and forces constrains human choice and resists our attempts to impose our will upon it. This chapter explores the capacity for theoretical positions often (but not exclusively) associated with the 'material turn' to enrich our understanding of the journey between wheel – or mould – and kiln. Such approaches provide a means to build alternative narratives that, rather than retroactively imposing a linear series of production steps upon the material that results in a standard artefact type, considers the agencies (both human and non-human) that become entangled through the production process.

It should be stressed that the central assumptions of the 'material turn' are not used here as blinkered ontologies, nor as lenses through which to view the data; an appropriate metaphor in this present context understands them as theoretical tools, picked up to reshape our conceptualisation of Roman making. The goal is less to revolutionise our understanding of ancient Roman wares as consumer goods structured by the vagaries of economics and style, than to highlight the eclectic and the non-standard, the innovative and the experimental; to refocus on the inherently material nature of making material culture, and the challenges therein. This chapter focuses on the context of a single, local, well-established industry during a particular period of its production and for which the available data are appropriately rich; that is, the late antique (fourth–sixth centuries AD) red-slipped ceramic industry at Sagalassos, a city located in the western Taurus mountains of SW Turkey.

Theoretical considerations

Theoretical approaches to craft production have a long history in archaeology. Some have considered development of craft technology and associated technological choices (Lemonnier 1986; 1992), technological systems (Lechtman 1977; Lechtman and Steinberg 1979), and behavioural archaeology (Schiffer 2004). Others have investigated the links between society and craft production through agency or practice theory (Dobres 2000; Flad and Hruby 2007), political economy (Sinopoli 2003), and social identity (Costin and Wright 1998). Yet others have stressed crafting in terms of artisanal skill (Bleed 2008; Apel 2008). In this context, Leroi-Gourhan's (1993) *chaîne opératoire* has provided one of the most prevalent models for the understanding of production process (from raw material, to finished product, and to deposition into the archaeological record), as well as for the understanding of the learned gestures and skilled hand of the craftsperson. The *chaîne opératoire* continues to inform discussions of skill, gesture, form, and process, and finds some intellectual crossover with more recent conversations on embodied practice and socialised learning. Such a linear sequencing of production steps and their associated gestures, however, fails to address the dynamism of slight improvisations in the process of forming and the encountering of fluctuating properties of material that influence and alter form.

More recent theoretical discussions deriving from the so-called 'material culture turn' in archaeology (Hicks 2010) have emphasised approaches to the material world that step away from anthropocentric ontologies based on assumptions of human subjects *vis-à-vis* material objects. Far from a cohesive theoretical movement, however, as Thomas (2015, 1287–9) has noted in his review on the future of archaeological theory, the current 'material turn' has taken a variety of different directions. One such direction has explored materials as dynamic entities in flux (Strang 2014; Bennett 2010, 6–8; Sennett 2008, 214–38; Ingold 2007; 2010; 2012). By emphasising the properties and forces of materials in addition to the embodied practice of the craftsperson engaged in a mediation of form and technique, this strand offers an attractive flexibility in resituating ceramics within their contexts of making. This genre of literature has informed the analysis of the Sagalassos production material; particularly, but not exclusively, the theoretical work by Tim Ingold concerning the *textility of making* (2010).

Some key emphases offer points of departure for the subsequent discussion of ceramic making at Sagalassos. First, from the perspective of specialised production, the artefact is the material manifestation of socialised training and the expression of skilled work practice. The process of learning a craft is a social experience, and its material products embody the negotiation between individual agency and wider cultural expectations. Second, artefact form is never an inevitable outcome of the production process. Ingold stresses that his conception of textility stands in contrast to what he describes as a platonic *hylomorphic model of creation*, which is based on idealised, fixed forms that are conceived for, actualised through, and imposed upon materials (Ingold 2010, 91–3). In this sense, preconceived form or desired attributes simply provide inspiration that inevitably is carried along unanticipated trajectories. This relates to the third point of concern: making, or (to use the terminology of Ingold) textility of making, is based on a forward-looking process that is relational between the spontaneous improvisation of embodied skill and materials of heterogeneous and fluctuating properties (Ingold 2010; 2007). In this way, craft skill is conceived as being neither mechanical execution nor a state of being; rather, skill is a practice overtaken by a 'rhythm between problem solving and problem finding' (Sennett 2008, 9), or a process of *becoming* to use the terminology of process philosophy. Thus, every process of making is a unique negotiation that cannot be *iterative* (simply reproduced and repetitive), but is *itinerative* (similar but variable) (Deleuze and Guattari 2012, as cited in Ingold 2010, 97). Grounded in experience yet encountering ever new circumstances, form therefore emerges from 'tactile and sensuous knowledge of line and surface' (Ingold 2010, 92).

Closer to the Roman world, a similar approach to the material properties in production can be seen in the work of Peter Rockwell (1990). His description of sculpting in the context of Roman-period Aphrodisias (SW Turkey), echoes similar concerns, particularly regarding the material/maker dialogue and the role of the tool as an intermediary negotiator in the production process. Yet the example used by Rockwell concerns what is described as a 'reductive' technological process (Miller 2009, 44), wherein the material is chipped or broken apart but its properties remain geochemically unaltered. This contrasts with what Miller has described as 'transformative' production processes, in which material undergoes alterations of its chemical or micro-structural state (2009, 101). While the conception of an active negotiation with a material's properties should not necessarily be restricted to manipulative techniques of plastic materials (such as pottery forming), they nonetheless involve a more direct, kinetic engagement between human and material that is more easily conceived through these ways of thinking. Yet, in the case of pottery making, the forming of vessels on a wheel or in a mould is only one segment in the production process, and, in the kiln, the same materials engage with a whole new set of forces, which are at this time mediated through heat, kiln structures, and draught. Thus, while this chapter (in keeping with earlier works on textility (Ingold 2010)) primarily focuses on issues of ceramic forming, it should be stressed that this is only a small segment in the trajectories of action that influenced the appearance and form of the ceramics at the production site.

These various theoretical approaches represent recent work at the crossroads of crafts production and material culture studies. For the purposes of this chapter, this arsenal of perspectives will be deployed to confront assumptions of rigid standardisation and mass production that are perhaps more often derived from consumption contexts than from production sites of Roman and late antique red slipped tablewares.

Craft tradition and learning in the Roman World

First, let us socialise the standardised. The production centre, as an archaeological construct, is often defined by similarly classified wares manufactured in a spatially restricted area; it is an imposed category. By contrast, from a social perspective, this same production centre is a community of individuals whose practices are defined and reinforced through traditions of crafting (and in some cases conservative adherence to such tradition may be expressed through what archaeologists conceive to be standardised goods). The archaeological remains of production, in this view, present a blending of socialised expectations developed through training, as well as individual experimentation in dialogue with material forces. Neither innovation nor tradition can be dissociated from one another, as an individual's innovation (*heterodoxy*) invariably references the established tradition (*doxa*) against which it innovates (Bourdieu 1977; for craft see Dobres 2000) and both rely on some form of learning and skill acquisition. Learning both within a contemporaneous community of artisans (horizontal transmission) and through generations of potters (vertical transmission) is contingent on individual actors internalising skill (*habitus*).

For the Roman world, various scenarios of socialised craft learning can be suggested and most relate to multigenerational (i.e. vertical) transmission of knowledge – from household instruction by family members (Saller 2011) to more formal apprenticeship arrangements (Westermann 1914a; 1914b). While it is often difficult to identify businesses run and operated by nuclear families in the archaeological record, apprenticeships, by contrast, are well known due to the legal nature of these agreements between parent and master craftsman that resulted in textual contracts. While most preserved examples derive from Roman and late antique Egypt, these apprenticeship arrangements appear to have been widespread. The contracts describe circumstances in which a parent entrusts their child to an established craftsman, and the youth, typically beginning between the ages of 12 and 14, is then professionally trained in the workplace for a particular occupation (e.g. weavers, scribes) during a specified period of time (Westermann 1914, 310). Details on the actual training accrued by such apprenticeship are rarely outlined in the contracts, but modern ethnographic work describes apprentice-style learning as a means of socialising younger generations into the culture of an occupation (Herzfeld 2003), and human cognition studies describe the development of muscle memory, cognition, and continually refined skill (Malafouris 2008). Emphasising repetitive practice, these learning patterns are very much in keeping with hands-on, apprentice-style training or what Malafouris (2008) might describe as the development of technical know-how.

Beyond the scale of the individual trainee, aggregated workshops of artisans might present other social dynamics regarding the training of new generations of craftspeople that serve to further reinforce community-level crafting culture and traditions. An example outlined by Liu (2016) highlights how apprenticeship arrangements might extend networks of trust among *collegium* (guild) members of a particular craft. Citing the example of a first century *collegium* of weavers in Oxyrhynchus (Egypt), she demonstrates that within the guild, two families, both well established in the local weaving industry and even residing in the same neighbourhood quarter, appear to exchange their children in apprenticeship (2016, 217–24). Such an arrangement might not only strengthen social networks among potentially competing professional families, as Liu rightly notes, but it might also serve to standardise the skills, techniques, and production expectations across workshops within a single production centre.

Unfortunately, examples of apprentice contracts specifically for potting industries are not preserved from the period. Other evidence suggests that the development of technical skill in potting may have begun at an early age in some instances. At Kôm el-Dikka (Egypt), for instance, a sixth century moulded lamp preserved a fingerprint impression within a pressmark that could be aged to a child between 10 and 14 years (Dzierzykray-Rogalski and Gezeszyk 1991), thereby placing a youth of apprenticeship age at work within a local potting industry. Moreover, at other sites in the eastern provinces, local potters are believed to have organised professional associations (*collegia*). Such a case has been proposed in Asia Minor, for instance, at Korykos (Cilicia) from the clustering of professional titles of potters within the funerary landscape of the city (Iacomi 2010, 29; Trombley 1987), and a potter at Myrina (Aiolis) inscribed his *collegium* officer title (*hymnoidoi*) on a terracotta figurine (van Nijf 1997, 167). While the evidence is currently patchy for Roman-period social structures framing ceramicist training, what is available nonetheless suggests that in some circumstances such social collectives were in positions to reinforce intergenerational potting tradition within communities.

Socialising the Sagalassos potting tradition within a nucleated industry

The red slipped tableware industry of Sagalassos presents a very particular social context of production for the Roman world through which to consider these social dynamics of craft learning and transmission. Concentrated in the eastern suburban area of the city and manufacturing a regionally distributed red slipped tableware for over seven centuries, the dozens of manufacturing workshops operating contemporaneously on the fringe of the city represent what Peacock described as a 'nucleated industry' (1982, 9). Conglomerate workshops of this sort are not unique to Sagalassos, and have been identified in the Roman East at sites of pottery production, for instance at Buto, Egypt (Ballet *et al.* 2007) and Zurrabeh, Jordan ('Amr 1991; 'Amr and al-Momani 1999). Such workshop nucleation creates circumstances in which numerous potters were not only competitors, but also neighbours. Consequently, in addition to spatial clustering, other evidence suggests close ties among workshops. Sagalassian potters, for instance, shared resource networks, specialised in manufacturing red slipped tablewares, and used similar technologies. The case of clay resources is of particular interest as the fabric clay was transported over eight kilometres from the valley of Çanaklı (Degryse *et al.* 2008) – the regular supply of which would have required considerable and sustained transportation costs. Also, regional use of these clay sources for pottery can be traced to the Classical and Hellenistic periods (Neyt *et al.* 2012), demonstrating that use of this costly material was deeply embedded in local craft knowledge. This suggests that some features of the Sagalassos craft traditions were maintained within the local potting communities through long-standing, intergenerational learning of the craft, and that these traditions concerned not only ideas on pottery forms, but also knowledge of potting technologies and the properties and availability of regional resources.

Poblome (2016, 392) has discussed the potential role of the extended family in providing such training environments for the Sagalassian potters; yet professional networks can also be considered. Professional associations are known in the epigraphic record of Sagalassos and through the possible identification of a guild meeting house (*schola*) (Poblome 2016, 398–400). While there is no direct evidence specifically for a potters' association, such nucleated workshop scenarios nonetheless provide the social context in which traditions of craft skill might be transmitted through time and between workshops through individual learning and skill acquisition. These contextual factors help to explain much of the standardisation observed and classified archaeologically through the seven centuries of production at the site (late Hellenistic to early Byzantine periods). As is the case with all traditions, however, the Sagalassos potting industry was neither static nor monolithic, and a closer investigation of processes of individual innovation are another part of this craft's story. Small-scale processes of failure, creativity, and innovation within potting traditions represent internal dynamics between trained individuals and wider potting communities at a production site.

Part I. Wheel throwing: improvisation and form

The fourth to sixth centuries AD ceramics presented in this study have been primarily recovered from production contexts in the city's eastern suburbium. Sagalassos' archaeological record presents ample evidence for the reconstruction of its tableware production – workshop structures, kilns, numerous tools, and extensive waste dumps of discarded ceramics and kiln furniture. The quantities of material found at the site can often be staggering, with many thousands of sherds being retrieved from a single production refuse deposit. Its exceptional quantitative and qualitative signatures render the Sagalassos record particularly suitable to explore theoretical perspectives that illuminate the production process in terms of perceptions of form, embodied practice, and material properties. For the purposes of this discussion of ceramic making at Sagalassos, two forming techniques frame the discussion: wheel-throwing (part I) and moulding (part II). The wheel thrown tablewares were primarily analysed from production refuse deposits, while the mould-made wares were recovered from both workshop contexts and production refuse deposits.

The most prevalent means of forming ceramics at Sagalassos was wheel throwing. Indeed, in contrast to a simple dichotomist interaction between matter (passively receiving) and form (actively imposing), potting, and wheel-throwing especially, is a process of making whereby the potter engages 'with materials that have properties of their own and are not necessarily predisposed to fall into the shapes required of them, let alone stay in them indefinitely' (Ingold 2010, 93). The dynamism and versatility of textility is perhaps best viewed archaeologically in instances of failure, when things went wrong and the negotiation between material and form resulted in discard. Such refuse deposits have been a rich testing ground for these concepts, as they demonstrate a multiplicity of techniques used by the potter in response to the material in motion.

Formal divergences and 'failure'

The numerous production dumps scattering the eastern suburbium, and the thousands upon thousands of sherds retrieved from them, attest to the regular failure of the Sagalassian potters and ceramicists in manufacturing marketable wares. Yet not all wasters are alike, and production refuse attests to an array of material-human entanglements that preceded the addition of the waster to the dump. Ethnographic studies reveal typical misfiring rates using simple updraft kilns, of the type used at Sagalassos: twelve- to twenty-percent loss-rates are not uncommon in such cases, with fifty-percent discard occasionally observed with major firing failures (Rice 1987, 173, tab. 6.1). Moreover, the archaeological sample likely under-represents the many itinerations employed by a potter when forming and drying a ceramic object, as many such 'problem pieces' could have been recycled, salvaging the clay through re-saturation and re-prepping. Therefore, the majority of identifiable problems concern misfiring (over- or underfiring, or partial firing) of the vessels in the kiln.

A smaller subset of the production refuse is composed of objects with physical traces of other types of material-human engagement, particularly those between the hand of the potter and the clay body. Moving beyond simple stages of vessel forming, drying, slipping, and firing, these traces demonstrate a series of negotiations outside of a rigid linear progression (from clay extraction to clay preparation, forming, drying, slipping, drying, and firing), and many of these diversions are archaeologically visible as alterations and repairs. Wheel throwing, particularly on a fast-turning potters' wheel, is an especially dynamic scene for the coming together of materials, forces, and embodied maker. Timing and speed are critical in the constantly changing interplay of rotating wet clay body with gesticulations and force of the hand. Malafouris has described the fluency of motion, force, and material: 'The hands are grasping the clay. The fingers, bent slightly following the surface curvature, sense the clay and exchange vital tactile information necessary for a number of crucial decisions that are about to follow in the next few seconds' (2008, 19). Throwing is an inherently tactile performance.

8. Rethinking standardisation through late antique Sagalassos ceramic production 109

This performance of human actors and material properties and forces can be seen at Sagalassos in instances of repair. Sennett describes, 'The simplest way to make a repair is to take something apart, find and fix what's wrong, then restore the object to its former state.' (2008, 200). Yet, when confronting materials in motion, such

Figure 8.1 Example of a clay disc applied across the exterior base of a jug that had been cut too thin. © Sagalassos Archaeological Research Project.

'simple fixes' are not always so straightforward. For instance, several examples of repair holes have been observed in the dataset, where the vessel wall was punctured and a small patch of clay was used to refill the hole (Murphy and Poblome 2017). These are likely instances where a clastic inclusion or air bubble was noticed by the potter. Deposits of cleaned Sagalassos Fabric 1 clay (used for the body of SRSW) have been found in the workshops, giving a sense of the properties of the prepared clay engaged by the potters. The very fine fabric, Sagalassos Fabric 1, has been described as 'detrital clays [...] the main clay minerals present are chlorite and mixed layers chlorite/smectite with smaller amounts of illite and kaolinite' (Degryse and Poblome 2008, 238). However, modern potters might more readily refer to such clays as 'fat' or 'rich', i.e. a clay that is highly plastic yet keeps its shape (Rice 1981, 61). While every prepared batch of clay would have its own specificities and irregularities, in general the properties of this fine, fat clay suggest that an inclusion or void of any significant size would have been perceived by a potter as a bump within the smooth clay wall when rotating on the wheel. Subsequent poking through the wall with a pointed tool would have served to either release the trapped air or to push an inclusion through the wall, leaving a puncture that was plugged with additional clay. Such motions and forces of the wheel, however, resulted in a disjunction between the original thrown surface of the vessel and the smoothing over with secondary clay. Thus, while the properties of the clay being applied and the hand working the clay may be the same, the forces being engaged had changed and resulted in a dimpled, irregular vessel wall that perhaps played a factor in its subsequent discard.

In other instances, repairs have been observed that seem to relate to different types of itinerative processes of production. Several instances of bases cut too thinly from the wheel have been observed, leaving the vessel structurally compromised for its intended use. Additional efforts were subsequently made to apply a second disc of clay across the outer face of the base to reinforce and thicken the surface (Fig. 8.1). These appliqués did not always affix to the surface, however, and became detached during firing. The properties of clay particles, their platelets and hydration, as well as the forces of the wheel and potter were unique actors in the making of both vessel and *appliqué*. Those properties and forces in some cases could not be easily enmeshed, and the transformative changes in the kiln's firing chamber caused the pieces to break apart.

SRSW forms and improvisation
So far, this chapter has discussed how materials in their heterogeneity and their variable malleability resisted or encouraged manipulation, or in other cases drove artisans to alternative choices and down different pathways. It is not the case that the potter imposes ideal forms on inert material, but rather compromise emerges between the goals of the potter and the properties of the material. Just as the processes of making result in dynamic renegotiations with materials and forces, textility

recursively influences the perception of idealised form (e.g. its size range, the subtle differences in rim shape and proportions), thereby rendering the conception of form perpetually dynamic. These improvisations are not related to the consumer function, but rather seem more closely tied to potting traditions and expectations. In this section, these relations are explored through typological variability and improvisation.

Artefact typologies based on idealised form, dimension, decoration, and finishing treatment only roughly capture the variability within its classification, and subtype variability can be extensive; issues which Van Oyen (2015) has investigated between production sites and ware groups (ITS, GTS, etc.). There is also evidence for innovation in intra-ware form and type, however. Indeed, these production dumps often include vessel forms that do not appear in contemporary urban (i.e. consumption) contexts and that do not readily fit into the ideal types outlined by Poblome's SRSW typology (1999). Archaeological typologies are fundamentally modern etic constructs, distilled from messy patterns in datasets, and imposed on materials in ways and according to structures that would have likely been unrecognisable to those that made and used them (Van Oyen 2015). As such, there also exist vessels at the interstices between types, more commonly described as 'hybrid'. The 'odd-ball' sherd or the typological variant occurs in the ceramic analysis of any site, either productive or consuming. When considered in the context of making, their occurrence is more prevalent and suggests a much greater range of experimentation and innovation taking place in the Sagalassos workshops than that which is represented in consumption contexts in the city. What is striking, however, is not the fact that outliers and variants are so common, but how they vary from other 'standard' types.

Formal characteristics
Taking a single such example, the profile shown in Fig. 8.2 demonstrates a large open bowl or plate form. In the general SRSW typology (Poblome 1999), this form would fall into the 1B000 or perhaps the 1C000 class, with 1 designating the fabric group (Sagalassos fabric 1), B and C designating the general functional category (bowl and plate, respectively), and 000 indicating an unknown morphology within the subtype class. For all intents and purposes, this artefact would be lost in the dataset as quantitatively insignificant (and therefore insignificant to the broader social patterning being tracked). The undoubted merits of quantified analyses notwithstanding, if we undertake a closer evaluation of the 000 class, we can begin to see this object in a wider context of technical versatility and formal innovation among potters working within a potting tradition. Indeed, the grooving of the outer rim face is suggestive of the 1B220-type, the shallow sloping wall is suggestive of a 1C140 plate, and the inner groove on the wall is reminiscent of a 1C180 plate. Such a vessel, from the perspective of an archaeologically retro-fit typology, therefore falls between types, representing a recombination of rim shapes, wall curvatures, and base treatments associated with types that are more widely recognised and made in greater frequency across the production site.

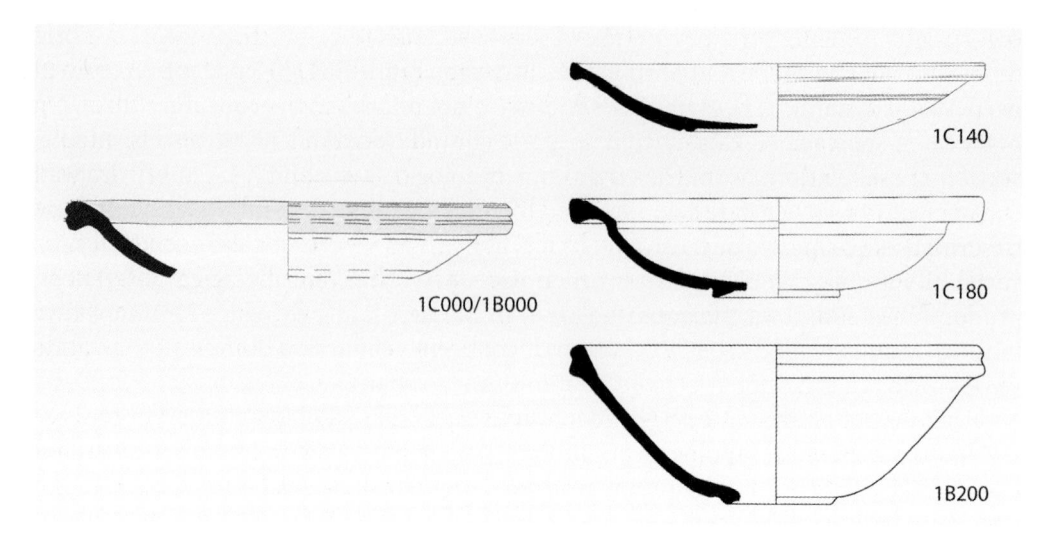

Figure 8.2 Drawings of an 'anomalous' SRSW 1C000/1B000 form, demonstrating similarities to 1C140, 1C180, and 1B220 forms.

While the typological segmentation of these features creates a sort of 'hybrid' form, by reconsidering this vessel in the context of textility and its forward-looking perspective on making, this vessel becomes the embodiment of versatility and improvisation. Rather than representing discrete building elements (rim, wall, base), textility highlights that in negotiating a widely-splayed wall, the rim must be shaped on the wheel with additional care to prevent collapse, particularly when the interior ridge was then cut into the lower wall, thinning it further. In this process, the wheel must be adjusted to differing speeds, and the tool and the hand must be applied with differing forces. Every force and every manipulative gesture is redefined, perhaps based on experience in making the so-called 1C140s, 1C180s, and 1B220s with this clay, yet the combination of each action and reaction would result in an entirely unique negotiation of materials and forces. In this case, textility highlights the skill, risk, and improvisation involved in innovative processes of making too often glossed over by catch-all typological categories.

Intra-form variability
At Sagalassos, other improvisations can also be found within the well-established morphological classes. The reconceptualisation of form through and with different materials with variable properties could result in other types of improvisation. For instance, beginning in the fourth century AD, a coaseware *lekane* form (typological designations 2F100, 2F110, and 2F120; Degeest 2000, 137–8, 361–2, fig. 126–9) began to be made in the workshops. These high-walled, coarseware vessels demonstrate close parallels to the rim shapes of similar types of SRSW kraters (typological

designations 1F140, 1F160, 1F170; Poblome 1999, 168–9, 172–5, fig. 78, 80–1) being made concurrently. Yet the large clastic inclusions in the clay (Sagalassos Fabric 2) used to make these coarsewares would have ripped the hands of a potter throwing on a wheel. Instead, the base and walls of the containers were built up on a turntable, the upper wall and rim were then quickly turned or thrown, and then the entire wall surface was smoothed on the wheel. In this way, the vessels display what might be described as composite or hybrid technical execution, whereby preconceived forms, while maintaining features that are reminiscent of other morphological references, are redefined and renegotiated with materials (namely clay) with differing properties that were engaged by the potter through different means with different strategies of making.

This discussion has attempted to highlight this aspect of fluidity in order to offer reflections on issues of standardisation, form, and artefact typologies. These divergent trajectories might be interpreted too readily as morphological 'hybrids', sub-type variants, or alternate fabrics, yet when conceived within the process of textility, those examples that too easily fall into the interstices of quantified typological analysis become the embodiment of material and technical improvisation and formal experimentation. In some cases, such as that of the 'hybrid' dish described above, the form never became popular and is known only from its discovery in the production dumps of the workshops. Yet, in other instances (such as the large coarseware containers), the use of these vessel forms became increasingly widespread at the site until the mid-sixth century AD. While the driving factors influencing why one variant might be adopted, yet another might not, are poorly understood at Sagalassos, both examples highlight similar processes of innovation within a well-established potting tradition.

Part II. Moulded wares: same, same, same?

Wheel throwing was only one technique of ceramic forming employed in the Sagalassos workshops, and in this section another forming technique is explored: late antique moulded ware production. Moulding offers an important contrast to the wheel-throwing discussion, as it involves an entirely different set of forces, temporality, and material engagement.

With the manufacture of relief decorated moulded wares, the implications for applying conceptual approaches such as Ingold's textility are particularly significant, as moulding concerns the reproduction of not only morphological artefact form, but also imagery with its own stylistic and symbolic implications. Thus, decisions were made not only concerning whether to produce a jug or a cup form, but also regarding which imagery was deemed appropriate (or at least marketable). As will be demonstrated in this section, the selection of object form and representational motifs and imagery was often negotiated by the properties of the materials and forces being engaged and the traditions in object form and embodied skill of the maker. Each of these factors influenced the choices by actors within the workshops (e.g. the types of imagery represented, the forms on which they appear, and their methods of production).

In addition to the typical refuse retrieved across the site, mould-made wares have also been well-studied in their workshop contexts. An entire workshop complex manufacturing these wares has been excavated in the eastern suburbium (Murphy and Poblome 2016). This complex has provided a significant amount and broad range of material, as well as a clearer picture of the context of their production. By the late antique period (particularly by the first half of the sixth century AD) this workshop complex comprised four discrete workshop units, all producing moulded and stamped red slipped ceramics. Although tightly built together and sharing abutting walls, each workshop unit in the complex appears to have been provisioned with a full suite of facilities and infrastructure to support the entire production cycle. The ceramics represent a cross-section of mould-made wares of the period that can be classified into four functional classes – figurines, oil lamps, cups, and juglets/*oinophoroi*. The common feature uniting all ceramic objects produced in the workshop complex is manufacturing technique (particularly the use of ceramic moulds), while form, function, and sets of iconography seem to have been of (relatively) secondary importance in terms of the workshop repertoire.

Mould-making: a 'standardised' practice?

It is important to begin this conversation by disentangling the concept of standardisation from the technicalities of mould forming. In archaeology, mould-made production has often been conceived as a means of standardisation – standardisation of both form and imagery. It has effectively been perceived as a method of mass-producing objects more efficiently by churning out the same, same, same (Roberts 1997, 190). Although the use of the mould in producing ceramic objects does result in the repetition of a basic form at some level, this is only part of the story.

Moulds and mould-making are not singular processes and can involve a variety of types and techniques. As evidenced in the workshop materials, different techniques were employed in making the moulds (i.e. hand-carved moulds, stamped blank-moulds, *surmoulage*-impressed moulds); different mould-making techniques were employed (i.e. one-part versus two-part moulds); and some moulded objects required the application of additional vessel parts (i.e. pulled handles and wheel-thrown necks). These production techniques presented different limitations and opportunities for variation and experimentation in both form and decoration, even within a single workshop.

All moulds and all stamps found at Sagalassos thus far are made from the same local clay as was used for SRSW (Sagalassos Fabric 1). It is assumed, therefore, that the moulds were all manufactured within the workshops, suggesting two phases of negotiation: (1) in the making of the mould (i.e. negotiation between maker, stamps,

8. Rethinking standardisation through late antique Sagalassos ceramic production 115

handtools, and clay) and (2) in the making of moulded objects (i.e. negotiation between maker, mould, scraping handtool, and clay); Simondon describes this dual process in the context of brick-making as '*demi-châines de transformations*' (Simondon 2005, 41–2, as cited in Ingold 2012, 433). Through these negotiations, improvisation and experimentation can occur, resulting in innumerable variations that reflect an incredible degree of versatility in the formal conception and technical execution of pottery making.

Improvisation occurred in the use of moulds in vessel forming. In these instances, the moulds were creatively readapted or redesigned in anticipation of different vessel forms. The vessels (as opposed to other types of moulded objects, such as lamps or figurines) present the use of similar techniques that are tweaked for different shapes. For instance, two-part moulds appear in both top-bottom (horizontally seamed juglets) and side-to-side (vertically seamed *oinophoroi*) configurations even within the same workshop. One side of a two-part mould might also be used to manufacture a series of different vessel forms. For instance, vessels depicting a bearded smiling face appear in two forms – either as a small juglet or a cup. When used for juglets (a closed vessel shape), two-part moulds with a vertical seam were pressed together to make the body of the vessel. The same moulds, however, were also used singularly as the rounded base of a small cup (an open vessel shape) (Fig. 8.3). In contrast to

Figure 8.3 Vessel mould depicting a smiling face (left) and moulded cup formed in a similar mould (right). The notch in the upper edge of the mould was used to cut the neck-hole for juglet forms. © Sagalassos Archaeological Research Project.

the juglet varieties, these cups were typically thrown on a wheel into the mould in a 'jolley' configuration, as evidenced by the interior wheelmarks and slip application, the thrown rim, and an occasional hook for hanging. While more often considered as a single means of manufacturing standardised forms, this case presents different means of making moulds, as well as several alternative uses from the originally conceived form of the mould.

Blanks and stamps: decoration and actors
In the case of juglets and *oinophoroi* as well each mould was a unique production: a 'blank' mould was thrown on a wheel and then impressed by hand-carved stamps. This production process afforded re-combinations of individual decorative and iconographic elements that could be creatively employed to produce different types of representation and could involve the assemblage of a variety of actors – both human and nonhuman.

Tracking such stamp impressions within the corpus of workshop materials offers a sense of the relationships between the workshops in the complex. For instance, these combinations of stamps were not restricted to a single workshop unit. Indeed, it seems that, despite the fact that each workshop was capable of functioning as a totally independent production unit in terms of the built environment and production infrastructure, some degree of collaboration was taking place among workshops in this production process (Murphy and Poblome 2016). In fact, in some cases, the figural and patterned stamps used on *oinophoroi* were likely manufactured in the workshops and appear to have been shared between workshops, as matches between stamps and stamp impressions on moulds have been identified between the work units, thereby extending the network of toolsets and material culture beyond a single architectural unit and workgroup. Collaboration between work units may have served to reinforce the use of certain types of production practice and iconographic repertoire, but it would have also offered a more diverse set of uniquely carved stamp motifs to the individual potter. In this way, the network of participants served to reinforce a level of consistency in the certain iconographic renderings on these objects.

While the sharing of stamps within and beyond the workplace suggests a fluid movement of some types of tools, the use of individual moulds, however, highlights a much more personal relationship between potters and their repertoire. For instance, a set of four lamp moulds, all of similar basic circular lamp form, was found on the floor of one room of the moulded-wares workshop complex (Fig. 8.4). Each of the circular lamp moulds, however, was then incised or impressed by hand with geometric designs or palm branches. Following traditional archaeological artefact typologies, it is tempting to simply consider the products of this group as being based on a fundamental 'archetype' morphological form (Bailey 1997, 168–9), with type-variants defined by slight decorative detailing (Fig. 8.5). Yet these variants also appear to have been perceived as different formal types by the potters, as symbols and letters were incised into the backside of the mould. The use of these 'tags'

8. Rethinking standardisation through late antique Sagalassos ceramic production 117

likely offered a shorthand to identify individual moulds, conceivably with their own properties and particularities. It might also be possible to suggest that these tags are tied to individual potters, as similar markings occur on other types of tools in the workshops, such as potters' rib scrapers and a pottery wheel fragment (Murphy and Poblome 2012, 206, fig. 3f). When considered within the broader corpus of workshop materials, the reoccurring personalisation of specific types of tools seems to have served to demarcate private implements within the larger workshop.

Thus, within the context of the workplace, the significance given to morphological variation might be seen in relation not only to the individual properties of the moulds, but also to individual potters who claimed their own tools – and, consequently, in the

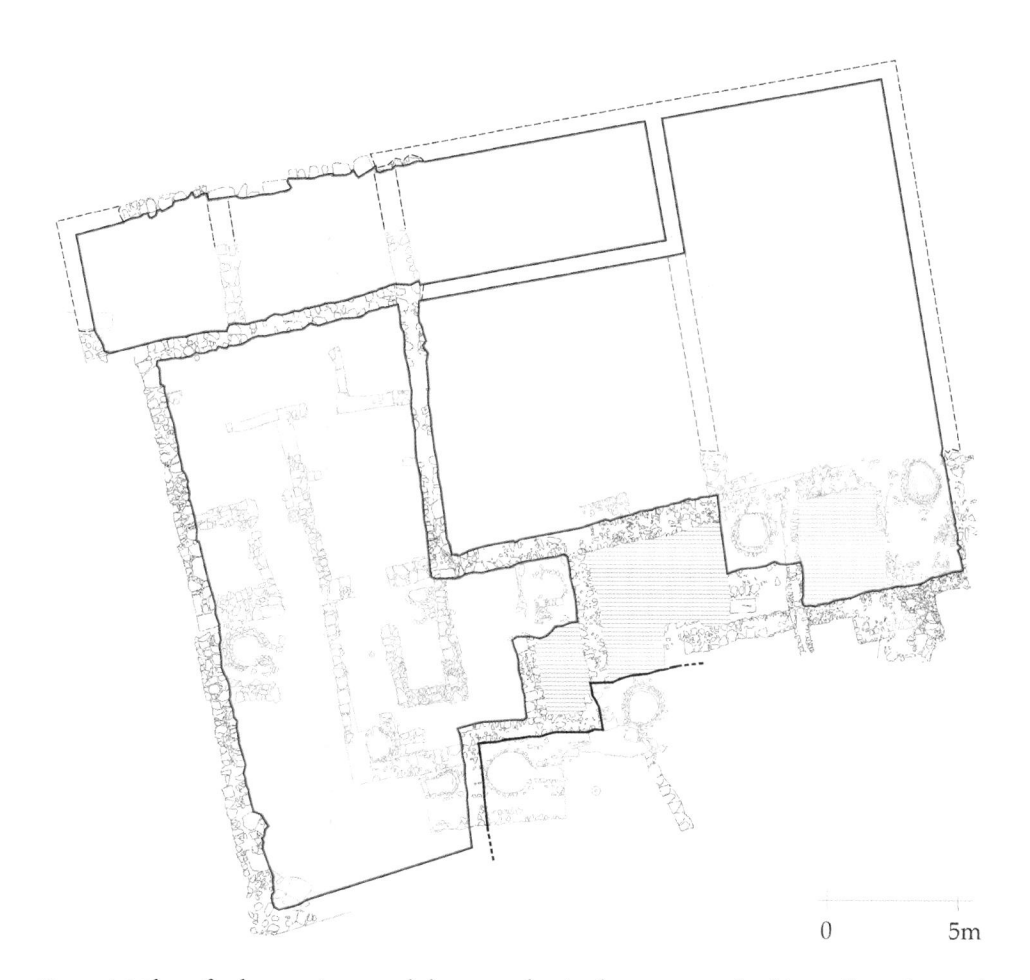

Figure 8.4 Plan of a late antique workshop complex in the eastern suburbium of Sagalassos that manufactured moulded wares. The north-east areas of the complex have been only partially excavated, and the dotted lines indicate walls inferred from geophysical prospections.

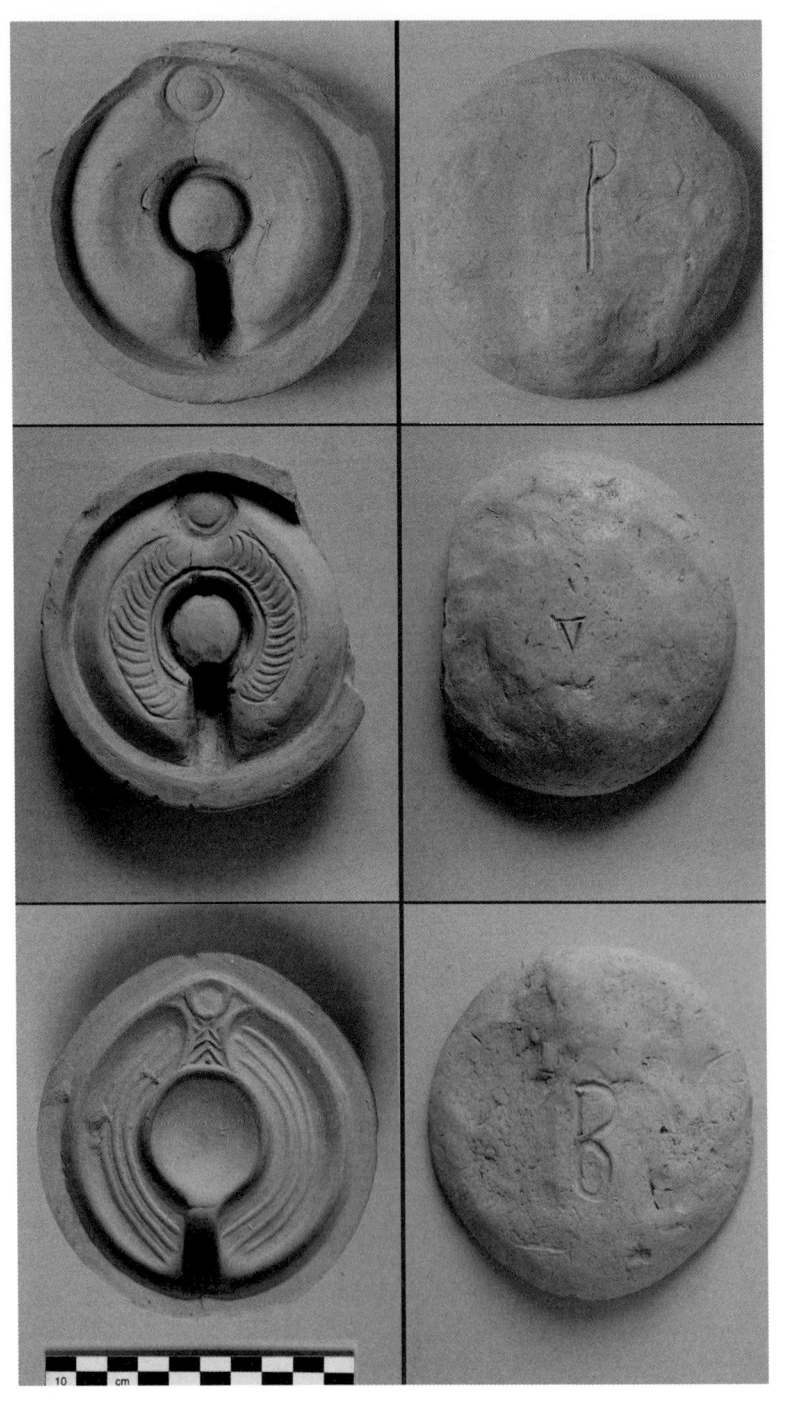

Figure 8.5 Examples of three lamp moulds found on the floor of a workshop. Interior of the mould (left). Exterior of the mould with incised tag (right). © Sagalassos Archaeological Research Project.

case of moulds, their own product repertoire within the workplace. This reconstruction situates the materials in relation to human actors, collective and individual, and demonstrates that in these *demi-châines de transformations* (i.e. making the mould versus making the object) different human and non-human agents were relationally assembled.

Temporality of moulds and figurine making
A primary tenet of Ingold's textility maintains that materials are not static; properties of materials, both the clay and the tools acting as mediators, are in flux. This is perhaps most notable through the surface wear of moulds. As noted previously, the moulds of *oinophoroi*, juglets, lamps, and figurines were made of fine clay (Sagalassos Fabric 1), which lent itself to detailed impressions, but also wore relatively quickly and dried slowly when compared with other types of moulds, such as stone or plaster (Bailey 1997, 168–9). More commonly described in terms of a mould-series, the incremental wear on moulds and use of *surmoulage* techniques (to reproduce an ever-smaller version of the mould from a finished object) can track the lifecycles of the moulds and phases of workshop production.

The evidence from the moulded wares workshops, however, demonstrates a much more complex temporality of moulds that were perpetually undergoing a gradual attrition of their surface through repeated abrasions by wet clay, i.e. what Ingold might describe as 'matter flow' (Ingold 2010, 94). Engaging with these transformations in matter, the potters seem to have adapted their production strategies at different times in the lifecycle of the moulds. Working with dynamic materials, in some cases the potter can be seen to have taken additional steps after removing the impressed ceramic form from the mould in an attempt to clarify its appearance and details. This entanglement is perhaps best evidenced in figurine production. Figurines were a common type of moulded object manufactured in the Sagalassos workshops during the late antique period. A range of animals, including dogs and horses, have been recovered, but the majority of the figurines depict an armed rider on horseback. The rider figurine was formed in a single, frontal mould while the horse is more commonly formed in a two-part mould. Both were composed of solid clay and subsequently red-slipped in the same manner as the SRSW vessels.

While manufactured in the same materials as the vessels and formed in moulds of similar type, figurines, by contrast, present different types of negotiation between material properties and the ceramicist, which involves the working (and reworking) of, not only the figures, but also the details of their appearance, through pinching, incising, stamping, and *appliqué*. For instance, trappings might be incised into the head of the horse (Fig. 8.6d–e), small circular stamps might be impressed into the chest of the rider, or the blurred face of the rider might be pinched into shape to better define the nose and chin (Fig. 8.6b–c). In other cases, attributes were applied with additional pieces of clay, such as an additional arm, a helmet, or shield. These demonstrate a conscious manipulation of the figurine from the original impression in order to alter or enhance details diminished throughout the life of the mould.

The reworking of the figurines focused on certain attributes and details, in particular defining the armour and faces of the soldiers, as well as the trappings of the horse. These themes of a horse and armed bearded rider also appear on other items manufactured in the same workshops and may represent a shared imagery. For instance, the head cups and juglets (which were used to produce both drinking cups and *oinophoroi*) share similar iconographic details of headgear with many of the horse and rider figurines (Talloen 2011; Talloen and Poblome 2005). In several cases the

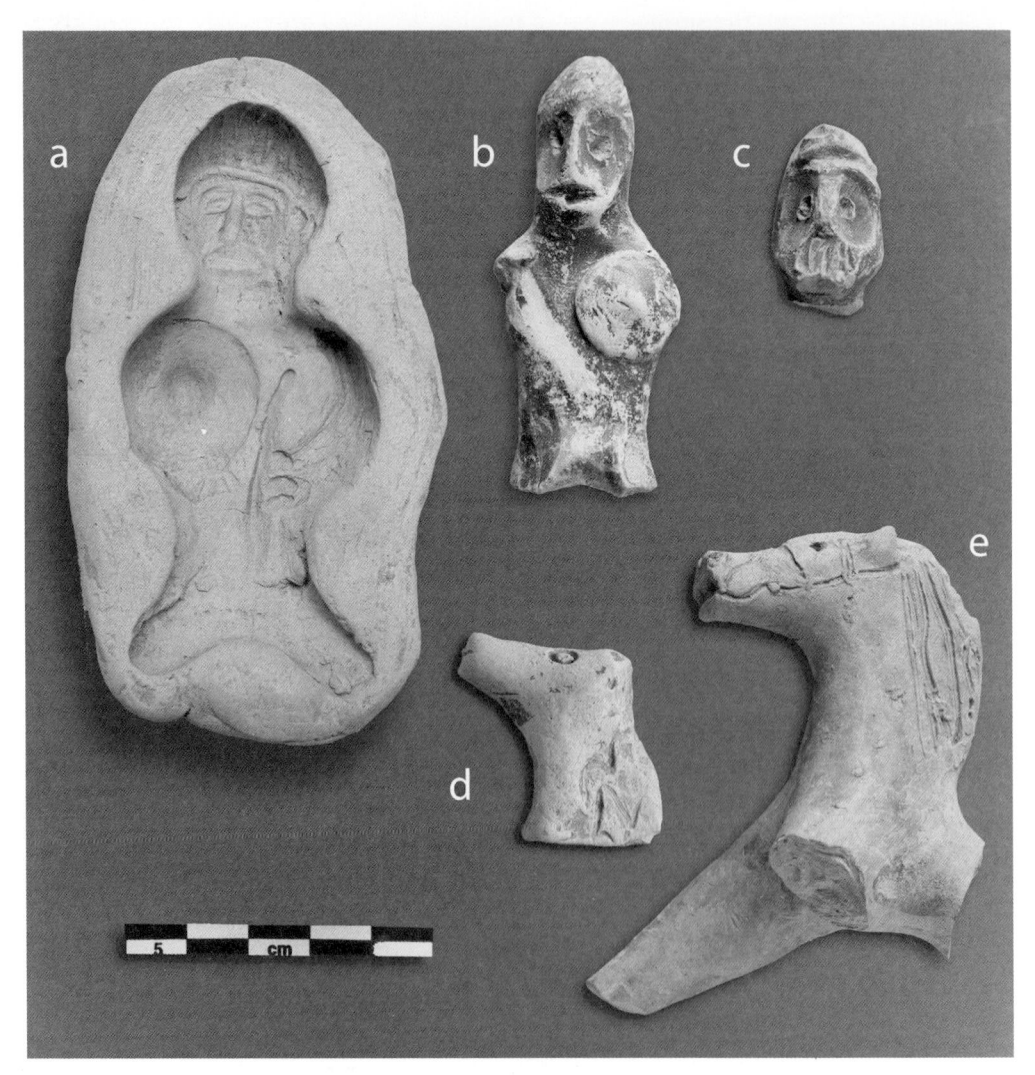

Figure 8.6 Mould and figurines with post-moulding adaptations: figurine mould (a), rider figurines with pinched faces and incised detailing (b-c), and horse figurines with stamped and incised detailing (d-e). © Sagalassos Archaeological Research Project.

headgear on the figurines was enhanced by secondary applications after the figurine was removed from the mould (Fig. 8.7), suggesting these details were important to the overall image represented. Likewise, *oinophoroi* decorated with relief images of warriors and hunters (in some cases on horseback) brandish similar weapons and armour as those depicted on the figurines.

It thus seems that the workshops employed similar sets of specialised visual references that cross-cut and in some ways superseded artefact functionality or basic morphology, but were also often renegotiated to the realities of working with different types of moulds with their own material properties. Moreover, when wearing of the mould's face failed to provide such details, additional steps were taken in an attempt to clarify what seem to have been central features to the figure. Yet, even in these cases, the materials were not always so easily manipulated, and several instances of what might be considered production failure with the appliqué becoming detached from the figure have also been noted, as evidenced in the case of the conical cap of a rider (Fig. 8.7). Moulding a vessel or a figurine into shape implies control; control over the manipulation of materials and control over the form they will take. Yet in all stages of this moulding process, different individuals, collectives of individuals, tools, and materials were assembled in the making of a multiplicity of images that were worked and then reworked to reference entangled imagery and forms, and resulted in divergent pathways of making that can be described as anything but the same, same, same.

Figure 8.7 Examples of post-moulding appliqués: rider figurine wearing an appliqué helmet (left) and figurine helmet that popped off during firing (right). © Sagalassos Archaeological Research Project.

Conclusion

The approach followed in this chapter offers insights into the relationship between learned traditions within craft communities and individual innovation by closely studying small-scale processes of making. In the case of late antique Sagalassos, a local community and its social dynamics sustained a craft tradition for several centuries, during which time generations of potters learned craft skills to manipulate and work with local clays. Despite wider expectations of pottery form and finishing, innovation was ongoing and dynamic. In some cases, formal innovations referenced other trends within the tradition, for instance recombining rim, wall, and base in new ways. In other cases, innovation was expressed in creative ways employing techniques or motifs typically used in the making of other types of product. These examples highlight the dynamic processes of heterodoxic innovation and doxic tradition present in any such ware group. By looking at how different actors (human and nonhuman) were assembled and how materials, forces, and makers were engaged in fluid and improvisational action in the textility of making, the overall picture that emerges is one of creativity, adaptation, and innovation that transcends simple categories of production techniques, operational sequences, artefact typologies, materials, and individuals. Throughout, itinerative processes can be observed by which individuals and collectives of potters came together and engaged material properties and forces in the action of making. Moving from past hylomorphic models of form to dynamic interplays of textility opens an interpretive framework for understanding the nuances and particularities of production assemblages that differ in so many respects from preconceived expectations of standardisation and the 'success stories' of consumption assemblages.

Acknowledgements

This research was supported by the Sagalassos Archaeological Research Project, a Belgian American Education Foundation Research Fellowship, and a Visiting Research Fellowship from the Institute for the Study of the Ancient World, New York University. Many thanks to Tom Leppard and Jeroen Poblome, who offered comments on earlier drafts of this chapter, to Bernard Knapp for allowing me to see an advanced copy of a manuscript that was particularly relevant to this topic, to the anonymous reviewers of the volume for their thoughtful edits and insights, and to Astrid Van Oyen and Martin Pitts for their kind invitation to take part in this volume and their especially helpful suggestions. All errors are, however, the fault of the author.

Chapter 9

Discussion. Material standards

Robin Osborne[*]

Why standardise? The advantages of standardisation are to us so patent, that the question hardly seems worth asking. But it needs to be asked since understanding the archaeology of Rome and the Mediterranean down to 200 BC is impossible unless we understand why one might not standardise, or might even resist standardisation. Standardisation enables people to have some confidence that the (class of) action or object in question reproduces in all essentials some other action or object. If the other action or object did something, this object that meets its standards will do the same. Standardisation is, therefore, good if one needs to be confident that the situation in which one finds oneself today reproduces the situation which has been or could be experienced at another time or in another place or by another (standardised) person. Standardised weights and standardised measures of value guarantee that the price per unit weight of a standardised commodity in a particular place and at a particular time will be the same. Standardised language guarantees that the identical sounds made, or words written, in the same place and at the same time by one person mean the same as those sounds made or words written by another person.

As my qualification 'in the same place and at the same time' indicates, perfect standardisation is impossible. Standardised language does not prevent the same words being taken to mean different things by different people at the same time or by the same people at different times. Standardised forms may carry different affordances because they were made at different times and places. Standardised actions regularly move from indicating that someone is au fait with the latest practices to indicating that someone is out of date. The ideal of standardisation in every respect is practically unattainable. Nevertheless, however imperfect standardisation may be, standardisation of forms and standardisation of practices facilitate exchanges of all sorts, material and immaterial, that would not be possible, or not be as easy were forms and practices not standardised.

---
[*] Faculty of Classics, University of Cambridge.

Since it is hard to think that since the creation of Eve there has ever been a human being who did not desire to effect exchange of one sort or another (words, goods) with another human being, measures that facilitate exchange might be assumed to be an unalloyed good – until we recall the apple in the Garden of Eden and that it is equally unlikely that there has ever been a human being who did not desire to prevent exchange of one sort or another with another human being. The need for secrecy follows close on the heels of the possibility of communication, the desire for differential sharing close on the heels of the first exchange of goods. The social and economic advantages of standardisation always stand in the face of the social and political advantages of non-standardisation.

The discussions of pottery in the eastern Roman empire by Poblome, Özden and Loopmans and by Murphy give us rich insights into the means by which and the extent to which standardisation was achieved and what a cultural *koine* might look like; but as Jiménez highlights the formation of a cultural *koine* was not the necessary result of cultural contact, and properly to understand the role that material standards play we need to understand not simply what happens within a cultural *koine* but the circumstance in which a cultural *koine* is created. In what follows I look further at the case of Rome, which for a very long period evidently rated the advantages of standardisation with the wider central Mediterranean world not worth having.

We owe a lot to the refusal of the Romans to standardise. Like the fact that we do not write in the Greek alphabet. The tradition recorded by Tacitus (*Annals* 11.24) has the Etruscans taught the art of writing by Demaratus of Corinth, who settled at Tarquinia (and was the father of Tarquinius Priscus, the fifth of the seven kings of Rome). Tacitus' story has got garbled in some respects, and the Latins may have acquired their alphabet directly from the Greeks, but the important feature is that neither Etruscans nor Latins took over exactly the Greek alphabet they encountered. They took the principle, and they took most of the letters, but early Etruscan alphabets are unstable in their precise letter-forms and they and the Latin alphabet, though in general closest to Euboian scripts, crucially take over the crescent gamma (i.e. letter 'c') from Corinthian (Cornell 1995, 103–5, 124; Cristofani 1979, 381). The Latin alphabet further adopts various Greek letters not used by the Etruscans, but uses some of them, notably 'x', to represent different phonetic values from those carried by the Greek equivalents. The universal is particularised. The idea of standard representation of phonetic values is adopted, but the particular standard offered is rejected.

The alphabet is worth dwelling on briefly because the whole significance of an alphabet is that it enables communication. Here, one might think, is an area where standardisation has clear advantages. What more confusing than to take signs from an alphabet used by others but assign new phonetic value to them? But of course that is what the Greeks themselves had done in adopting the letters used by the Phoenicians, and that again is what the speakers of Latin do. The implication must be that the communication enabled by the alphabet was to be local, and only local, even that barriers to communication beyond the locality were desired. This is perhaps less surprising given that being able to read the writing is of little use to those who do not know the language that is written: while languages remain distinct, the pressures to standardise the alphabet used are reduced. Rome and Latium were far from being alone in not adopting a standardised alphabet. Even within the Greek world, where local distinctions in language were slight enough not to impede mutual intelligibility, it was not until late in the Classical period that alphabets became standardised.

The absence of any desire simply to take over their alphabet from the Greeks from whom they acquired the idea of writing goes closely with a Roman lack of interest in copying Greek material culture. Not only has a wide range of Greek pottery dating to the second half of the eighth century been excavated from the Sant'Omobono sanctuary in Rome – Euboean, Cycladic, Corinthian – but Greek potters seem to have set up in Rome or perhaps nearby in Veii before 700 BC (Holloway 1994, 166–7). Other sites in Latium are equally well connected to the Greek world – above all Gabii (modern Osteria dell'Osa) and Castel di Decima. There is no reason to think that Greek material culture and Greek ideas were any less familiar in archaic Rome than they were among the Etruscans, whose own products display a detailed familiarity with Greek mythology from the seventh century on, and perhaps even a particular familiarity with the *Odyssey* (Snodgrass 1996, 96; True and Hamma 1994, 182–7). Nevertheless, while the material culture of archaic Rome and Latium shows many signs of awareness of Greek as well as of Etruscan traditions, in a pattern that will later be repeated across the Roman empire, it constantly modifies and adapts those traditions, rather than simply imitating them. This is visible, for instance, in the series of miniature *kouroi* from the votive deposit beneath the *Lapis Niger* and at Gabii (Cristofani 1990, 3.1.23–29, 7.3.1–20). Within the Greek world miniature *kouroi* are found only on the southeastern fringes – in Knidos, Rhodes, Cyprus and Naukratis; the much smaller Roman tradition (ht. 6–8 cm rather than 15 cm) is quite independent (cf. Bartman 1992, 34). It is visible too in the use of the satyr in architectural terracottas – a familiar figure put to novel use (Cristofani 1990, 3.4.1, 3.6.1, 4.1.4, 8.4.3, 8.5.2, 9.3.4, 9.6.71, 10.1.4) – or in the replaying of the bull-headed man iconography of the minotaur outside the context of the story of Theseus (Cristofani 1990, 3.2.13). This is in contrast to Etruscan attempts to imitate, as well as import, very large quantities of Corinthian pottery and Athenian black- and red-figure pottery. Particular qualities that are universalised here, as the general appearance but not the detailed iconography of the Greek pottery is imitated, identify the standards that it was felt important to match.

The much discussed 'Hellenisation' of Rome from around 200 BC (Wallace-Hadrill 2008), aspects of which are explored by Jiménez, is not a story of Rome's discovery of the Greek world, for the Romans had discovered the Greek world at least half a millennium earlier, it is the story of how Rome and Italy came to embrace, rather than to resist, standardisation with the central and eastern Mediterranean. From this point on, being seen to emulate Greek culture was a potential source of admiration, as is most obvious in Latin literature with its ever-expanding embrace of the various genres of Greek literature. But it is apparent also in artistic styles and even in pottery, where, as Jiménez points out, the *terra sigillata* tradition has firm Greek foundations and sells a variation on a Greek product, the so-called 'Megarian bowls'.

The question of what had happened to make standardisation a desirable goal for the Romans is a crucial one for this volume and its aim to get beyond instrumentalism and representation, and Jiménez rightly stresses the role of archaeological categorisation of material in this. It is easy to tell the story of standardisation as a story about politics and identity, where standardisation essentially follows empire, and the central Italian city-state which had long striven to maintain a distinct identity realises that not only is such a distinct identity no longer needed, it stands in the way of making the empire work. This simply assumes that archaeological classifications map onto Roman categorisations, but it is the process by which things are put in the same category that is part of the story of standardisation in the first place. Given political unification, standardisation of categories was the crucial first step to increasing the profits of empire by lowering transaction costs and by creating a sense of underlying cultural unity – all the stronger for this being the culture of the conquered, not of the conqueror – that would discourage bids to renew independence. But for Greeks newly caught up in empire, standardisation was equally attractive; not only did the adoption of their cultural products as standard offer prospects of economic gain, it also offered a route to power. If we tell the story like this, then material culture becomes instrumental in achieving political and economic ends and standardisation comes to represent a particular socio-political identity at both the individual and collective level.

Can we, and should we, tell the story in a way that gets beyond representation and instrumentalism? The chapters by Poblome, Özden and Loopmans and by Murphy in this section have explored how standardisation works within the world of the early principate, a world that has long been expected to have been standardised. They both show the extent and the limits of 'local' standardisation, that is of standardisation within the products of the potteries in a single place, and the way in which broad standardisation can be driven by a set of stylistic preferences that are widely shared and may exist independent of any material object substantially realising them. In this long-standardised world, where standardised objects are the norm, the material environment, from the town plan and architecture through to the pots and coins, entangles individuals in such a way that any variations around the standard potentially reveal more about the user of the object than the user might wish.

It is here that the impossibility of total standardisation becomes crucial. As Jiménez points out, 'The type is created through the selection of certain characteristics that are crucial in contrast with others that are accessory', that is types are conventional. But the conventions are never fixed and always subject to negotiation and change – the attractions of Wallace-Hadrill's image of standardisation as an organic process must not be allowed to obscure this. Given the differences between human individuals and groups, both inherited and constantly being generated, any 'standardised' action or item may be turned into an outlier, because in particular circumstances or by particular groups or individuals additional traits are considered crucial. We might speculate that, for instance, those possessing a skilled eye could detect the pot described by Murphy which had had inclusions removed and patches inserted, and might form a (low) view of those who purchased such 'seconds'. Objects and expressions which pushed at the boundaries of a cultural *koine* had the potential to present, or represent, an individual or indeed a whole community as failing to conform, in a way that might signal, for example, 'rusticity' or 'hyper-urbanity' – either of which might, in different circumstances, be admired or derided. In part, the material environment does things to the individual and the group because it represents them to others in a particular way, but equally it does things to them because it has shaped their own *habitus* – and indeed their *doxa*, the system of classification producing so perfect a 'correspondence between the objective order and the subjective principles of organization' that 'the natural and social world appear as self-evident' (Bourdieu 1977, 164).

In the world of the third and second centuries BC, where standardisation is only newly being adopted, what a thing does, its material agency, is particularly hard to plot. There is, in a sense, so much variety in what different people want to do with things that assessing the part played by the material affordances of one type of house or style of portrait statue or shape of pot in limiting or enabling a particular behaviour becomes very hard to assess. As Van Oyen and Pitts point out in their introduction to this volume, 'competition is only enabled in relation to a material environment already characterised by a certain degree of standardisation'; for things to be in a competitive relationship demands that those who use them are using them to do more or less the same thing. When there is a high degree of variety in what people are using things for, it ceases to be clear that the same physical objects are serving the same ends. The degree of variety in what people are using things for makes a difference because few affordances are in the end entirely determined by physical features and their practical consequences – a lot of different pots can be drunk from, used to store liquids, etc. What matters is as often what a particular pot shape (or whatever) is perceived to do (i.e. what it represents), as it is what can actually be done with it.

An example will clarify the point. The standardised glossy surface of *terra sigillata* was arguably more important because it was perceived by some to make this pottery 'like silver', not least because this *was* a standardised quality of this pottery, than because sigillata *was* significantly more like silver, in terms of what it could and could not do, than other pottery. Its competitive advantage relied on the perception that it was 'like silver' being widely shared; for those who did not see it that way, or who did not value silverware in the first place (i.e. those who had not bought into a certain set of standardised values) the glossy surface offered no special advantage. 'Material culture is not ... so easily separable from mentality, habit and moral culture' (Woolf 1998, 242): what things do and what they represent turn out not to be separate or separable. Modern advertising relies exactly on this – the creation of standardised values and the representation of particular standardised commodities as peculiarly good at satisfying those values. Just as modern consumers as often want to acquire the image as the thing, so when the Romans decided to acquire, rather than resist, the high cultural products of the Greek world they did so in order to ditch one image, one set of values, and acquire another. Standardisation itself is as much about standardisation of values as about standardisation of things.

But who were these Romans who decided to ditch one image and acquire another? As soon as we ask whether this process is top-down or bottom up (cf. Millett 1990; Woolf 1998; Spawforth 2012; Osborne 2012), we are forced to look again and more closely at the affordances of what was acquired. When Plautus and Terence turned Greek New Comedy Roman they certainly did it for an audience who knew their Greek myth, but hardly for an elite audience (Feeney 2016, 180, 184). Comedy afforded fun, and the comedy of Plautus and Terence afforded fun in relation to the wider world that was opening up. To laugh at these comedies was to feel that one could take on the Greek world into which Roman military activity had expanded. The desire to speak the (cultural) language of the wealthy Greek East, to be entangled in the wider Hellenistic world, will have been widespread across Roman and Italian society – and it is unlikely that Greeks will themselves have been reluctant to push their cultural products, material and immaterial, so as to extend their entangling web. Standardisation builds networks and building networks does not merely increase information flow, it frequently also increases the flow of money (Morley 2015). One of the things that things did was to bring in profits, and profits not just at one point of cultural transfer, but repeatedly, at all the nodes of the network.

As Poblome, Özden and Loopmans's discussion of LRD demonstrates, individual objects create demand for other objects of the same category, just as *terra sigillata* travels in sets. Indeed, what standardisation does is to make it easier to acquire other objects in the same category. It is not surprising, therefore, that the story of Roman engagement with Greek culture is essentially one of heavy resistance, with no single item of Greek origin acquiring a central place at Rome, followed by complete capitulation. As soon as people engage with things at all, indeed in order to engage with them, they classify them, making them representatives of something wider. In doing so they may well enable them to do things that their makers never envisaged – just as LRD describes a tableware that users knew and loved but that no one set out to make.

To focus a discussion on the mature Roman empire is to focus a discussion on a world where politically very little was at stake – something that Gibbon stresses when he picks out the Antonine age as a uniquely golden one: 'The vast extent of the Roman Empire was governed by absolute power, under the guidance of virtue and wisdom. The armies were restrained by the firm but gentle hand of four successive emperors, whose characters and authority commanded respect. The forms of the civil administration were carefully preserved by Nerva, Trajan, Hadrian and the Antonines, who delighted in the image of liberty, and were pleased with considering themselves as the accountable ministers of the laws' (Gibbon 1909, 86). Arguably the standardisation explored in this section had a significant part to play in maintaining that stability – indeed the globalisation of material goods and of institutions and patterns of action was one of the things that served to make the globalisation of political power unsurprising. In such a context, what things do may seem to be shaped primarily by economics. We should be wary, however, of imagining that this golden age provides a model for standardisation in antiquity more generally.

If we reflect rather on the last two centuries BC, when politically a great deal was at stake, both locally and across the whole Mediterranean, and build on Jiménez' observations, what was at issue over standardisation appears much more clearly. The opportunities offered by standardisation were and are also threats. If we do not keep an eye on instrumentalism and representation we risk being swallowed up by empire, repeating the same story. Instrumentalism and representation are not rival approaches that need to be replaced by emphasis on standardisation, for it is only against a more or less standardised background that the dynamics of instrumentalism and representation can be assessed. When they long-resisted standardisation, the people of Rome and Italy knew what they were doing. Their political independence depended on their not-conforming to the standards of Greece and the Hellenistic kingdoms. Only once they were politically dominant could the common culture of the Hellenistic world become the instrument of their own domination and serve to represent Roman imperial power. As long as instrumentalism is a feature of human behaviour, it is folly to move too far beyond it; rather, we must go behind, for only if we understand the economic, social and political possibilities offered by standardisation will we be able to appreciate the importance of the instrumental representation of those material standards.

Part 3

Matter

Chapter 10

Finding the material in 'material culture'. Form and matter in Roman concrete

Astrid Van Oyen[*]

The relation between form and matter is a fraught issue in archaeological analysis, expressed most vigorously in the style/function debate. Traditionally, formal change has been the empirical identifier for historical trends – including the development of a 'Roman cultural revolution' – leaving matter as its mute twin. But even after the 'material turn' in archaeological thought, matter continues to be 'socialised' or written out of historical narratives altogether. This chapter explores different models for writing truly 'material' histories. It does so through the case study of Roman concrete or *opus caementicium*, one of the few materials recognised to have been developed in the Roman period, and to have been granted its own formal revolution in architecture.

A material-cultural revolution?

At the start of the Roman imperial period, new ideas, styles and forms were drawn to the heart of the empire, where they were recombined and redefined in an Augustan 'cultural revolution' (Wallace-Hadrill 1989; 2008; Jiménez, this volume). The cultural revolution initiated a subtle dialogue between old and new; between legitimacy and status; between tradition and fashion. Material forms were crucial in this balancing act: furniture, tablewares, houses, and cities all took on new forms (Wallace-Hadrill 2008). The appearance of new forms has traditionally also been the empirical identifier for the provinces' enrolment in this cultural revolution (Woolf 2001). Following the 'Romanisation' paradigm, formal change in material culture was equated with the spread of a new, 'Roman' culture. More recently new material forms have become linked only indirectly to changes in practices, identities, and connectivity in this empire-wide process of redefinition.

---

[*] Department of Classics, Cornell University.

In the developments sketched above, the primacy of formal aspects in charting cultural change continues to be taken for granted. The cultural revolution is traced via proxy evidence such as shapes of pots, styles of wall painting, or plans of houses. This is in sharp contrast to prehistory's 'revolutions', which tend to be based on the development and use of new materials (especially the 'Neolithic Revolution', see most recently Hodder 2012). At least since Thomsen's Three-Age System, archaeological periodisations are grafted on material novelty: from Stone Age to Bronze Age to Iron Age. According to this classification, all of 'history' is squeezed into an extended 'Iron' Age, in which material change was supposedly negligible, until, perhaps, the twentieth century 'plastic age' or anthropocene (Waters et al. 2016). The implication seems to be that material change happens at a different rhythm than formal change, and that its historical impact pans out on a macro scale.

Such a separation of the character, scale, and rhythm of the material and formal aspects of material culture is inherently problematic. It harks back to the Cartesian separation between nature and culture – or matter and mind – that has come under attack from various directions (Hodder and Preucel 1996; Latour 1993), and often equates nature with processes happening at a slower rate on a bigger scale, as in Braudel's *longue durée* (Bailey 2007; Braudel 1972). At a smaller scale, the materials of material culture tend to enter the picture only as passive matter subject to the whims of human ('cultural') action. Material properties at the scale of artefacts or assemblages are charted as functional characteristics (behavioural archaeology's 'performance characteristics': Skibo and Schiffer 2008), harnessed for a predefined purpose: a hammer is in stone because it needs to be hard; a cooking pot is tempered to maximise its thermal properties, etc. Material properties, then, are interpreted instrumentally, often within a matrix of efficiency and maximisation. This implicit apparatus for analysing and interpreting the physical properties of objects in turn reinforces the tired style-function debate (Sackett 1985; Wiessner 1983) by ascribing anything that does not fit the parameters of efficiency (of energy, time, or resources) to 'cultural' factors, to be found in the design, decoration, colour, surface, meaning, patterning, etc. of objects. The upshot is a dual instrumental/representational strategy of writing history from material evidence that is *at best* partial (Van Oyen and Pitts, this volume).

One exception to a strictly instrumental approach to matter is a tradition of historically situated accounts that grant a formative role to specific material categories: porcelain, the Chinese empire, and Europe (Gerritsen and MacDowall 2012); gold and the Spanish conquests; or sugar and the slave trade triangle (Mintz 1985). In those 'material culture histories' (Gerritsen and Riello 2015a), matter is positioned centre stage, shaping historical developments. And yet ontologically, matter is still fundamentally ahistorical: once discovered (e.g. gold) or produced (e.g. porcelain), it becomes a commodity, a resource that might change history but does not itself change. As a consequence, the implicit picture of material change in much of archaeology and history remains one of occasional revolutions at the scale of geological epochs

10. Finding the material in 'material culture'. Form and matter in Roman concrete

(e.g. the Anthropocene) or archaeological eras (e.g. the Bronze Age), interspersed by long periods in which the available materials simply present a stock of resources to be drawn upon as and when needed (cf. Misa 1994; critiqued in Boivin 2008, 161–2).

The recent material turn has moved beyond the style/function dualism, and more generally beyond instrumentalism and representation (see Van Oyen and Pitts, this volume), but it is still at a loss when writing matter into history. The last decade has seen several calls to do justice to the physicality of material culture, which was threatening to slip away entirely by a privileging of social and constructivist aspects (Boivin 2008, 20; Ingold 2007; Olsen 2010). The term 'material culture' itself is, of course, of no help, suggesting as it does that objects are a mere crystallisation of culture and that the world is composed of two separate but combinable spheres, one material, one cultural (Prown 1996).

Several alternatives to this model of 'material+cultural' have been proposed (see most recently Hodder 2012), and in this chapter I single out two in particular. Ingold (2000, 2007) has long critiqued the notion that artefacts arise out of the imposition of form or design on passive matter (cf. Murphy, this volume). According to Ingold, matter is everywhere and not just below the surface of artefacts; it includes bodies but also the air we breathe, the rain in the air, etc. We are always both *in* and *of* matter; and therefore it makes no sense to talk of a surface or interaction where the cultural meets the material. While Ingold's critical analysis identified a weakness in the material turn that has not yet been remedied, his alternative model of an organic growing through 'currents of the lifeworld' or 'generative fluxes' (Ingold 2007, 12) has two flaws. First, it does not acknowledge the fact that in making sense of the world, categories do emerge (although they are not inherently stable), boundaries are made, and change ('growing') is, at times, halted (cf. Van Oyen 2015, 73). Secondly, using the metaphor of storytelling to reconstruct this growing, Ingold's model steers clear of history with its specific political, economic and social formations. More recent theorisation, in particular by Barad (2003), indirectly continues Ingold's project of restoring life to matter but addresses these two problems. Barad replaces Ingold's 'generative flux' with the notion of performativity: the world and its differences are created 'in the doing'. This allows for differences and categories to emerge from practices and to be historically meaningful.

The work of Ingold, Barad and others (Deleuze and Guattari 2012, 468–70) invites us to fundamentally rethink the way we write matter into historical narratives instead of merely filling the lacuna of materials in histories, including histories of the Roman empire. Materials do indeed tend to be written out of Roman history as well. Granted, the importance of grain, for example, is a recurring trope in the history of the Roman empire, which relied on managing the flow of cereals from the rich arable lands of Sicily and North Africa to its large urban and military populations. But 'grain' itself – aside from changes in its cultivation and variety in or modification of its subspecies – is generally seen as an unchanging resource, known and available in the Mediterranean since the Neolithic. Some materials did however come into being

136 Astrid Van Oyen

in the Roman period. The example discussed in this chapter is Roman concrete (*opus caementicium*), a mixture that could be poured in fluid form and then set to become a strong structural building material. Its supposed emergence in the Roman period makes concrete into a productive exemplar with which to rethink how to write material histories. *How* did matter 'come to matter' (Barad 2003) in the Roman empire? How did concrete help produce an imperial Roman world?

Three material histories of concrete (*opus caementicium*)

Roman concrete or *opus caementicium* was a new, composite material used in the city of Rome by the second century BC (Coarelli 1977 and Mogetta 2015 for debate on date of origin; Torelli 1980 for later dates *opus reticulatum*). Mortared rubble had been in use in the Mediterranean before, but Roman concrete is traditionally differentiated on the basis of specific ingredients (Fig. 10.1; Blake and Van Deman 1947, 324–7). Most typically, its fine aggregate consisted of volcanic ash from different sources in Central

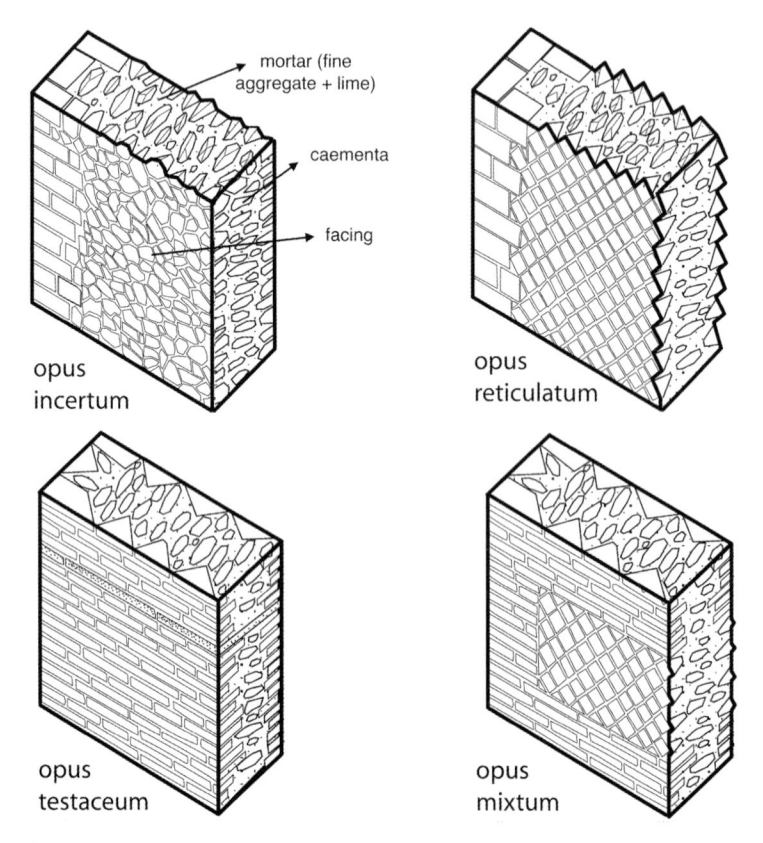

Figure 10.1 Schematic representation of different masonry types of concrete walls. Drawing by Lynne Lancaster.

Italy (Lancaster 2015, ch. 2 on different fine aggregates employed in the provinces). This fine aggregate was mixed with lime to form a mortar, into which *caementa* were laid – chunky pieces of stone or other building material. *Opus caementicium* has long been associated with a so-called architectural revolution in the first century AD (Ward-Perkins 1981; MacDonald 1982, 41–6) – almost three centuries after the supposed 'invention' of concrete as a material. As with the wider (and possibly slightly earlier) Augustan cultural revolution, identification and definition of this revolution are predicated on the appearance of new *forms* – new construction forms such as vaults (Lancaster 2005) and apses, and new building forms with wider, open internal spaces.

When an attempt is made to consider the material and not just the formal signature of the architectural revolution, this winds down to narratives of increasing efficiency and maximisation (Quenemoen 2014, 80). Blake wrote that 'concrete was the result of a long period of development', in which chance led to the use of the right ingredients in the right proportion to move from 'pseudo-concrete' with limited binding power to concrete as a structural material (Blake and Van Deman 1947, 327). But further developments and adjustments to the composition of *opus caementicium* or to building techniques using this material are explained by an 'interest in optimizing structural performance and expediting the construction process' (Quenemoen 2014, 65; after Coarelli 1977; Torelli 1980, 156 for 'mechanisation' through the shift to *opus reticulatum*) or as 'enhancing the strength and durability of monumental construction' (Jackson and Kosso 2013, 283).

The template of 'history' that informs traditional stories about a new material such as concrete is a mechanical, not an organic one. The underlying assumption is that once the material is 'invented' or has originated, it is generally present and available as a resource. While it is acknowledged that changes continued to occur in the different elements making up the composite *opus caementicium*, these are not considered anything like the organic development of biological species that 'grow': they are seen as originating from *outside* rather than from an evolutionary dialogue between internal and external dynamics. In this case, much is to be gained from an Ingoldian account of the organic 'growing' of *opus caementicium* – the first material history developed in this chapter.

This chapter limits itself to central Italy, and in particular to the city of Rome, as a case study for the development of a specific material history in a geopolitical centre with unique access to knowledge and resources (Lancaster 2015 hints at how this story changes when expanded to the provinces).

A micro-history of physical change: concrete's 'growing'

One way in which Roman concrete can be said to have 'grown' organically is through its physical transformation from a fluid to a solid state. This material transformation made concrete as a building material radically different to the spectrum of preceding building materials: rocks, stones, and wood could be cut and their shape could be modified, but their fundamental material states would not be altered.

Concrete was a composite material, and its characteristic material change played out on the level of its individual constituents as well. The gradual hardening of concrete when used in buildings was in large part dependent on the nature of the mortar, which consisted of lime and a fine aggregate. In Roman Italy, the fine aggregate was catered for by ash from various volcanic deposits on the Tyrrhenian side of central Italy (often called 'pozzolana', see Lancaster 2015, ch. 2 for terminological clarification). In geological terms, concrete started to grow several hundreds of thousands of years ago, when the volcanic deposits of central Italy were formed (Jackson and Kosso 2013, 270). It was this volcanic ash that reacted chemically with slaked lime (i.e. lime combined with water) to transform previous substances of various compositions into stone-like mortar.

The lime component equally resulted from a process of material transformation. Calcium oxide (CaO) had to be created by burning stones containing calcium carbonate ($CaCO_3$) (Adam 1984, 69; Lancaster and Ulrich 2014, 173). To this effect, limestone, travertine, or marble were fired at temperatures up to 1,000°C. Water then needed to be added to the resulting quick lime to produce slaked lime that would react with the silica (SiO_2) and alumina (Al_2O_3) in volcanic ash. In imperial Rome limestone was the major source for producing lime. It could either be imported as newly quarried stone or recycled from preceding constructions. Turning limestone into lime was a fairly *ad hoc* process. But slaked lime was not a readymade resource available as such at the time of construction, in contrast to volcanic ash. As a result, lime was more expensive than volcanic ash in Roman times (Faventinus 4; DeLaine 1997, 112–4; Lancaster 2005, 17). This shows that while based on current scientific understanding we might consider volcanic ash as the 'key' ingredient in the success of Roman concrete, with lime being the more 'banal' and easily available resource, these differences and their valuation cannot be retroprojected.

To obtain concrete, *caementa* were laid into, and covered by, the matrix of the mortar. The choice of *caementa* was extremely flexible, and could consist of any chunk of solid material, usually between 10 and 30 cm in size (Lancaster 2015, 19): various kinds of stone, rock, or ceramic material. In some cases, *caementa* with special properties (especially light weight) were imported, but generally locally available stones and rubble were used, often in the same materials as the facings, or recycled from preceding constructions. The *caementa*, then, came with their own biographies, which usually involved formal (e.g. chipping of stone fragments) and material (e.g. firing clay into brick) transformations.

Concrete walls are often contained by a facing. By the second century BC, this was provided by irregularly laid small stones (*opus incertum*), and later by diamond-shaped stones whose flat fronts could be organised in a net-shaped pattern and whose pointy ends were anchored in the mortar core of the wall (*opus reticulatum*) (Fig. 10.1) (Adam 1984, 139–47; Coarelli 1977; Torelli 1980). From the second half of the first century BC, tiles and bricks were used as facing alongside or instead of stones (*opus testaceum* or *latericium*): first the flanges were broken off of roof tiles to be laid as facing on the outside of the walls (Blake and Van Deman 1947, 161; Lancaster and Ulrich 2014, 167); later purpose-made bricks of standard sizes were used, either broken diagonally or whole. Much like the *caementa* in the concrete core, the components of the facing came with their own biographies, including material transformations.

Not just each individual component of concrete as a composite material resulted from a process of material transformation. On a larger scale, each individual concrete building had a history of material 'growth' in an Ingoldian sense: a specific process by which the material transformed, which occurred at a different pace and in different ways depending on context. Unlike modern concrete, Roman *opus caementicium* could not simply be poured into the formwork. Instead, the *caementa* needed to be laid in with the mortar, in a repetitive sequence. The pozzolanic mortar would set within hours, by which time the concrete would attain a solid state and a new layer could be laid on top. Facing and concrete core would rise simultaneously, layer by layer (Blake 1959, 160; Lechtman and Hobbs 1986, 102). The 'growing' of concrete walls would therefore not have necessitated a conceptual leap from the laying of stone walls, course by course. The process was different for concrete vaults and structures other than walls, which did not have facings, and were built using wooden formwork (Lancaster 2005, ch. 2). Here the fundamental physical transformation characterising concrete as a material altered the nature and conception of the construction process, which relied on the creation of temporary wooden formwork that was then 'filled' and materialised with mortar and *caementa*.

Within this generic sequencing of concrete construction, different concrete buildings developed along different paths. As already mentioned, Roman concrete would set within hours, transforming from a fluid to a solid state and reaching about 10–20 per cent of its full strength, but it would not attain that maximum strength until days, months, or even years later (Lancaster 2005, 52; Lechtman and Hobbs 1986, 99). This process of curing and its outcome were highly contextually dependent. The pozzolanic mortar, for instance, requires water for the chemical reaction to occur between the elements of the lime and the volcanic ash. Moderate temperatures were preferred, and hot conditions in particular would have made the water evaporate before the chemical process had taken place. Roman builders understood that curing was a contextual process. The Lex Puteolana (*CIL* X 1781; dated to 105 BC, early in the development of concrete construction) specifies November 1 as the last date in the year to build in concrete (or, at the time, a rubble and mortar mix). Frontinus (*De aquis* II 123) limits aqueduct repairs to the period between April and November, with exception of the hottest periods (Blake and Van Deman 1947, 352). The future material behaviour of a concrete building was not fully determined by its material components or its design. Roman concrete buildings would often have exhibited cracking, shrinkage, and creeping even within years of initial building. Such post-building material transformations, for instance, often caused vaults to be flattened, in a marked divergence from the original design and shape of the formwork (Lancaster 2005, 9).

Now to return to Ingold (2000, 172–88), who distinguishes between 'building' and 'dwelling': the former as an imposition of form on passive matter, given meaning post-hoc ('representationally') by humans inhabiting it, the latter as an always already meaningful engagement with the world out of which form emerges. This section has shown that concrete as a material has a particular history of 'growing', both on the scale of its components, and on that of the whole. But a material history of concrete's 'growing' leaves much out of the picture. In particular, by seeing everything as interrelated, the analyst does not have the tools for distinguishing between different *kinds* of growing, with different rhythms, transformations, and consequences. The following subsection therefore complements this history of organic 'growing' with discussion of how differences – material and historical – were made and maintained.

A history of concrete as a material: standardisation and categorisation
Material transformation occurred with every single instance of making the composite of volcanic ash, slaked lime, *caementa*, and facing; but on a larger temporal scale concrete also transformed physically from its initial use in the Republican period to its deployment in the early and later empire.

Initially, constructors in Rome excavated the volcanic ash of concrete locally, near the building site. Later projects, such as the Forum of Caesar, show experimentation with mixtures from several sources (Jackson and Kosso 2013, 19). Vitruvius, writing in the first century BC, distinguished between two additives for the production of concrete: the *harena fossicia* or 'pit sand' (as opposed to river or sea sand) originating from volcanic deposits in the Alban Hills and in the Colli Sabatini, respectively to the south and to the north of Rome; and the *pulvis puteolanus* from Pozzuoli in the Bay of Naples.

The *pulvis puteolanus* was used and proven effective from the second century BC onwards in underwater concrete constructions (cf. later Vitruvius *De Architectura* 2.6.1). The two types of additives (which we now know are variants of volcanic ash), *harena fossicia* and *pulvis puteolanus*, were never considered to be the same kind of material: Vitruvius (*De Architectura* 2.6.6) explains the different behaviour of the additives from Campania and Tuscany (Jackson and Kosso 2013, 273). He concludes that both are very useful for building, the former underwater, and the latter on land. It is likely that skills developed in underwater concrete construction were never translated to the technical development of above ground concrete construction (Blake and Van Deman 1947, 42 and 341; Lechtman and Hobbs 1986, 89–92). This categorisation had real consequences. While (land) construction projects in the city of Rome never used the Campanian *pulvis puteolanus*, Claudius imported it for the waterworks at the port of Portus (Jackson 2014; Pliny *Historia Naturalis* 16.202), and it was even exported beyond Italy for construction of ports, as at Caesarea Maritima in Israel (late first century BC) and Chersonesos on Crete (probably Augustan) (Hohlfelder and Oleson 2014, 224–5; Oleson et al. 2004, 206). What we consider a single category of 'concrete', therefore, were really different things for the Romans with different properties and different possibilities for action. Historical possibilities – such as the development of harbours – emerge from trajectories in which the properties of materials interact with their social categorisation.

The categorisation of different kinds of volcanic ash, or pozzolana, and what it could be used for went hand in hand with a progressive treatment of the pozzolana before it was mixed with lime to form a mortar (Jackson and Kosso 2013, 280–1; Lancaster 2005, 56–7). In the late Republic, the pozzolana was not separated from any soil that surrounded it at its point of mining before becoming part of the composite concrete. In the Augustan period, coarse sieving of the pozzolana seems to have taken place, although small soil particles were not washed off (Blake and Van Deman 1947, 314). It was not until the later first century AD that the volcanic ash used in concrete buildings in the city of Rome appears not only to have been sieved finely but also to have been washed. Over time, then, not only were different kinds of pozzolana defined in relation to their use (for construction underwater or on land); what pozzolana – the 'useful' material that would form concrete in combination with lime and *caementa* – really consisted of was reconsidered and refined as well.

This process of redefinition was no doubt steered by experience, but it would also have been aided by the physical properties of the material. The good quality pozzolana around Rome was variably red or black in colour and originated from two distinct geological horizons. Increasingly the red variants (Pozzolane Rosse) were selected, as in Trajanic public construction (Bianchi *et al.* 2011, 77). The volcanic ash from the Bay of Naples, instead, was greyish in colour (Fig. 10.2). The colour difference with the surrounding soil matrices would have facilitated practical and conceptual separation (Blake 1959, 159). Vitruvius (*De Architectura* 2.4.1), in turn, suggests other methods to identify the 'useful' material: it should not leave stains on a white cloth in which it had been wrapped; and it should make a grating noise when rubbed in the hand. The sharp particle edges producing such a noise would indeed have been characteristic of the volcanic scoria from which the pozzolana eroded (Lancaster 2005, 56). The physical properties of different grain sizes and colours thus actively contributed to their own categorisation, and to the establishment of differences both between 'soil' and 'fine aggregate to produce mortar', and between different 'fine aggregates'.

Just as the fine aggregate used in concrete was progressively (re-)defined, the *caementa* changed over the course of the first centuries BC and AD. Monuments dating to the second century BC generally have coarse *caementa* 'laid without regard to order' and with individual pieces exceeding 40 cm in size (Blake 1959, 160; Jackson and Kosso 2013, 280). From the reign of Augustus onwards, the sizes of *caementa* in concrete buildings more generally averaged 10–30 cm, and they were laid in regular horizontal layers.

In addition to this sorting on the basis of size and horizontal layers, the density and weight of *caementa* became increasingly adjusted to their structural position within a building. In the Republican period, *caementa* consisted of various kinds of locally and regionally sourced stones (be it derived from preceding structures or not), often the same materials as used for the facings; and were generally undifferentiated throughout the building. By the Julio-Claudian period, the use of recycled materials or waste from preceding building projects as *caementa* was increasingly complemented or even replaced by imported stones with specific qualities (Blake and Van Deman 1947, 346, 349). Denser materials such as travertine were preferentially used in foundations and lower parts of walls; whereas *tufo lionato* became the 'standard' type of *caementa* (Jackson and Kosso 2013, 280) and exceptionally lightweight stones such as Vesuvian scoria or pumice formed part of the concrete used in vaults and domes (Fig. 10.3) (Lechtman and Hobbs 1986, 102; Lancaster 2005, 59–62 for examples of this strategy as applied in individual buildings; Lancaster *et al.* 2011; Quenemoen 2014, 65; Wilson Jones 2000, 187 for the Pantheon). As with the *pulvis puteolanus*, specific lightweight scoriae and pumice from regions around the Mediterranean equally circulated, via regional and/or imperially organised trade routes (Hohlfelder and Oleson 2014, 224–5; Jackson 2014, 150–9; Lancaster *et al.* 2010; 2011).

Caementa were thus sorted both in relation to one another (within the layers) and in relation to the structure and its loadbearing requirements. These relations defined

Figure 10.2 Comparison of volcanic ash from the area around Rome (left) and from the Bay of Naples (right) (Lancaster 2015, Web figure 2. Reproduced with permission).

Figure 10.3 Baths of Caracalla, Rome: concrete wall and dome with brick facing (bottom), tufa caementa (middle), and lightweight pumice caementa (top). Photo by Lynne Lancaster.

subcategories within the *caementa* used for concrete building: such as specific new lightweight stones to be used in vaults; or dense varieties for use in foundations. The resulting categories remained flexible, however: even in imperial times, less finely sorted *caementa* could be used for concrete building, depending on need, funds, and other contextual parameters. But by introducing a possibility of choice, the definition of increasingly narrow subcategories also changed the way these choices would be valued. For example, *not* opting for lightweight stones in vaults had now become a *lesser* option. In historical terms, the point is not to chart a linear evolution of 'progression' or increasing 'efficiency', but to trace how choices (in the use of *caementa*) became *potentially* much more specialised and relationally defined, and to acknowledge that this changed the relative valuation of such different choices.

The nature of the facing changed as well. In the Republican period, stonework provided the facing of concrete walls. As with the *caementa*, stone facings went through a process of standardisation and specialisation, from the irregularly laid stones of various sizes of *opus incertum* to the late Republican *opus reticulatum* with its highly standardised stones cut in a specialist pyramid-like form, to be used only for the purpose of concrete wall facings (Fig. 10.1). Explanation of the uptake of *opus reticulatum* usually emphasises its functional advantages (although Torelli 1980, 153–4, 158 for its aesthetic relation to an ideal of *urbanitas*): the pyramid-like shape of the stones would have facilitated structural bonding with the concrete core of the wall; and their standardised shape would have sped up the building process and enabled the use of unskilled slave labour (Coarelli 1977, 18; Torelli 1980, 155 envisages large firms overseeing the entire, subdivided, construction process). Labour investment thus shifted away from the assembling process on the building site to the preparatory stages of stone-cutting (Adam 1984, 141). Taking place in conjunction with this functional reorganisation of the building process, however, was a process of conceptual (re)categorisation. Cutting stones to a specialist shape *only* for use in concrete building demarcated the latter as a conceptually distinct type of material process. By facilitating the assembling of concrete buildings, the shift in workflow in the production of *opus reticulatum* stones would have emphasised the unity of concrete as a material over the heterogeneity of its constituent components.

The stonework used as facing in concrete buildings of the Republican period was gradually superseded by terracotta *opus testaceum* or *latericium* (Fig. 10.1). Initially concrete walls with tile facing exclusively used broken tiles as *caementa* (Blake and Van Deman 1947, 294–5; Lechtman and Hobbs 1986, 104). This can be read as conceptual continuity with the previous practice of stonework: somehow the material used as facing and the material used as *caementa* were meant to be drawn from the same category (stones with stones; bricks with bricks). The correlation was then abandoned and arguably 'material for facing' and 'material for core' became independent categories. This goes to show that categorisation is a historically orchestrated reality, which shapes possibilities for action (in this case, the instrumental question of which resources can be used for which purpose).

10. Finding the material in 'material culture'. Form and matter in Roman concrete

Roof tiles were gradually replaced by purpose-made bricks (which could not double as roofing material!) as the facing of concrete walls. Although bricks were produced and used earlier, the Neronian fire of Rome and the subsequent massive rebuilding of the Urbs tend to be seen as the watershed for the brick industry in Rome (MacDonald 1982, 25–31; DeLaine 2000; Bianchi 2004 for later imperial ownership of brickyards). Bricks occurred in three standardised sizes, which could then be broken into smaller triangles or squares (which, by deduction, were also of a standardised size) (Lancaster and Ulrich 2014, 170). While the shapes of bricks were highly standardised, their material composition varied, depending on the clay sources and matrix used.

As for *opus reticulatum*, the formal standardisation of bricks and their sizes assured compatibility between the different stages and parties involved in the process of concrete construction. Brickyards could churn out bricks that would be useable for a variety of building projects (MacDonald 1982, 152; Wilson 2006, 228). Surplus bricks from one project could be used in the next. In the case of the facing, compatibility thus hinged on form and its standardisation.

But the materials of concrete and their biographies also generated compatibility. While we have seen that the material properties of concrete's individual components – volcanic ash, lime, *caementa* – became increasingly definable and subdivided, variability could and did persist. This variability was partly absorbed by separating the production of the constituent elements of concrete buildings from the process of their assembling into a new whole. But it was also enabled by the very composite nature of concrete and its inherent process of material transformation (from fluid to solid state), which made compatible materials, forms, and units that were otherwise incompatible (and in turn facilitated the re-use of 'demolition materials': DeLaine 2006, 249). Things of forms, materials, and origins as different as pit sands from the Alban Hills, scoriae from the Vesuvian area, slaked lime produced from travertine from the foothills surrounding Rome, bricks, and *ad hoc* recycled components were brought together and transformed into a single new unit: a concrete wall, vault, or building. The physical transformation on which concrete building relied not only guaranteed its literal solidity but also its conceptual unity.

In sum, a narrative of Ingoldian 'growing' does not suffice to make matter historically relevant, and, vice versa, to write a truly *material* history. This section has explored the interplay between material and conceptual transformations: how the notion of what constituted (or could constitute) concrete changed over time, and what the role of materials was in this changing categorisation. Material properties such as colour, grain size, or weight actively steered a process of standardisation, for instance in the definition of suitable fine aggregates (volcanic ashes) or in the relative sorting of *caementa*. Such standardisation went some way to enhancing compatibility; a process further facilitated by the sequencing of the workflow and by concrete's materially transformative nature. Material properties, however, were also at the basis of increasing differentiation, for example between the black and red ashes, or between *caementa* with different weights. These differentiations had real historical consequences, as exemplified by the cost of importing special *caementa* from the Vesuvian area in Rome, or shipping *pulvis puteolanus* to ports across the Mediterranean. As a result, such differences became the basis for statements and judgments of value (and of economic cost: DeLaine 2006, 241).

While the move from Ingold to Barad – from matter to concepts – should at once have brought people back into the picture, the rhetorical effect of the passive voice in this section shows how difficult it is not to reduce human agency in material histories either to a faceless generality ('Roman constructors') or to identified historical figures ('Vitruvius'). Moreover, the passive voice is not only a pitfall for the role of human agency; it also threatens to reify the instrumental approach to matter from which this chapter seeks to move away. How a material 'grows', then, is still crucial to its historical importance. But this 'growing' never happens in a historical void; instead, relations between materials (volcanic ashes and soil), objects (one brick to the next), and practices (stone-cutting or brick-making and assembling) create boundaries. It is the differences emphasised by these boundaries that end up shaping history. Ingold's (2007) 'growing' cannot exist without Barad's (2003) 'material-discursive phenomena', and vice versa.

A history of concrete building: how concrete forms 'grew'

So far I have sketched how concrete and its constitutive components came with specific biographies of material transformation; and how concrete as a building material developed along a trajectory of redefinition, categorisation, and differentiation. This section shows that only by making these two processes speak to one another it is possible to show how concrete shaped Roman history. In the process, it becomes clear that matter and form are co-constituted.

How did the form of concrete buildings emerge? Concrete as a material was essentially shape-less. It had to be moulded or cast into form, by supporting the fluid material until it set. The wooden centering and formwork (for vaults) and masonry facing (for walls) were thus paramount in deciding on the final form of concrete structures (Lechtman and Hobbs 1986, 102) – even if concrete eventually made visible and tangible what wooden formwork could only suggest (Lancaster 2005, ch. 2 for discussion of centering and formwork for vaults and domes). In one way, then, concrete seems to epitomise Ingold's (2000) notion of the 'building perspective', imposing form on matter, in diametric opposition to the dwelling or growing perspective, which sees form emerge out of a more authentic engagement with matter. In theory, Roman concrete came with 'a potential of form' (MacDonald 1982, 153) that could be passively adapted to any predetermined design.

Initially, concrete building reproduced the traditional 'trabeated' (i.e. using post and lintel) architecture of the Roman Republic and early empire, which was characterised by spaces separated by walls (in concrete), columns and piers providing necessary structural support, flat ceilings (in wood), and façades oriented outwards

(Wilson Jones 2000, 65). This was essentially the architecture described by Vitruvius in the first century BC, who showed a noted conservatism to form and apparently deliberately ignored the few concrete buildings that by his time had already gone beyond the trabeated canon such as the sanctuary of Fortuna Primigenia at Praeneste with its impressive concrete vaulted terraces (MacDonald 1982, 10; Wilson Jones 2000, 34).

In the Augustan period, concrete was used widely in building, but new forms, vaults, and domes remained limited in number, scale, and shape, especially in the public monuments in Rome itself (allowing for their possible archaeological invisibility through later replacement by large-scale building projects). One of the examples of Augustan date often cited as precursor to the architectural revolution, the 'temple of Mercury' at Baiae with its large dome with central *oculus* spanning a section of a bath complex, was part of a private luxury villa on the Bay of Naples (MacDonald 1982, 11). It was not until the later Julio-Claudian period that the formal architectural revolution of concrete building took off with Rome at its centre. Nero's *Domus Aurea* – the new imperial palace constructed after the fire of AD 64 – is traditionally seen as the watershed of formal change in concrete vaulted construction. Its extant remains on the Esquiline demonstrate new principles of communicating spaces, internally unobstructed passageways through sequences of volumes, vaults and domes, and the establishment of a new world closed in on itself, cut off from surrounding 'nature' (MacDonald 1982, 31–41; most recently Ball 2003). Why then did these new forms only appear at least two centuries after the 'innovation' of Roman pozzolana-based concrete?

An explanation for the apparent lag between the development of Roman concrete and the formal architectural revolution of concrete building tends to be sought in the instrumentalist assumption that matter is a mere 'passive' resource, waiting to be used. Asking why concrete did not trigger a formal revolution earlier would be like asking why the Iron Age did not take off earlier than it did, as iron ores had been available throughout world (pre-)history. MacDonald (1982, 5) ascribes the architectural revolution to 'immanent cultural forces', with the material of concrete and its structural techniques as 'the mechanical servants of a new imagery'. More specifically, the revolution would have been caused by 'Nero's taste for novelty' and 'imperial ambition' (MacDonald 1982, 42–3). This presents a model of history in which matter is at the whim of design; in which causality lies solely with volition and individual will; and in which innovation is a self-contained, essential phenomenon, identified on the basis of formal change. More specifically, such an explanation implicitly sees the new forms of the architectural revolution as 'just another form' imposed on the endlessly malleable concrete.

Instead, the plasticity of concrete did not mean that as a material it was not predisposed to specific forms; that concrete forms did not 'grow' in a particular way. Concrete quickly transformed from a medium of replication of previous architectural forms in stone into a driver of innovation, as builders gained confidence, and discovered the material's internal dynamics. In concrete buildings, the loads and their horizontal thrusts were distributed through sequences of vaults, and were often contained and directed further by applying masses above those vaulted structures. As a result of the different channelling of loads in concrete vaulted buildings, the walls, piers, and columns that had been the traditional structural supports in trabeated architecture now lost their functional necessity. Once those structural supports were omitted, internal spaces could be continuous – even if externally defined by separate volumes – and uninterrupted vistas could be established through the length and width of a series of rooms. The fact that concrete *had* to be used as a vault – flat concrete ceilings were structurally impossible – set in motion the development of a whole new spatial vocabulary.

These new kinds of concrete vaulted spaces fostered new kinds of interactions with and between their occupants (Fig. 10.4 for an example of how concrete could be 'sculpted'). A dome, for instance, directs vision and movement to its centre, the unique point in the space with maximal height (MacDonald 1982, 44). Communicating spaces unobstructed by vertical supports allowed the development of new patterns of axiality

Figure 10.4 Aula, Trajan's Markets, Rome: a new type of vaulted space enabled by concrete. Photo by Lynne Lancaster.

10. Finding the material in 'material culture'. Form and matter in Roman concrete

and directionality. The lateral support of concrete shapes apparently contradicted the effects of gravity (MacDonald 1982, 177) – parading the ultimate domination of nature. The inside-out logic of concrete vaulted construction meant that concrete spaces became 'domesticated' worlds in themselves, focused on interaction inside rather than with the outside. In addition, concrete allowed for a dramatic increase in the size of many stock urban building types such as amphitheatres, basilicas, and baths (Quenemoen 2014, 68–9). Combined, concrete buildings' interior focus and size increase spurred new modes of urban interaction, defining social constituencies of urban and imperial citizens (cf. Lechtman and Hobbs 1986, 82; MacDonald 1982, 183). The regularity of the new *insulae* with apartment blocks, aided by the modular nature of 'moulded' concrete building, in turn exuded order, control, and would not have been without its psychological consequences for inhabitants (*sensu* Foucault 1975). The material histories of concrete branch out into histories of imperial identities (e.g. differently valued subcategories), economic development (e.g. sped-up building with standardised components), control (e.g. modular apartment blocks), and citizenship (e.g. interaction in large, contained spaces).

The material properties of concrete thus made certain kinds of architectural forms possible. But these forms did not develop automatically out of the mere use of this material. Instead, the right context needed to be established, and this was a cumulative process over time. Elements of this context and its trajectory have been described before: population growth and influx of slave labour in the second century BC, large-scale Republican building, a broader Augustan cultural revolution, and, eventually, a megalomaniac and autocratic emperor in the first century AD. But this chapter argues that another key part of this context has been hitherto overlooked, and consists of the gradual categorisation of the material, its components, their properties, and their proper usage. This process of categorisation went beyond mere 'familiarity' with the material (although this would of course have been important as well). Although no formal evidence is available, it is likely that engagement with material, planning, and designing the new concrete forms was very different from the previous trabeated architecture, so that thinking in section (charting loadbearing relations between concrete vaults on different levels) had to prevail on thinking in plan (establishing relations between a plan and its direct vertical supports) (Quenemoen 2014, 70–1). More specific than material engagement and know-how, categorisation describes how *opus caementicium* became 'knowable', how it became a specific material with well-defined components and ways of assembling them.

As discussed in the previous section, Vitruvius already distinguished between different types of additives (fine aggregates) from different origins (the Alban Hills versus Pozzuoli), to be used for different purposes (construction on land or underwater). But evidence of differentiation within the *harena fossicia* based on colour and grain size, and of extensive sieving and washing of the volcanic ash to separate it practically and conceptually from the surrounding soil does not occur until later in the first century AD. Sorting of the *caementa* both in relation to one another and to their structural position in the building had to wait until the late Julio-Claudian period. It was not until that time that 'concrete' had become a clearly defined category, with standardised options reflecting contextual possibilities that mapped onto a spectrum of difference (and its valuation). It was precisely when concrete was categorised as a singular material that the architectural revolution's new concrete forms gained momentum.

Paradoxically, then, in order for 'form' to emerge out of 'matter', the latter needed to be defined as a stable resource. Put differently, concrete as 'matter' impacted most on form when defined instrumentally. The difference with the 'standard' instrumental narrative critiqued in this chapter is not just that matter *is* made to matter; but that its status as an 'instrumental' well-defined resource was a historically specific stage in its trajectory of transformation and redefinition, and not a natural way in which the world of materials presents itself to us.

Nevertheless, the key to the early imperial context for the development of new forms of concrete buildings is usually sought in dramatic political protagonists, first and foremost the megalomaniac emperor Nero. As has long been noted, the fire that destroyed large parts of Rome in AD 64 provided a *tabula rasa* of previous architecture and created space for new buildings on a scale unseen before in the densely-built centre of the city. This tends to be read as an opportunity either seized or created by Nero's 'taste for novelty' described above (MacDonald 1982, 42 and 25–31), who promptly started construction of a new, massive personal palace (*Domus Aurea*) in the heart of the city, as well as of systematic apartment blocks – all in concrete. Because for a proverbial split second in Roman history space in the centre of Rome was less of an issue, architecture could be conceived of from the point of view of its internal dynamics instead of the space it had to fit within. In combination with concrete's predisposition to defining interior space, this context triggered the creation of 'very large unobstructed spaces' (MacDonald 1982, 5), internal vistas and carefully orchestrated circulation pathways; in contrast to the previous focus on frontal, outside façades, making the biggest impact possible in a limited space. In addition, concrete greatly accelerated the speed of rebuilding (cf. Wilson 2006), allowing construction of the new 'Rome' within the span of a single imperial reign. The historical footprint of Nero, then, would not have been possible without concrete – without the possibilities of speed and shape it afforded. These possibilities emerged from concrete's much longer material history of transformation and categorisation. Material histories shuffle causality, situating traditional protagonists firmly within their historical entanglements.

Conclusion

How, then, did matter come to matter in the Roman empire? Material histories cannot start from an instrumental perspective, seeing matter as a passive resource and describing the imposition of varying historically determined forms. In instrumental

10. Finding the material in 'material culture'. Form and matter in Roman concrete

narratives, matter merely has an origin, but is denied redefinitions, transformations, and a biography. In search of an alternative, this article traced three material histories of Roman concrete.

As a narrative of Ingoldian 'growing', material history no. 1 described the processes of physical transformation that characterised both concrete as a composite material and its individual components. These transformations played out on different temporal and spatial scales, defined the building sequence, shaped the nature of skilled engagement, and helped identify and rank different components (e.g. slaked lime as more expensive than volcanic ash). But a strictly Ingoldian narrative does not get at the stuff of politics, decisions, tensions, identities, etc. Moreover, while it sketched micro-histories of physical transformation, it does not speak to a diachronic development of 'concrete' as a material.

Material history no. 2 therefore drew on Barad's emphasis on how material assemblages create differences to trace how concrete as a material was redefined. Concrete, its individual components, and their assemblage gradually became standardised. Different subcategories were created – from finely sieved Pozzolane Rosse and regularly laid special lightweight *caementa* to coarser mortars combined with undifferentiated *caementa*; shaping which choices were possible and how they were valued vis à vis other possible choices. This categorisation was often steered by the very material properties of the components, as for instance when fine aggregates were differentiated on the basis of colour and grain size; or when concrete's physical transformation facilitated conceptual unity of concrete as a material. The history of the redefinition of concrete not only affected practices (e.g. the choice to import *pulvis puteolanus* for harbours across the Mediterranean) and their valuation, but also informed the very concept of instrumentalism: which material was suitable for which purpose and what exactly it was that was defined as a material 'resource'.

A combined emphasis on physical transformation and its skilled engagement (material history no. 1) and on redefinitions, categorisations, and the creation of differences (material history no. 2) is necessary for material histories to develop to their full breadth, and for matter to speak to form. A traditional history of concrete building emphasises the shift in architectural form from reproduction of previous trabeated architecture to new possibilities of domes, vaults, and open interior spaces. Concrete features as passive matter, instrumentally at the whim of changing historical conditions and their formal expression (Ingold's 'building' perspective). Material history no. 3 showed that only when the definition of concrete as a material (in itself partly steered by its material properties) was stabilised, could its forms be allowed to grow 'organically' (as per Ingold's 'growing' or 'dwelling' perspective) and make history by facilitating rapid rebuilding of Rome after the Neronian fire and by shaping particular kinds of spaces, interactions, and identities.

An 'instrumental' approach to matter, then, is shown to be a historical construction, with real historical effects, and paradoxically to have been a requirement for the 'growing' of concrete forms: in order to use something as passive matter, one needs to have decided on its categorisation (what it is) and its properties (what it includes and what it can do). Neither Ingold's 'building' perspective nor his 'dwelling/growing' perspective is more authentic than the other; both are historically specific 'material-discursive' formations *sensu* Barad. And instead of being exclusive options, they are mutually implicated. Conversely, the instrumental framing of concrete in the early imperial period can no longer be considered a universally shared (i.e. ahistorical) approach to matter. Instead it was a factor of concrete's long material history, and a facilitator of the period's historical footprint, enabling for instance Nero to enter history books as Rome's rebuilder.

This chapter set itself the seemingly impossible task of 'finding the material' in material culture: if matter is not a separate ontological domain, then its contribution to history cannot be singled out as such (cf. Morton 2013, 91–2). The solution can therefore not be to fill in the gaps left by the almost exclusive reliance on form in charting historical change. Instead, a more fundamental rethinking of matter's historical role is needed, in the form of material histories. Material histories are relational (they cross scales and ontological domains), performative (they create their own differences) and emergent (they have no single, direct cause). By combining attention to processes of physical transformation and social differentiation, material histories can trace the modes in which form related to matter, and in which people engaged with the material world. Such modes are *always* historically specific: they have a history and they make history.

Acknowledgements

I am greatly indebted to Lynne Lancaster, whose generosity and unsurpassed knowledge on Roman concrete have done much to improve this argument. Lori Khatchadourian, Martin Millett and Martin Pitts kindly read and commented on previous versions of this chapter. Any remaining errors are mine.

Chapter 11

Design, function and everyday social practice. Artefacts and Roman social history

Ellen Swift[*]

In recent years, and as discussed in the introduction to this volume, theoretically informed approaches to Roman material culture have become mainly concerned with the themes of identity, representation and consumption (e.g. Eckardt 2005; Greene 2008), while synthetic studies of the Roman period show a limited engagement with artefact studies (e.g. Millett 1990; Woolf 1998; Mattingly 2006). Functional studies of individual artefacts and their assemblages make a valuable contribution to Roman social history, yet one that has been persistently neglected. In part this is because of the focus of synthetic studies on political and economic questions and the 'Romanisation' debate. It also stems from the misperception that studies of functional artefacts have little to contribute to investigations of cultural change. This chapter outlines a theoretically informed approach to functional studies, particularly in relation to the design function of artefacts. Drawing specifically on design theory, and using Roman dice and Roman finger-rings as short case studies, I investigate the relationships between the physical features of artefacts (their form and material), everyday social practice and experience, and wider cultural traditions of behaviour.

Artefact studies are particularly suited to an exploration of the diversity of changing social experience in the Roman world. This has been well-demonstrated in a number of analyses of pottery forms, which explore for instance cultural or regional diversity in foodways, or chronological changes in dining habits. In such studies, pottery forms have been used mainly to document variation in social behaviour, rather than exploring how the objects actively enable or foster such behaviours and their maintenance or attrition (e.g. Cool 2006, 39–41; Hawthorne 2000). As regards 'small finds' studies, while there have been previous considerations of regional and chronological diversity, generally the aim has been to investigate aspects of identity and representation (e.g. Eckardt 2014; Jundi and Hill 1998). These approaches have

---

[*]Department of Classical and Archaeological Studies, University of Kent.

yielded important results, for instance with regard to the construction of identities through material culture, but there is much potential for more in-depth exploration of discrepant social practices and experience. This could be done, for instance, by exploring how cultural traditions and beliefs were embedded within and contested by wider society through material culture, and investigating the key role of artefacts in enacting cultural change and development.

Theoretical approach

Design theory uses a particular term, *affordance*, to describe the perceived properties of an artefact that make possible, and incline people towards, a range of uses (Norman 2002[1988]; see also Knappett 2004). Often these are uses intended by the maker (for instance sitting on the seat of a chair). Some objects also have affordances that make them suitable for divergent uses that are different to those envisaged by the maker (for example keeping a door open by using a chair as a prop). Affordances can be considered to be relational, in that they emerge within particular contexts of use, and can thus vary with different usage.

Many studies of artefacts intuitively make use of the concept of affordances in order to reconstruct possible functions. This concept can help us to refocus on the materiality of objects, that is, the physical properties and qualities of both form and material, by examining how their practical features intersect with various possible actions and behaviours. An informed viewpoint is necessary, in which critiques of the associated concept that 'form relates to function' are taken into account (Hodder 1995, 86–9; Miller 1985, 51–74; Swift 2017).

A useful exploration of artefact function is that made by Beth Preston. She suggests a dialectical relationship between what she terms 'proper function' and 'system function'. Proper function refers to the use for which an artefact was made, and 'system function' to the way that an artefact is actually used. These may coincide, for instance a woodcutter's axe used to cut down a tree, or they may be different, for instance a woodcutter's axe used as a weapon. As she explains, archaeologists in recent years have tended to focus on the 'system function' definition, using contextual archaeology to examine, particularly, the end-use phase of an artefact's life. The end-use phase is often constituted by a secondary or discrepant function as compared to the original purpose for which the artefact was made (its proper function). However, it is useful to consider both proper and system functions and the way that they are interrelated in much more depth. New uses for objects may develop, influenced by wider social trends, and these may then influence adaptations in the design of future examples (Preston 2000; 2013, 152–60; Swift 2017). Objects, or features of objects, may also move between practical and representational uses (Swift 2014, 231) or simultaneously fulfil both types of uses. A practical use for an object can form either a proper or a system function for that object, and the same is true of representational uses. This complexity in the ongoing development and use of artefacts is something that has been rarely considered in Roman small finds studies. Yet it is essential to take it into account if we are to successfully address the relationships that exist between artefacts and various aspects of human culture and behaviour in the Roman period.

Roman finger-rings with engraved motifs

As a brief example to illustrate the relationship between proper and system function, and the utility of analysing the detail of material properties such as object affordances, I consider Roman finger-rings with engraved motifs. It has been suggested that in the later Roman period the use of such rings to stamp seals was a declining practice, and instead engraved images on rings were used purely decoratively. The argument is made on the basis of the affordances of the stones within seal-rings in the earlier and later Roman periods, although the term is not used explicitly. Stones set into early Roman rings are more transparent and more convex, meaning that the engraved design is difficult to see until it is stamped into wax, while later stones are less transparent and flatter, so that the motif shows up more clearly on the ring itself, and thus they would increasingly be suited to decorative uses. The trend has been suggested to relate to declining levels of literacy in the late Roman period, although any necessary association between seal rings and writing practices has since been questioned by new research that shows that seals were also used in other ways (Zienkiewicz 1986, 121; Johns 1996, 78; Cool 2010, 305; Andrews 2013). Notwithstanding this proviso, the possible trajectory from a practical tool to a representational object, which in this case shows the dialectic between proper and system function uses and the development of a new proper function, can be evaluated further by examining additional details of object appearance and affordance.

As an example, I examine one particular type of engraved motif on finger-rings, the *Chi-rho* motif, that usually occurs engraved on a metal bezel rather than on a stone set into a ring. This late Roman motif, as the name suggests, is composed of Greek letters. When it is depicted on a ring used as a seal-ring, it thus needs to be represented backwards so that the motif appears correctly, and is readable, when stamped into wax (Fig. 11.1). Conversely, if the intention is to use the motif purely as a decorative feature of the ring, it should be depicted frontwards, and the ring will have a mainly representational function. In both cases the ring may be used to display Christian allegiance, or involvement with the late Roman state by the user (Petts 2003, 103–14), but in the first case, the object has a specific practical function in creating a separate stamp that will act representationally. The backwards facing motif shows only slight divergence from the 'correct' motif, and this may mean that it simultaneously held a representational and practical function in some instances.

Examining the orientation of the motif allows us to evaluate the suggestion that rings with engraved motifs lost their function as seal-rings by the late Roman period. Data on extant rings (mostly without provenance) show that the motif occurs depicted both frontwards (14 examples) and backwards (13 examples). These trends exist

Figure 11.1 Bezel from finger-ring with representation of Chi-rho motif (shown backwards), Portable Antiquities Scheme LEIC-5FC533 (Worrell 2008, cat. no. 10). © Leicestershire County Council, licensed under a Creative Commons Licence.

irrespective of materials, with both frontward and backward-facing motifs occurring on both gold and copper alloy rings.[1] In representations of *Chi-rho* motifs in other contexts such as mosaic floors, on silver spoons and plate, on belt fittings, on coinage, etc. they are invariably shown correctly. If, despite facing the wrong way, the motif had become purely representational on rings, or if it were simply a case of mistakes being made, one would expect more instances of backwards facing motifs in these other media. Instead, backwards facing motifs correlate strongly with contexts in which they could function as seal stamps. In conclusion, examining the evidence of potential affordances shows that there is indeed a change towards representational uses for this type of finger-ring, but there is also evidence that a function for an engraved ring to create a seal stamp persisted in the late Roman period.

In addition to demonstrating the relationship between proper and system function, the example is illuminating in a number of ways. Firstly, it shows how affordances are already used intuitively in archaeological interpretation. Clearly, a more explicit approach is desirable. Secondly, it illustrates the way that practical and representational functions for artefacts may fluctuate within one category of material. Thirdly, it shows that the study of affordances provides evidence that contributes to established debates, for instance that concerning cultural change in the late Roman period. More generally, the evidence of artefacts like these allows us to examine daily practice across a wider spectrum of society than might otherwise be possible. There are of course potential problems. This example also shows that affordances must be used with caution, as the change in potential affordances visible in stone-set rings is only partially borne out by evidence of those in which both bezel and hoop are made of metal. We can also see that it is difficult to avoid over-simplification when attempting to incorporate artefact evidence into explanatory narratives.

Dice and the social experience of gaming

For a more detailed example I examine Roman dice in relation to the affordances of the object and how they relate to the social experience of gaming, gambling and divination in the Roman world. Data have been collected as part of a wider

11. Design, function and everyday social practice 157

Figure 11.2 Examples of amber and crystal dice, British Museum acc. nos. 1772,0311.224 (amber) and 1772,0311.220 (rock crystal). © The Trustees of the British Museum.

project on the design and function of everyday Roman artefacts, mainly through museum visits that have provided an opportunity to examine and record details relating to how the dice were used in everyday activities. The data are evenly split between Roman Britain and Roman Egypt (ca. 100 from each area), with a scatter of material from other places. The dice, including those in luxury materials, show much evidence of normative use, for instance, chipping to corners and wear to surfaces, so we can be confident that for much of their lives they were used for the purposes for which they were made. In terms of assessing the material qualities of the object I was fortunate enough to be allowed to roll many of the dice and so evaluate how the qualities of dice may have affected play at first-hand (see Swift 2017 for a full presentation of some of the material discussed below).

Dice were used in gambling games, board games similar to backgammon, and in divination practices (for these see Graf 2005; Klingshorn 2002; 2005). Ancient sources tell us something about these games and their social and cultural context, and archaeological evidence of course exists in the form of game boards, counters and dice shakers, as well as the dice themselves (on gaming and equipment, see Toner 1995; Carbone 2005; Purcell 1995; Schädler 1995; May 1991).

At one level, dice as material agents enacted the will of the goddess Fortuna in the human world. They also express the concept of randomness or probability and there is some evidence from ancient texts that the Roman elite understood how these concepts related to dice games: Cicero for instance shows an awareness of probability with regard to successive dice throws (David 1962, 24; Cicero *On*

Divination, 1, 23 [transl. Wardle 2006, 53–4]). Dice are particularly interesting objects from a material perspective, because the material qualities of the object directly affect the experience of play and are used to enact and contest particular social rules. For instance, a small number of Roman dice are weighted with lead to always land on a six. For two examples, from Arles and Nîmes, see *Artefacts online encyclopedia* type DEJ-401, http:/artefacts/mom.fr. Another unfinished example comes from Rome (St. Clair 2003, 114 cat. no. 597), dated to the first to second centuries AD. In this way, weighted dice contest the convention of fairness of outcome seen in the design of cubic dice.

Although this is of course a broad-brush approach, I examine what the objects 'do' in the social context, and trace consequent possible diversity in social experience, by comparing dice made from luxury materials to those in more everyday materials. Elite gamers may sometimes have participated in games alongside lower status people, for instance in taverns, and thus also have used dice made in more ordinary materials. Based on literary evidence, however, Toner suggests that gambling and gaming normally occurred in peer-groups (1995, 95). Such a comparison has not previously been made, since extant studies of dice focus only on bone, the most common material.

Luxury materials: amber and rock crystal dice

The luxury materials under study are amber and rock crystal (often inlaid with gold leaf). Fig. 11.2 shows examples of each. Although many are without provenance, dice in these materials retrieved in excavation contexts support the Roman date that has been assigned to them in museum collections (e.g. rock crystal die inlaid with gold leaf, Koster 2013, burial 4 at Nijmegen, dating to the late first to early second century AD; amber die from Roman London, context dated to the second half of the fourth century AD, Glyn Davis pers. comm.).

Dice also occur in ivory, but since this material can be difficult to visually distinguish from bone it would not be a very effective marker of luxury and as such it is not considered here. Luxury dice are likely to have been used in private games among the urban elite. The only example with details of a burial context suggests it was owned by a wealthy member of the provincial elite (Koster 2013, 186–7, Burial 4). Examples in the British Museum collected by Sir William Hamilton, Ambassador to the Kingdom of Naples, are likely to have been acquired in Italy.[2]

How far the dice conform to the ideal of a perfect cube (and thus an equal likelihood of all outcomes) can be examined by classing as 'regular' all those dice where the lengths of each face measured within 5% of each other. The number of rock crystal and amber dice for which accurate measurements are available is quite small (8 examples). All except one were regular cubes using the 5% measure. Some further examples of Roman amber dice shown in photographs (accurate measurements not available) appear to show similar trends (Calvi 2005, 134–5 and Tav. 94–6). All the rock crystal and amber dice studied show high production standards, for instance in the regularity with which the spots are arranged, and the uniformity of the treatment of edges and surfaces. Standardisation in design would have been used as a reference point for quality, implying that the object was trustworthy, and the qualities of the dice attempt to foster a uniformity of gaming experience. Of course, different users would still be affected by the material qualities of the objects in different ways, for instance transparency or translucency would make the dice more problematic for some user groups, such as short-sighted people, since the numbers are quite difficult to make out even where filled in with an opaque material. It is evident that the affordances of the object affect different users differently and potentially exclude some categories of users (Swift 2017).

Unusual or expensive materials, although probably chosen for status reasons, would also have functioned to deter crooked practices. Obtaining biased dice in these materials, which could be substituted for the originals during the course of play, would be more difficult than accessing dice made in commonly available materials like bone. The hardness of rock crystal would also be a useful affordance as it would inhibit tampering with the shape of the dice. Other properties of these particular materials, such as the transparency of the rock crystal dice and translucency of amber, help guarantee that these dice are not weighted.

Overall, the design features and material qualities of dice in luxury materials suggest that the various types of games played with these dice developed on the principle that there was an equal chance of throwing one through six, and that elite gamers and gamblers knew that a die should be a perfect cube in order to achieve a fair game.

Everyday materials: bone dice

I focus in this section mainly on the data pertaining to bone dice, as this is by far the most common material (others include opaque glass, pottery, wood, stone such as steatite or limestone, and copper-alloy). Classing as 'regular' all those dice where the lengths of each face were within 5% of each other, only 20% of bone dice were uniform on this measure. The fact that 20% are good cubes does show some awareness of the concept that uniformity and equality of outcomes are desirable. However, the fairly low incidence of good cubic dice makes clear that the norm for players will actually have been irregular-looking objects. The most common type of irregularity is shortness on one axis ('flat' dice in modern gambling terminology), usually that between the one and six face (Fig. 11.3 shows some examples). This phenomenon has already been noted by previous scholars, who suggest that it is mainly an accidental feature relating to production methods and the available dimensions of bone suitable for dice-making (Schmid 1978, 58; Greep 1983, 243–7; Poplin 2004, 62). Additional evidence can also be adduced, which there is not space

Figure 11.3 Examples of bone one-to-six flats, Petrie Museum, acc. nos. UC59202 and UC59217 from Egypt. Courtesy of the Petrie Museum of Egyptian Archaeology, UCL.

Figure 11.4 Examples of five-to-six flats in materials other than bone, Petrie Museum, UC59244 (stone), UC59226 (ceramic), UC59240 (stone), and UC59236 (stone), all from Egypt. Courtesy of the Petrie Museum of Egyptian Archaeology, UCL.

to consider here (Swift 2017). Recurring features of objects, which were not necessarily intended by the makers, but which have come into existence as a result of particular constraints on production processes, demonstrate the agency of materials and are a reminder that artefact form results from many interrelated factors of which design intention is only one. Bone dice also tend to be much more irregular in their other features (arrangement of spots; treatment of edges and surfaces) than those in luxury materials considered above.

Although many non-cubic bone dice were probably not deliberately produced, dice that are shorter on one axis also occur in materials other than bone, such as ceramic, stone, and wood, showing that not all examples result from constraints in relation to the available dimensions of the raw material (examples in Fig. 11.4). Feugère and Picod also note that there are some bone dice of non-cubic form that have been deliberately made in different shapes; for example, a lozenge-shaped dice from Boscoreale (Feugère and Picod 2014, 30, 41). Further instances of lozenge-shaped dice can also be identified.[3] In addition, I have been able to distinguish some instances of dice that have been broken and renumbered (see Fig. 11.5). They have changed shape from a cube to a much flatter form, but the re-numbering suggests

11. Design, function and everyday social practice 161

that they continued to be used as before and that the alteration to their shape was not felt to be problematic. We can also look at contextual evidence of dice found together as part of gaming assemblages, for instance in burials with counters, game-boards, and other equipment. Individual burial assemblages include both good cubic dice and those of more irregular form.[4] This suggests that dice of variable shapes were used together in the same games and differences between them were not considered important.

One particularly 'flat' dice form found in bone does appear to be something of a special case. The form consists of an oval plaque only a few millimetres deep, numbered on both the two principal flat sides and the narrow edge faces (example in Fig. 11.6; the spots on back and edge faces confirms they are not to be confused with furniture inlay in bone). Feugère and Picod cite one instance from Claydon Pike, and several further examples have also been found (see Table 11.1).[5] The dice have only four possible numbers, in two cases 3, 4, 5, and 6, and so it is likely that they were used for different purposes than normal, six-sided dice forms. Experimental rolling of two of the examples shows that they are strongly biased to the flat surfaces, as one would expect, but do occasionally land on the edge faces.[6] Dated contexts suggest a likely second century AD date (Table 11.1).

Figure 11.5 Examples of dice broken and renumbered, National Museum of Ireland, acc. no. 1904.548 from Oxyrhynchus (one uppermost), photo taken with the permission of the National Museum of Ireland and reproduced with the permission of the National Museum of Ireland, and Verulamium Museum, acc. no. 2002.25 (broken and renumbered) from St. Albans (six uppermost), photo author, courtesy of Verulamium Museum, St. Albans.

It was proposed by Feugère and Picod that this dice form can be linked to pre-Roman Iron Age dice of parallelipid shape which also have only four faces numbered three, four, five, and six (example in Fig. 11.6) (Feugère and Picod 2014, 38). The larger number of examples now documented, including an additional one numbered three, four, five and six, support this interpretation. Firstly, the social distribution of the material can be considered. All the known examples come from Romano-British sites, and so this form of dice would appear to represent a localised cultural tradition specific to southern Britain. Three of the examples come from Roman rural settlements, one from a small town, and one from a Roman fort. In general, rural settlements and small towns have less 'Roman' material culture profiles than major towns and military bases, and sometimes feature material culture that can be linked to indigenous traditions (e.g. Eckardt 2005). Secondly, the decoration of these dice can be investigated. The Richborough and Claydon Pike oval plaques

Table 11.1 Oval plaques with numbering.

Site details	Reference number/ publication details	Spot arrangement	Dated context
Claydon Pike, Whelford, near Swindon, Wiltshire. Iron Age and Roman period rural settlement	Miles et al 2007, fig. 5.28, cat. no. 40. See also Feugère and Picod 2014, 41	5 opp. 6, (flat sides) 3 opp 4 (edges) Six spot made up of two semicircles of three spots	None
Wanborough, near Swindon, Wiltshire. Roman small town	Ashmolean Museum acc. no. AN1955.260; See also Passmore 1922, 272-80.	5 opp. 6 (flat sides) 3 opp 4 (edges) Six spot made up of three rows of two spots	None
Richborough, Kent. Roman fort	English Heritage Archive, Dover, acc. no. 4052; see also Wilson 1968, 106.	7 (flat side) 5 (edge) other sides unnumbered Seven spot made up of two semicircles of three spots plus one in the middle.	ca. AD 90
Stonea, Cambridgeshire. Roman rural settlement with villa; also thought to have had a military presence in relation to supply of goods	Greep 1996, cat. no. 65, fig. 198.	7 (flat side) 4 (edge) other sides unnumbered Seven spot made up of horizontal rows of two, three and two spots.	Late 2nd/ early 3rd century AD
Brentford, Essex. Roman roadside settlement	Cowie, Wardle and Thorp 2013, cat. no. <S22>, fig. 62.	1 opp. 6 (flat sides) 4 (edge) other edge unnumbered Six spot made up of rough square with one dot either side.	Late 2nd/ early 3rd century AD

show derivation from Iron Age traditions in that the spot arrangement is the same as that on some Iron Age parallelipid dice (two semicircles of three spots each at either end of the face, see Fig. 11.6), and different to the Roman norm (two parallel rows of three spots each along the length of the face).[7] Finally, the arrangement of spots across the different faces can also be considered, with examples of both Iron Age parallelipid dice, and oval counters, featuring an arrangement in which five is placed opposite six and three opposite four (Table 11.1). Some Roman influence percolating into the design of these items is clearly evident: the example from Wanborough for instance shows a 'Roman-style' six spot, and the example from Brentford features numbering with one opposite six, which is the Roman norm. Taken as a whole, therefore, there is strong evidence that these oval plaques in bone show the survival and continuing development of pre-Roman cultural practices in the Roman period in Britain.

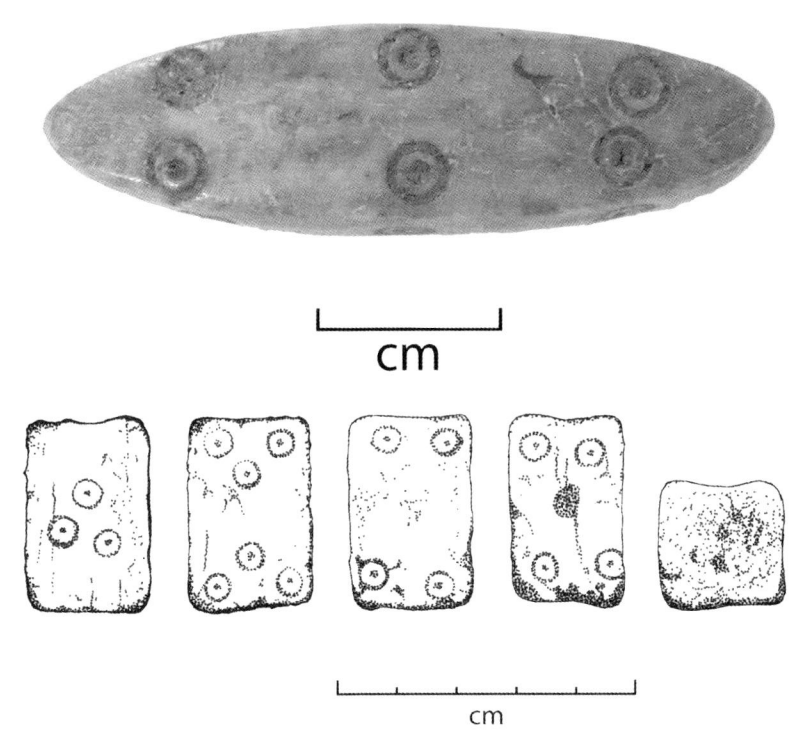

Figure 11.6 Example of oval plaque, from Wanborough, Ashmolean Museum acc. no. AN1955.260 © Ashmolean Museum, University of Oxford, and parallelipid die from Knowth, Ireland, redrawn by Lloyd Bosworth after Eogan 1974, fig. 31 no. 150.

Discrepant experience in everyday gaming

It is evident that the trends displayed by dice in non-elite materials are somewhat different to those of their more luxurious counterparts. The survey of bone dice above shows that this material does not foster a uniformity of gaming experience – indeed quite the reverse. The existence of unusual, specialised forms such as the oval plaques implies a variety of usage including, perhaps, different games or divination practices derived from pre-Roman traditions.

Even when considering only the dice with six faces, which are likely to have been used to play games of Roman origin, there would still be considerable diversity of gaming experience among everyday players. The likelihood of the dice falling on particular numbers would be different from one game to the next according to whether more cubic or more rectangular dice were used. The common occurrence of dice shorter on the axis between one and six would mean that in many dice games, these numbers (the most favoured and disfavoured in Roman gaming), would be the most likely to be thrown, and the game would be more exciting as a result, offering more gains and reverses than a similar, elite dice game. There might also be discrepant knowledge between different individual players. Some might have been more aware than others of how the shape would affect the throw, and could place their bets accordingly.

The concept of a die as an object that ensures an equal likelihood of six different outcomes is much less well-established in dice made from ordinary materials, and it seems likely that ideas of what a die should be, or do, are affected both by the agency of materials (inadvertent drift in the features of dice as a by-product of particular material choices and production processes) and by other concepts of gaming equipment that co-existed with the concept of a cubic die. In Britain this will have included concepts based on parallelipid dice. Divergent dice forms that are developments of pre-Roman traditions can also be identified in other provinces such as Roman Egypt (Swift 2017).

In the case of games or ritual practices derived from Iron Age traditions, exact modes of use and any attendant rules cannot be elucidated, yet the material evidence is still important in suggesting that such activities existed, and provided a means of continuing and affirming non-Roman cultural traditions through daily practice. For the Roman games, some details of their structure and conventions of play are known from written sources, yet it is the archaeological evidence – particularly, the concept of affordances in combination with a detailed analysis of the objects – that sheds light on the experience of using the dice, and the relationships between human and material agencies that exist in their uses.

Discussion: how does studying artefacts change Roman social history?

Artefacts have an obvious contribution to make to Roman social history in providing information about everyday social practice and behaviour. However, in addition to reconstructing aspects of Roman daily living, this case study has also illuminated a number of ways in which artefact study can address broader questions of interest to social historians. These include how culture is assimilated and maintained, how it develops, and what cultural diversity exists, both regionally and across different social groups within the Roman empire.

In previous scholarship, provincial Roman material culture has been interpreted mainly from the perspective of assertions of/transformations in identity, and this is persuasive (e.g. Mattingly 2006; Eckardt 2014). Although some scholars, such as Eckardt, recognise the importance of daily practice (see, for instance, her (2014, 210) emphasis on variant practices that are indicative of regional identities), artefact usage in relation to modes of behaviour and habits of daily practice has not been sufficiently stressed. The focus has tended to be on the potential of material culture to outwardly represent and communicate identities (Pitts 2014, 71), rather than the instantiation of culture through the materiality of actions and experiences, which is clearly crucial both in producing/maintaining a particular worldview and associated cultural conventions, and in bringing about cultural change.

Roman material culture that is found across the empire has usually been discussed from the perspective of cultural homogeneity and similarity (Mattingly 2006, 472). Studies have emphasised that Roman-style material culture could also be used in a multiplicity of ways within provincial society, and needs to be seen within the context of the negotiation of power relations (Webster 2001, 217). This has been explored with the greatest success from the point of view of religious and ritual practice, an area which offers some of the best evidence, although much of it relates only to social elites (e.g. Mattingly 2006, 480–7; Webster 1995; 2001; James 2001, 199–201 discusses the problems with this). Webster stressed, however, the importance of everyday domestic material culture in understanding provincial experience, particularly of the poorer sectors of society (Webster 2001, 223). The present study shows that there is much potential for further investigation of ordinary everyday artefacts, illuminating a diversity of practice and behaviour not available to us from textual sources, and allowing a focus on the non-elite levels of provincial Roman society. Furthermore, focusing on the areas of behaviour and experience allows us to consider to greater effect the discrepant experiences of different social groups. New material culture provided the possibility of different ways of living (Hingley 2005, 106–7, 118; Laurence and Trifilò 2015, 104). The scope for new leisure pursuits provided by gaming equipment was apparently, judging by the quantities of such material found throughout the empire, taken up enthusiastically by provincial populations. Yet a detailed study of the material culture shows that gaming practices at elite and more ordinary levels of society were quite different experiences.

Richard Hingley has noted the way in which new behaviours are informed by past materialities (Hingley 2005, 74). The converse is also true, that introduced artefacts can be used within previous cultures and traditions (Webster 2001, 218). Yet interpretations of artefacts that stress their divergent meanings within differing contexts of use sometimes appear to treat the artefacts themselves as unchanging (e.g. Keay 2001, 130–6; James 2001, 203–6; Mattingly 2006, 470–3), and overlook the way in which changes in usage or understanding of the artefacts in turn impact on the production of new versions of the artefacts (which themselves continue to contribute to behavioural practices). The evidence discussed here reveals more of the *process* of interaction of new objects with established cultural habits – the way in which, over time and within different contexts, different versions of objects develop that are the product of the intersection of new material culture, such as cubic dice, with previous habits and traditions developed in the context of a rather different material world.

By studying ordinary everyday items such as dice or seal-rings, I have attempted to examine the extent to which introduced mental concepts, which might be termed 'Roman', or 'global' if a less culturally loaded term is preferred (Pitts 2014, 79), were or were not assimilated into everyday provincial practice and behaviour, or how they were ultimately rejected or subject to an ongoing process of modification. In this way, it is possible to document the gradual abandonment of what had once been established behaviour, and the failures as well as the successes of cultural transmission (a process termed 'glocalisation', see Pitts and Versluys 2015b, 14; Robertson 1992). The example of bone dice also shows that the establishment and/or maintenance of cultural norms can be affected by material constraints on production (which could be termed the agency of materials), that may have a significant impact on the production and reproduction of artefacts, associated cultural behaviours and user experiences. From both points of view (the agency of users, and of materials), material studies illuminate the often incremental nature of cultural change. The process of the reproduction of artefacts inevitably introduces unintentional change that has an impact on daily experience. Even with regard to cultural change brought about by the negotiation of power relations, or by the reframing of cultural phenomena within new contexts of use, there is a large component to culture change that is incremental, and worked out through the practices of material living at all levels of society.

Acknowledgements
Grateful thanks to the Leverhulme Trust for supporting this research with a Research Fellowship, and to all the museums and other organisations who made available their collections for personal study. I would also like to thank Michael Marshall for drawing my attention to a publication reference on oval plaques, and Glyn Davis for providing context information on an amber die from London.

Notes

1. *Chi-rho* motif represented backwards: British Museum acc. nos. 1872,0604.309 (Dalton 1912 cat. no. 25); 1984,1001.1 (also published in Sas and Thoen 2002 cat. no. 232); 1983,1003.1, AF. 215 (Dalton 1901, cat. no. 75), AF.213, AF.214, and AF. 216 (the last three also published in Dalton 1912, cat. nos.29, 30 and 31); Chadour 1994, cat. no. 452; Chadour and Joppien 1985 no. 110; Henkel 1913 cat. no. 1004; Henkel 1913, cat. no. 1864; Worrell 2008, 361, cat. no.10 (Portable Antiquities Scheme LEIC-5FC533).
    Chi-rho motif represented frontwards: British Museum acc. no. AF.211 (also published in Dalton 1912, cat. no. 28); Chadour 1994, cat. no. 456; Chadour and Joppien 1984 cat. nos 106, 112 and 118; Henkel 1913 cat. nos. 106, 402 and 1867; Sas and Thoen 2002 cat. nos. 233 and 234; Mawer 1995 nos. D3.Si.5, D3.Si.6, D3.Br.3, D3.Je.1 (*Rho-cross*).
2. British Museum acc. nos. 1772.0311.220; 1772,0311.224; and 1772,0311.228.
3. From London, London Archaeological Archive and Research Centre OPT81[483]<637>; from Brancaster, Norwich Castle Museum 2011.336.2; probably from Caesarea, Hecht Museum, University of Haifa, Lessingimages.com no. 08-05-09/.
4. E.g. in a burial assemblage from London with a game board, counters and four dice, the percentage difference between the shortest and longest sides was different for each dice; for one the difference was only 7% MSL87[1837]<716>; for the others it was 19%, 28% and 39% (Museum of London MSL87[1837]<714>, <715>, and <717>). Another burial assemblage from the same site contained two dice in a box, one with the shortest side within 5% of the longest side, and so very accurate; the other with the shortest and longest sides different by 14%. Museum of London MSL87[252]<560> and <561>. See Barber and Bowsher 2000 for the burial assemblages. Two dice found in a burial at Ospringe with a set of gaming counters were more similar to each other, both showing one axis shorter by 12% (Maison Dieu Faversham Group XXXVII no. 81006026). See also Whiting 1925.

5. Cowie, Wardle and Thorp (2013, 82) list the known examples (apart from the Claydon Pike plaque). See Table 11.1 for further references to the individual sites. Those from Wanborough and Richborough were personally inspected including experimental throws, see below.
6. In 120 throws, both English Heritage archive Dover no. 4052 from Richborough and Ashmolean Museum AN1955.260 from Wanborough landed 111 times on either the flat upper or lower surface and nine times on one of the edges.
7. E.g. an example from Burrian, see MacGregor 1984, fig. 71a; three examples from Knowth, in a grave dated to 40 BC–120 AD, Eogan 1974, 76 and fig. 31 (for the more recently carried out carbon-dating, see Hall and Forsyth 2011, 1330). All of these feature five opposite six and three opposite four.

Chapter 12

Object ontology and cultural taxonomies. Examining the agency of style, material and objects in classification through Egyptian material culture in Pompeii and Rome

Eva Mol[*]

Introduction: objects' turn beyond representation

This chapter discusses the agency of objects in cultural and stylistic classifications (or taxonomies) and the consequences of modern and ancient categorisation for the interpretation, use, and perception of objects in the Roman world. Both within modern scholarship and in antiquity, the role and agency of objects in classification is vital, albeit on different levels. It should be stipulated that material agency in this chapter is not meant as bestowing life, personhood, or intention on objects. Instead, material agency is proposed as the power that style or objects have to affect human intentions and behaviour. Stemming from their apparent role within cultural classification schemes, Egyptian(-styled) objects in Roman Italy are used as a case study to highlight the complex role of object agency in categorisation. Furthermore, as the objects found in domestic contexts are less subject to imperial-political decision making, these are considered a good way of elucidating agency and categorisation processes. It could be suggested, moreover, that Egyptian artefacts (Aegyptiaca) in Roman houses have suffered exponentially from the traditional symbolic, historical, political top-down interpretations, in which they were taken as religious or exotic, and treated as a distinct collection on the basis of stylistic properties. In this respect, it is not only important to re-evaluate the process of classification, but also to investigate the effect that such artefacts themselves could instigate. I argue that our understanding of objects in the Roman world can be significantly improved through a critical application of methods and theories from the recent material turn in archaeology.

---

[*] Faculty of Archaeology, Leiden University.

The 'material turn' is now approximately a decade old, and by fits and starts a number of critical voices have emerged (e.g. Barrett 2014; Gardner 2004; Graves-Brown 2013; Lindstrøm 2015. See Robb 2010 for a historiography of 'agency'). Although a few scholars have discarded material agency altogether as a flawed social theory or a re-invented empiricism after post-processual archaeology (considered overtly anthropocentric by its opponents), most critical voices warn against one-sided views of how agency as a term is applied, against the reductionist approach of object-oriented philosophy focusing too much on material, and against the sometimes simplistic and conflicting views on the relations between objects and human beings (Lindstrøm 2015, 207–38; Harman 2015, 94–110; Fowler and Harris 2015, 127–48; Sørensen 2013, 1–18). Such criticisms are useful for their realisation that it is not only the object that moves people, and for drawing attention to the particularities of different socio-physical environments. The agency of objects should never be accounted for in isolation, nor should we conceive agency as having only one significance in terms of power and directionality when human-object relationships are concerned (Mol 2013; 2015). In fact, object agency may be a dangerous theory for archaeology, running the risk of granting too much power to the material remains of past societies. Objects have the power to shape and move people, but human beings are not slavish followers of material constraints; they find ways of using them differently, alter their meaning, appearance or physical workings (Knappett 2005). Their relationships are more complex and multifaceted than a term like 'symmetrical' suggests (Webmoor and Witmore 2008, 53–70; Graves-Brown 2013), and although society is built up from things, things do not exist or act out agency without people, they rather co-exist in complex and dynamic networks of being and becoming.

To date, Roman archaeology has not been at the forefront of the debate on materiality; but it has lots to gain from it, and to offer to it. In contrast to many other 'archaeologies', Roman archaeology has a dominant historical basis, and has only recently begun to explore other avenues. The historical knowledge of the Roman past is exhaustive, and it is human agency that forms the principal framework for this knowledge. Roman archaeologists must therefore weigh the value of words and ideas, both in history and historiography, when making interpretations. *Materialising Roman Histories*, as the book title proposes, is therefore not only a useful initiative, but a necessary one, as it balances the prevailing human agency in the writing of Roman history. However, because of the existing conceptual burden, a different view can only be brought about by carefully integrating the power of objects into the present frames of textual and visual knowledge. Can we understand Roman history from objects? Using theories from the material turn is not only valuable to Roman history as counterbalance to the written word; because Roman archaeologists are continuously forced to take a nuanced approach due to the existence of texts, images, and objects, they are able to add to the general theory of materiality and object agency in archaeology. In other words, Roman archaeology might be able to 'soften' the material turn. This book and its contributions do not promise to re-write history, but to materialise it, to show where objects and environmental processes outside human intentionality mattered and what objects did while people made decisions.

Classifying the Egyptian and the agency of style

In order to evaluate object agency – i.e. how objects shape our minds and influence Roman history – it is useful to analyse the emergence of mental classification and categorisations. Classifications or taxonomies are cultural constructs made to describe the external world, and are at the same time influenced by the world itself, in a process also called 'ecological hermeneutics'. Although classifications are perceived as static bounded entities (otherwise they would not function), in effect they are a continuously changing network of links. As classifications are used to understand the world, exploring their dynamics and the influence of form and matter on this process is able to inform both about existing and changing worldviews. This starts with the scholar him- or herself: when considering relationality and object agency it is important to acknowledge that the object of study is not detached from the study itself. A 'thing' is what it is because of the precise configuration of relations that comprise it at any moment, and the investigator is part of that configuration too. For this reason, the scientific entanglement with Egypt forms an important part of the analysis (see Barad 2007, 91–2).

Cultural labels are powerful guiding elements when studying Roman material culture: Greek, Etruscan, Egyptian, Archaic, Classical; these classifications are based on form and appearance, on stylistic properties. The main problem is that such labels seem to have slowly concealed how objects were categorised by their users, thereby obscuring how cultural styles might have played roles in the past. Another issue is that categorisation, both modern and ancient, is an automatic process that occurs largely unconsciously. This makes studying classifications not only significant to learn about the Roman world, it also becomes relevant on a historiographical and methodological level. Our current knowledge about the Roman world was shaped through these unconscious existing taxonomies, by academics and non-academics alike. As Bianchi Bandinelli aptly put it, 'The art of the Roman period, like Greek art, is part of a widely disseminated cultural pattern. It is precisely for this reason that the underlying historical truths have acquired such a thick incrustation of commonplace judgements, affecting the specialist as much as the man in the street' (Bianchi Bandinelli 1970, ix). For these reasons scholars often fail to correctly classify something from a Roman viewpoint, mainly because of two causes: (1) automatic reliance on modern categories or (2) arguing from scientifically constructed classification schemes. Neither of these represent Roman perception, but nonetheless they often cause an emic/etic confusion in which the scholarly classification becomes equated with Roman use. The elusive category of 'Egyptian' has suffered substantially from both types of errors in cultural classification.

How can this be overcome? Cultural taxonomies present an inherent difficulty inherited from their original counterparts developed in biology (invented by Linnaeus), which were not only seen as a useful ordering of the world, but as describing its truthful nature. However, even biological classifications are creations that do not fit all dynamics of nature (see Dunnell 1986; 2001, xiii–xxiv; Hurt and Rakita 2001). An ecological approach as emphasised in this chapter holds that things (objects in this case) are not determined by their logical relations within a classification scheme, but by their working relations with other things in their environment, in which the relations are prior to the things related, and the systemic 'wholes' are prior to their component parts (Baird Callicot 1996, 199–200). It therefore strongly emphasises relationality and perception of the environment as the basis for categorisation. When carefully dissecting categorisation schemes, it might be possible to design a new way of looking at style, and point to some of the dangers involved in classifications made on the basis of cultural styles. These dangers, however, also prove to be important, because they illustrate the large influence that objects and their appearance have had on the human mind outside of human awareness.

Another important point that arises from this chapter on object agency is that although *some objects* move us (emotionally and consciously such as art works, or physically like walls), it can be argued that *all objects* shape us. This means that not all objects have a conscious effect on human behaviour, but that they do affect human beings in some (not always tangible) way. This less tangible impact of objects on humans becomes most evident when regarding categorisation as a neurological aptitude. A wine glass is a mundane object that does not catch immediate conscious attention – in our everyday use it goes un-interpreted. However, the material and form of the glass elicit a certain mental concept of a glass; its form dictates how to drink, and thereby unconsciously affects how we use it (Gibson 1979), but also how we think of it. It affects how different drinking vessels and different glass objects are valued and thereby aids in the creation of a category. This shows that categories such as 'drinking vessels' are usually formed from what can be observed in a person's immediate surroundings. When unknown things are encountered, they become automatically added to the category or discarded depending on whether they fit the category. In some cases, depending on certain factors that will be discussed below, objects might even stretch the category. Categorisation is an ecological feature showing that we understand the world through objects and therefore objects form our view of the world. For this reason, it is of considerable importance to take Roman material culture into account when regarding its conceptual history. Can Roman ontology be understood better by looking at objects?

Although not often featuring explicitly in literary sources, scholars have connected Egyptian-style objects to political and historical events. This begins with Augustus' defeat of Marc Antony and the annexation of Egypt, which was physically commemorated through raising an obelisk on the spina of the Circus Maximus. During the reign of Augustus an alleged wave of Egyptian objects (commonly described as

'Egyptomania') reached Italy due to the easier transfer of objects after Egypt became a Roman province. All things Egyptian-looking in Italy were either interpreted by scholars to belong to the Isis-cult or to Augustus' capture of Egypt, including Egyptianising wall paintings, the pyramidal grave monument of Cestius, the miniature obelisk copied from the Circus Maximus in the *Horti Sallustiani* and countless smaller artefacts imported from Egypt or made to look that way (Van Aerde 2015 for an overview). The objects and influences assigned to this Egyptomania were automatically labelled by scholars as 'Oriental', 'exotic', and 'Other'. Augustus' negative reaction to the Isis cults added to these ideas and reinforced the connection between the concepts of Egypt and Isis in relation to material culture (Orlin 2008, 231–53). Another prominent historical point in time concerning Egyptian objects is the Flavian period, especially illustrated through the refurbishment of the Iseum Campense by Domitian after the great fire of AD 80, which again linked the use of particular objects to a clear historical event. Under his auspices, the sanctuary not only saw the erection of a multitude of obelisks, he also imported a tremendous number of statues of Egyptian deities and animals from Egypt to redecorate the sanctuary. Through this particular event it is argued that the Flavians purposely re-Egyptianised the temple and forever changed the concept of Egypt in Rome (Versluys 2017a, 8–9; 2013a, 252).

As can be noted, in all these cases the objects clearly function to symbolise representational concepts, such as political power or elite status, and explanations depend on human intentions and historical individuals. Did Roman classifications change after the influx of different objects, and can we trace that through studying how objects were used? Of course, the obelisk of Augustus fell within the category 'Egyptian' at the moment of its installment, as it was literally inscribed on the object itself (for the use of obelisks see Parker 2007, 209–22; Curran *et al.* 2009; Versluys 2010, 7–36; Swetnam-Burland 2010, 135–53). A more harmful effect of the preoccupation with historical evidence, however, is the tendency of an event such as the Iseum Campense reconstruction to somehow dictate the use and meaning of all other objects that look Egyptian. This is why it is important to investigate how objects were used and how they behaved in ancient classifications, when analysed apart from the scientific cultural label Egyptian. The main question in historical terms is therefore not what Augustus or the Flavians intentionally did to the image of Egypt or of Isis, but what the objects did in the Augustan and Flavian period that could accommodate such decisions.

Classification and objectification

Before moving to the objects in question, it is important to further elucidate some of the scholarly problems concerning classification, the act of classifying, and the role of the object herein. As briefly discussed, two types of classification (although linked to the same neurological principles) are used to interpret Roman material stylistically. The first are scientific sequential period styles, first introduced in

Classical Archaeology by Winckelmann for classical sculpture (in which he made an ordering according to style instead of location, later redefined by Wölfflin: see Winckelmann 1764; Wölfflin 1915). Winckelmann and Wölflinn's work, and the works they inspired throughout art history and archaeology, made style and stylistic analysis an inherent part of the archaeologist's vocabulary. Criticisms of these cultural styles are part and parcel of the vocabulary too. However, both through use and through criticism they have shaped a framework that still guides how ancient art is viewed today. In this vein, it is especially problematic that these art historical classification schemes of Greco-Roman art slowly became equated with a Roman perspective. Mapping small stylistic differences in isolated objects that are studied in a museum-context, as Winckelmann did, produced different perceptions and categories to the Roman emic ones (although Winckelmann's schemes were nonetheless based on comparable neurological principles in terms of perception in ecological use-contexts: the objects at his disposal and the room in which he made his observations hugely influenced his final categorisations – see Pommier 2003; Harloe 2013).

The second type of categorisation that complicates emic object analysis in Roman archaeology is the influence of the modern analyst's internal classification systems, as shaped by automatic responses to modern environments in everyday life. This can be illustrated in a conceptual network constructed on the basis of questionnaires, which in this case shows the modern concepts to which Egypt is associated. Fig. 12.1 depicts the network of associations (semantic network) concerning the concept 'Egypt', based on interviews with students from different disciplines in the central library of the University of Amsterdam in May 2014, as mapped in the network software program Gephi. Although the survey contained no proper statistical analysis, it serves as a useful point of departure to explain how classification principles work and how objects and the environment play a role this process. It shows the difference between modern associations and those of the past concerning the concept of 'Egypt'.

The most frequently occurring concept linked to 'Egypt' (the most central node) listed by all participants was 'pyramids' (Fig. 12.1). 'Mummies' and 'desert' also occurred often. Secondly, the reference to 'General Sisi' and the 'Muslim brothers' are the only contemporary concepts covered in the news at the time of the questionnaire. Looking closely at all the answers, there are very few abstract concepts ('violence', 'dry', and 'magic' occur, but are not directly related to the concept 'Egypt'). Most are objects or visual images, derived from our knowledge through books, travels, museums and movies. This shows that visually based entities principally created our image of Egypt. What is the role of objects? Concepts of course are not given entities, like physical objects, but are actively derived from the world of objects via abstraction (Klaus 1973, 214). Any concept formation and any semantic relation has an ecological foundation (Hjørland 2009, 1519–36). The immediate physical environment is of fundamental importance in the creation of classifications, something which also increasingly has been established by studies from linguistics, cognitive science,

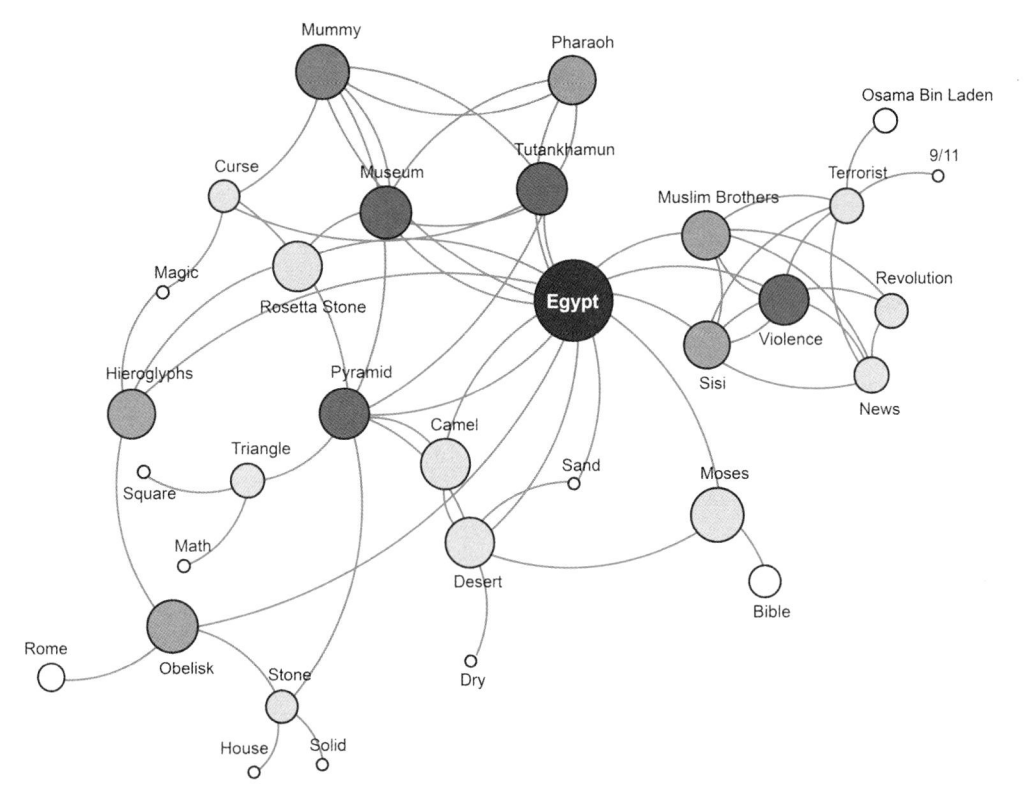

12. Object ontology and cultural taxonomies 175

Figure 12.1 Modern semantic network of the concept 'Egypt'.

psychology, and biology (Rogers et al. 2003, 625–62; Hjørland 2009; Noë 2004; 2009; Gibson 1979). However, the small survey teaches something more about classification in general, the role of objects, and its relation to Egypt. Although the world is more complex and dynamic than humans can cope with, the fact that humans constantly categorise and try to make their world less dynamic is significant in itself. Through the storage of mental representations (concepts) and the subsequent categorisation of these concepts, the world may be made sense of. These are cognitive brain functions without which humans would not be able to cope with new information.

The encounter of a new unseen marble statue would be an impossible task if it could not be stored in a mental category of other objects. Concepts do not exist independently of one other, but are interlinked. The relations between such concepts are known as 'semantic relations' (Stock 2010, 1951–69; Khoo and Na 2006, 157–228; Storey 1993, 455–88). These semantic relations in the brain work through a complex set of storage capabilities, linked to hierarchies, symbolism, and visual input. On the most superficial scale semantic relations can be defined on the basis of a couple of premises: resemblance (Wittgenstein 1953) and co-occurrence. When things resemble each other, they are likely to be linked, such as cats and panthers, for instance. When things do not resemble, but usually occur together they are also linked, as for instance water and boats, or bacon and eggs. Wittgenstein argued in his *Philosophische Untersuchungen* that things formerly thought to be connected by one essential common feature were in fact connected by a series of overlapping similarities, where no one feature was common to all (Wittgenstein 1953).

The relations *between* concepts are more complex and dependent on different types of existing relations that can vary in different contexts. According to Barsalou there exists a wide variety of relational concepts, including spatial relations (e.g. between seat and back in the frame for chair), temporal relations (e.g. between eating and paying in the frame for dining out), causal relations (e.g. between fertilisation and birth in the frame for reproduction), and intentional relations (e.g. between motive and attack in the frame for murder) (Barsalou 1992, 35–6). The greater the similarity, or the more often they occur together, the stronger the association between them. These workings are universal but the associations are very much environmentally and culturally based. If someone has never seen a panther, this will not become an association, no matter how much it looks like a cat, and the same goes when one is not used to eating bacon with eggs (Storey 1993, 455–88). Although archaeologists tend to be very much focused on the phenomenon of resemblance within classifications, co-occurrence usually receives less attention, while it plays a large role in the creation of categorisations – not only in antiquity, but also in historiography (work has been done in the context of contextual ecology, e.g. Butzer 1982, and on analytical correspondence and its consequences for social practice, e.g. Pitts 2010b).

Through the highly evolved and automatic classification system of the human brain, co-occurrence facilitates the creation of links that were not present in the past, which has a huge effect on the modern interpretation of objects. This becomes pointedly apparent in museum exhibitions, in which Egyptian objects used to be physically separated from other cultural styles, helping to create the impression that these objects were categorised as a single discrete group. The physical separation of objects from their use-contexts is effectively an altered co-occurrence on the basis of resemblance that influences how people view the past. The process of this alienation of objects is called *artefaction*: the transformation of objects from material culture in use and finds contexts to isolated artefacts in museums (Colla 2007). This shows not only how 'Egypt' as a style was created for the modern world, but also the way concepts and objects could become 'enframed' as static bounded entities within academic reasoning, and the further consequences this had for the interpretation of past objects.

Framing Egypt? 'Egyptian' objects in Roman classification schemes

With the Battle of Actium in 31 BC, the relation between Egypt and Rome changed significantly, resulting in what was believed to be an 'exotic crave' for Egyptian leading element within these classifications, but that use and material played a crucial role. Does this mean that style only has an unintentionally shaping agency and never a consciously moving one? While one of the main arguments of this chapter is that style need not have been the primary characteristic on which Romans categorised their material culture, this does not mean it should be completely dismissed. There are cases in which cultural style was the defining element of its classification and where Egyptian style was intentionally applied to express certain values. An example of this might be the Egyptian-style sphinx made of local red clay that featured in the Iseum of Pompeii (Fig. 12.5). It is generally assumed that the coarse red clay was purposely used to resemble Egyptian granite and therefore appeared more genuinely Egyptian. Emphasising the Egyptian as such was presumably more important for Isis priests than for the average Pompeian citizen. However, here it is apparent that the agency of style (how the object appeared) was more important than its physical provenance, for it evidently did not matter whether the sphinx was from Egypt, only that it looked that way. This suggests that Romans dealt with concepts of authenticity in a very different way to modern western society.

Figure 12.5 Terracotta sphinx from the Iseum of Pompeii, found in the Sacrarium. MANN inv.no 22572. From De Caro 2006, fig. III.135, p. 211.

Egyptian-styled wall painting

The second case study in this chapter concerns Egyptian-styled wall paintings. These paintings show a 'typical' Egyptian style with a flat rendering of human figures (with the head and legs displayed *en profil* and the shoulders *en face*), depicting pharaohs, offering scenes, or Egyptian animals. There are not many surviving paintings from this category, but Egyptian- or pharaonic-styled wall paintings have been attested in a number of houses in Pompeii such as the Casa del Frutteto (Claudian, around AD 40) and in the Villa of Postumus in Boscotrecase (Augustan, around 10 BC). The paintings of the so-called 'Black Room' and 'Mythological Room' of the Villa of Agrippa Postumus, *cubiculi* overlooking the bay of Naples, show panels with Egyptianising offering scenes (Fig. 12.6a–b). The Casa del Frutteto in Pompeii was a modest house, but its first *cubiculum* after the entrance in the atrium space housed lavish scenes comparable to those at Boscotrecase: an architectural frame depicting Egyptian offering scenes and animals. The scenes were traditionally interpreted as part of the Egyptomania wave and its taste for the exotic, 'reflecting a fashion which became especially popular in the decorative arts after the annexation of Egypt in 31–30 BC' (Ling 1991, 39). Like the sphinx statues, the paintings received a historically based top-down interpretation, making it equally useful to explore their semantic relations.

Egypt is present in the Second and Third Pompeian Style, the latter connected to Augustus. The Second Style, also referred to as the architectural style, was characterised by an interest in creating illusionistic architectural vistas and ran approximately from 60 to 20 BC. The Third Style is dated between 20 BC and AD 40. Egypt in the Second Pompeian style can be observed in the Villa of Livia and the Aula Isiaca in Rome (between 30 and 25 BC), in the form of Nilotic scenes, vegetalised columns, Egyptian crowns, lotus flowers, a frieze with *uraei* and beaked water jugs; possibly perceived as Egyptian subjects, but never explicitly rendered in a pharaonic-Egyptian style (see Rizzo 1939 for the paintings of the house of Livia; for the relation of Nilotic scenes to Egypt and the re-interpretation of them in terms of this new methodology see Mol 2015, 256–91). Egyptian-related images in the Third Style are represented in the Villa of Agrippa Postumus, Villa della Farnesina (around 20 BC) and in the Casa del Frutteto (Late Third): the Frutteto and Agrippa Postumus examples display Egyptian styled wall-paintings, and the Villa della Farnesina (the alleged house of Agrippa and Octavia) shows a representation of an Isis figure emerging from a vegetal candelabrum (for the paintings of the Villa della Farnesina, see Mols and Moormann 2008; for Casa di Augusto see Carettoni 1983, 373–419; for details of Alexandrian influence on Roman art see Pensabene 1993, 140).

The imagery inside these residences contained artistic references that related to Egypt in different ways but have all been interpreted as closely connected to Augustan politics. Was this difference in rendering, in displaying style, related to a change in the way in which Egypt came to be perceived after Augustus? I argue that it was not, and that it instead has more to do with style perception and the medium of wall painting. It is generally accepted that the overall purpose of Roman wall paintings was to make allusions to larger worlds and scenes, both physically by means of painted vistas and symbolically by means of mythological related images, resulting in the exclusion of human figures or scenes from everyday life (Wallace-Hadrill 1994,

12. Object ontology and cultural taxonomies

material culture in Rome and Italy. This is, however, based on modern classification systems of what Egyptian entails. A semantic graph such as shown in Fig. 12.1 is impossible to construct for an ancient situation due to the lack of conceptual data; however, realising how dependent categories are on the visual and physical environment, a detailed contextual object analysis might be able to retrieve some comparable semantic relations. This section provides two case studies of objects that were traditionally classified to belong to the conceptual category 'Egyptian' – sphinxes and Egyptian-styled wall paintings, and analyses of their ecological-semantic networks to see how they informed Roman emic categories.

Sphinxes

The Egyptian sphinx is usually differentiated from its Greek counterpart by its reclining pose, male identity, absence of wings, and pharaonic headgear (*nemes*); it features regularly in Italian contexts in the Roman period, is sometimes linked to Isis in the Iseum Campense in Rome or the Iseum in Pompeii, and in other cases far removed from cultic use, such as the sphinx statues in Hadrian's villa in Tivoli

Figure 12.2 Marble Sphinx from the Casa di Octavius Quartione (II 2,2), Pompeii. Soprintendenza Pompei, Inv. 2930. De Caro 2006, fig. III.134, p. 211.

Figure 12.3 Painting of a marble sphinx statue from the north wall of the peristyle of the Casa del Peristilio (VII.6.28), Pompeii. PPM VII, fig. 6, p. 187.

or in the gardens of Roman Pompeii. Egyptian sphinx-materialisations in Roman Italy were occasionally imported from Egypt, but could also be made locally, and appeared in a variety of materials such as greywacke, granite, marble, terracotta, painting, or bronze. The large variety of size, material and settings should already caution against a single meaning and purpose; and whether the sphinx was in all cases experienced as culturally Egyptian should be questioned. A telling example is the small marble sphinx-statue found at a canal in the garden of the Casa di Octavius Quartio (II 2,2) in Pompeii (Fig. 12.2). After it was stylistically identified as Egyptian, and through a small peripheral painting of an Isis priest located in a very different section of the house, the whole canal was consequently interpreted as symbolising the Nile and the inhabitant of the house as a priest of Isis, despite the many other attested statues that had no direct connection to Egypt in either style or subject (Della Corte 1932; Maiuri 1947). Although this view has been nuanced in recent research (Tronchin 2011; Mol 2016), it remains a recurrent interpretation in publications on the house.

Did sphinxes belong to the category of 'Egyptian'? Looking in more detail at the object-network that made up the visual environment of Pompeians shows quite a different image. This becomes notably clear regarding sphinxes in Pompeian wall painting, which accommodate a popular tradition of depicting marble sphinx statues in garden settings (Fig. 12.3). The sphinxes painted on the walls have a few recurrent characteristics: they are all depicted as statues instead of living creatures, they are portrayed to convey white marble, and they all were without exceptions connected to water features, either painted on the wall, or real features in proximity such as fountains, canals, or nymphaea.

As sphinxes were either positioned near a fountain or painted as fountain themselves, a cognitive relation between the concepts of sphinxes and water therefore seems evident (Mol 2015, 246–50). In style, however, sphinxes are quite varied: there are Egyptian sphinxes (in the Casa di Bracciale d'Oro), more Classical-styled sphinxes, Greek Archaic sphinxes and sphinxes that combine multiple styles. Wherever the original basis lies for the strong semantic connection between white marble sphinx statues and water, it was strongly present in first century AD Pompeii. This connection makes it much more understandable why a marble sphinx statuette ended up alongside the canal than through the top-down understanding of the scholarly classification of Egypt. The object is therefore also not particularly used to 'exoticise' the garden or to show religious preferences; placing the sphinx at this specific location derived from a Pompeian tradition that linked water to marble sphinx statues. The statuette, being displayed among other marble sculptures such as a young Hercules, a river god, a herm of Dionysus, and several animals such as dogs and lions, was selected for its material (marble), and its subject, and was clearly not classified according to cultural style.

A different sphinx-object that was likewise identified as both Isiac and as an exotic expression of Egyptomania is a bronze Egyptian sphinx that functioned as a table foot in the Casa dell'Ara Massima (VI 16,15) (De Vos 1980, 93; Mol 2015, 251) (Fig. 12.4). The modest middle class house was named after a large painted altar in the centre, which did not feature Isis or anything else related to Egypt. The bronze sphinx table foot, probably imported from Alexandria in Egypt, was placed in one of the *cubiculi*. If the category 'Egyptian' is discarded in favour of attempting to retrieve Roman semantic networks, can its use be explained?

As with the painted statuettes, tables in Pompeii also have a long history in which the sphinx as a subject plays a substantial role. It can be observed that decorated Roman tables all display so-called '*mischwesen*', otherworldly creatures such as griffins, lions, phoenixes, and sphinxes (Moss 1988; Mol 2015, 251–4). Again, the tradition might be much older than Roman tables, because the sphinx as a creature was present on the Italian peninsula already from the Archaic period onwards, when so-called 'Orientalising' motives appeared due to contact with the East, which ultimately culminated in diverse appropriations of the influence in Hellenistic and Roman material culture. Such Orientalising motives also had a long history of cultural exchange between many societies in Greece, Egypt, and the Levant before they reached Italy (Riva 2006).

Figure 12.4 Bronze table support in the form of an Egyptian sphinx. From Casa dell'Ara Massima (VI 16,15), Pompeii. MANN inv. no. 130860. From De Caro 2006, fig. III.133, p. 210.

The result in Roman table-decoration is that a mixture of all kinds of these creatures in a variety of styles and materials became present throughout Roman Italy (Moss 1988). Many of them, especially the marble tables with two slabs as feet, also render the creatures in an Oriental style, but this is not a general rule. The marble table found in the Casa del Fauno (VI 12,2) displays a sphinx foot in a distinctively classicising style (according to Zanker an expression of political loyalty towards the Augustan regime: Zanker 1988, 269), and a Hellenistic-styled bronze table with sphinxes could also be found (for example a bronze tripod table with sphinxes from Pompeii: *MANN inv. No. 72995*). The reason to choose a table with a sphinx-decoration in the Casa dell'Ara Massima seems to have stemmed from a time-honoured Roman tradition in table decoration, not from Isis-worship. It can most likely be excluded that the furniture was considered exotic or out of place on the basis of style (although the fact that it was an import of precious material and high level artistry might have played a role within social value systems). The category of perception was created not in terms of its cultural style, but in terms of its function, use, and subject.

These examples demonstrate that ancient classifications and associations can be retrieved when paying attention to ecological context and different networks of physical and visual objects. This does not mean of course that the objects did not also function in other networks, but it does show that this semantic network created a category decisive for their implementation and use. It also demonstrates that cultural style is not always a

17–28; Zanker 2008, 23–33). In spite of this aim to create fantasy worlds, there had to be some realism in order to convey and communicate the symbolic; to make the fantasy work as an allusion. What the development of the Third Style brought as an innovation to the Second was the implementation of isolated frames and panels in the form of architectural features. In such panels one could easily apply more divergent styles and subjects, as it was no longer part of the 'real' scene and did not represent something 'living' but something abstract or architectural. These frames therefore allowed painters much more artistic freedom to play with styles such as the Egyptian. It could be recognised, used and copied, but was never considered realistic or integrated in the main frame.

An important deduction can be made with regard to Egypt as the alleged 'Other', which might put the historically based argument of Egyptian material culture in a slightly different perspective: Egypt was not seen as the embodiment of the 'Other' *per se*, and for that reason adopted in wall paintings, but was visually externalised as a result of a Roman development in wall painting. This alienation of Egyptian style in wall painting is reflected in the architectural frames of the villa of Agrippa Postumus in Boscotrecase as well as the Casa del Frutteto in Pompeii. However, this seems to be a result of the development of painting styles rather than political ideas surrounding Egypt, a view which is sustained by the paintings from the Villa della Farnesina. While a painting of the goddess Isis in this case was rendered in a non-pharaonic style, as she was part of the 'real' scene, the paintings of the Villa did depict similar architectural frames as the Egyptian frames in the Boscotrecase Villa and the Casa del Frutteto, with a similar composition showing deviant styles on externalised architectural features. In this case however, it was not Egyptian but Greek style that became framed: archaising images within a golden frame and a white background, supported by means of winged female figures standing on pedestals (Fig. 12.7). The painting technique (pale colours on a white background) recalls archaic lekythoi, and the style was deliberately applied in order to establish a stylistic contrast to the regularly (Roman) styled background. This example serves to underline that it was the use of style in Roman wall painting that externalised Egypt as something different, not a prior concept of Egypt as foreign.

Historical implications: Egypt in concept, style and object

All things that were regarded as 'Egyptian' or 'foreign' by scholarly classification schemes, appear in this analysis to be part of various categories, involving more complex relations not always based on style. Depending on the context, cultural style could still matter, but at many other occasions different concepts structured the semantic network and subsequent use and perception. Whether intentionally used as Egyptian or not, all uses were dictated by resemblance in relation to co-occurrence in local traditions and were locally established understandings. It is possibly too large a leap to connect this finely developed network of associations to the city

Figure 12.6 The Egyptianising paintings from the villa at Boscotrecase. Top: Black Room (19), upper section, left panel north wall, in Boscotrecase. Metropolitan Museum of Art, inv. No 20.192.2. Bottom: fragment from the Mythological Room (15), upper section west wall. Inv. Metropolitan Museum of Art No 20192.13.

Figure 12.7 Greek archaising scenes in the two white-coloured panels, from the Villa della Farnesina. Moormann and Mols 2008, fig. 28, p. 29.

of Rome. Nevertheless, the small-scale patterns that are witnessed in the towns of Campania might well reflect broader trends, and can in this way be used as a micro-environmental case study for an exploration on a wider scale.

I now return to the public domain of human agency and history – a domain in which Augustus places dedicatory obelisks in Rome, bans the Isis cults from the *pomerium*, and yet has his house and that of his inner circle decorated with Egyptian and Isiac imagery. As discussed above, it was a development in Roman wall painting that made it possible to connect Egyptian-Pharaonic style to the concept of the exotic or alien. This development is therefore more informative about traditions in Roman wall painting than that it reflects contemporary thoughts on Egypt or Augustus' political influence on art and culture. However, in the context of the historical implications in relation to object agency it must be added that the development also *did* something. The possibility of playing with styles and images in wall painting under Augustus added something important to the allusion of the exotic and the otherworldly desired in Roman wall painting of this period (Zanker 2008), which urgently raises the question of object agency. Even when the use of Egyptian-styled painting should be regarded a less intentional and less political phenomenon than previously believed, with these new developments in wall paintings, the artistic externalisation of Egypt together with its change in style had consequences for how it became perceived in the Augustan Age. The effect of using style in this way was that Egypt became isolated and separated, allowing it to become foreign, exotic, and strange within Roman perception. This means that the style itself sometimes had the agency to change the concept of Egypt into something deviant, and not the other way around.

The appropriation of the sphinx in the Roman world showed that it could be used in various styles for various purposes, and that seeing an Egyptian sphinx did not necessarily fall within the cultural frame of 'Egypt'. It seems to fit into a pre-Augustan category of an already well-integrated subject to which new but similar objects could be automatically added. Pompeii shows countless examples of sphinxes used as fantastic creatures. It is valuable to compare this ingrained local Roman tradition witnessed at Pompeii with the refurbishing of the Iseum Campense in Rome, geographically apart, but executed in more or less the same time frame – two or three years after Pompeii was destroyed by the Vesuvius (for a discussion on Domitian and the rebuilding of the Iseum Campense see Sorek 2010; Versluys 2017a; Boyle and Dominik 2003; Galimberti 2016, 92–108; Gallia 2016, 148–65). What did the emperor Domitian (or his workforces) choose from the available Egyptian material?

Many obelisks, imported and locally made, were recognisable for Roman citizens because they had adorned the city for almost a century after Augustus. It is likely that the obelisks were consciously selected (albeit in a larger quantity) because they did not signify 'Egypt' as much as the power of the emperor – in this case the choice is therefore an intentional political decision playing upon the category of 'Egyptian'. However, there are also a notably large number of statues of lions and sphinxes – the same *mischwesen* already largely present within a Roman mental category shaped by tables, paintings and statues.[1] So was it intentionally re-Egyptianised? Perhaps, but the work executed under the rule of Domitian was not original, nor did it *change* the idea of Egypt: it acted upon an already slowly developed semantic network that was afforded by the material culture present in Roman Italy and interlinked through co-occurrence.

It seems that the choices that were made for sculpture have been influenced by subjects that fitted into a Roman classification of material culture, unintentionally recognised because they already existed through objects in Rome and on the Italian peninsula and not because they were Egyptian or appeared Egyptian *per se*. They were imported as something new, but not as something completely alien. This means it was a category of Egyptian that was created, stretched, and transformed by the available objects in Rome: a Roman category of the Egyptian which existed next to countless other categories that included Egyptian objects that were never part of this classification.

Returning to the role that style played and the influence it had on people, a different picture emerges of Egyptian objects in the Roman world than that based on historical narratives. Style plays a role, but not in the way it is usually classified by archaeologists. Style indeed has a form of agency in categorisation, but in particular circumstances and within specific object-networks, and is therefore a far more intricate phenomenon than the simple application of modern stylistic categorisations suggests. A continuous historical framing of these objects as one distinctive category has furthermore obscured their Roman use and perception, creating on the one hand a stylistic foreignness and exoticism that was not always present, and on the other too anthropocentric a view on its development and integration. The analyses of Egyptian artefacts in the Roman domestic contexts of Pompeii demonstrate how complex and dynamic networks of materially and visually based projections, classifications of materials, style and concepts lie behind the everyday (aesthetically and socially guided) choice and use of objects. The choice for certain Egyptian objects and styles, or the implementation of it, was derived from existing mental categories. However, the influx of Egyptian objects could affect Roman classifications and stretch them; ranging from 'tables', 'fountains', and 'garden decoration' to 'aesthetics', and eventually (and unintentionally), also to 'Egyptian' and 'Roman'.

What does this say about agency of style? Did Egypt as a style change things in Rome or Pompeii? First of all, it should be noted that a possible agency of style can only be regarded in cultural ecological terms. Under certain circumstances Egypt was used as a style, both in an intentional (moving) and unintentional (shaping) manner. Different networks of objects and concepts were changed in this way. It can additionally be stated that the concealed agency of Egyptian artefacts was able to change what was Roman, by not residing in semantic networks connected to the foreign, but in tables or water features; co-occurrence in social environments is able to affect categorisation to a crucial extent. Domestic units therefore might be the best way to illustrate how these processes work on a subconscious level, how they integrate and mesh within local frameworks without political intentions playing a decisive role. It is important to include these examples when studying material agency and not exclusively focus on imperial public buildings, because the latter were decorated with strong political intentions. A slight reappraisal is made in this case of Bianchi Bandinelli's important theory on '*arte plebea*', however, not as stylistic differences between the patrician and plebeian classes, but as a different bottom-up development through domestic use (Bianchi Bandinelli 1970, 51–105). It is the domestic contexts that show a more intuitive handling of things, and therefore might present a better view of unconscious but widely supported internal classification systems.

Conclusion: the agency of representation

This chapter argues that objects play a significant role in mental classification systems and that the study of Roman history can be aided by acknowledging this more explicitly. Two important observations on the analysis of Egyptian artefacts emerge from the analysis to sustain this idea. First, a category of Egyptian was created in Roman Italy from local understanding and presence of objects that were not always Egyptian in the true sense. Second, objects circulating in scholarly categories of Egyptian might not have been used and perceived as such in antiquity. This gives a different understanding both to Egyptian material culture and its presumed relations to historical narratives, and to what 'foreign' and 'internal' material culture entailed for Romans. Studying domestic contexts alongside imperial uses of Egyptian style and objects shows this well, because the domestic contexts act from use, and are able to illuminate the undercurrents of object and style associations and perceptions.

This chapter also shows material agency to be a force that can work beyond that of conscious human agency. While this example of cultural classifications has focused on how Egyptian styles and objects might have affected human agency, it has broader significance for cultural and technical styles in the Roman world. The Classical, Oriental, Etruscan, Plebeian, Archaic, Provincial, Dacian, Indian: stylistic cultural-historical categorisations that made and transformed Rome might all be aided by a network re-evaluation that focuses on co-occurrence and resemblance in an ecological use-context. Initial deconstruction of how modern cultural taxonomies are obscuring networks of the past is thereby considered particularly useful. Before we materialise history, we need to know how concept and objects relate, and how the gap between the agency of matter and that of historical narrative can be bridged.

Using relationality and network theory to reveal the co-dependencies of the world of objects and the world of ideas avoids categorical interpretations in favour of relations, and sketches a more dynamic (and therefore more realistic) picture of object-human relationships, spread of techniques and artefacts (Mol 2013; 2015; Mol 2014; Brughmans 2013; Knappett 2011). The world is not an organised whole in which objects bend to human creation – humans (and human agency) are partly made through their dealings with objects. To materialise the Roman world therefore, it is necessary to realise that objects are real entities that enter into relations, but are also constituted from these relations. Furthermore, network theory in combination with object agency brings a new realism to scientific arguments by acknowledging that there is a world beyond the human grasp, the complexity of which might be better captured through the use of networks and the mapping of different ontologies.

The material turn has aided the realisation that overarching concepts of typological thinking and grand theories should be avoided, and that the focus should instead be on the dynamic practices and flows of becoming, complex assemblages, and heterogeneous relations (De Landa 2002, 42). This, however, should not dismiss human categorisation as a powerful tool and a constructive force. The focus on classification systems in this chapter shows clearly that human projection, which is concentrated on stasis, order, control, and boundaries, affects the understanding, use choice, and creation of other objects. Not everything is beyond representation. Trying to empirically integrate the dynamic nature of objects in complex systems as a source and force of creation with those of human classifications as a bounded perception is a daunting task, and one that Roman archaeology, with its complex and self-conscious historical, material, and historiographical entanglements, is perhaps best positioned to undertake.

Acknowledgements
I wish to thank the editors, Astrid Van Oyen and Martin Pitts, for inviting me to the symposium to share my ideas with such a diverse, stimulating, and knowledgeable audience, and for their incredibly useful critique on my paper during the publication process. For this latter point I also wish to express gratitude to my Leiden colleagues Marleen Termeer and Rogier Kalkers. I want to thank Martin and Astrid especially for the inspiration that the two of them – together and individually – have generated by setting up an important new agenda in Roman archaeology, and for their attempt to transform the study of Roman material culture in such a critical, ambitious and intelligent way. By papers, articles, and conferences – and with this publication as the most recent example – they have shown that Roman archaeology is taking a new turn, a turn which gives room to material culture as a vital instrument to understand the Roman world, but from an integrative perspective that embraces historical and art historical challenges, and is taking advantage of both the empirical and conceptual richness that the field has to offer. I hope there will be more future occasions to witness and be part of this development.

Note

1. From the imports: five lions (nos 10–14 from the catalogue of Lembke), three sphinxes (nos 15–17), statues of deities (18, 19, 22, 23, 24, 28), baboons (20, 21) and other fragments of statues and naophorae (nos 25, 26, 27, 30–5). The statues that were produced locally contained three baboons (nos 36, 37, 38), a crocodile (39), three lions (41–3), two sphinxes (44, 45) and Domitian portrayed as a pharaoh (Lembke 1994, 221–53). For a discussion on style and material of the Iseum Campense, see Müskens 2017.

Chapter 13

Discussion. Object-scapes. Towards a material constitution of Romanness?

*Miguel John Versluys**

Innovating objects

History evolves through the particular relationship between objects and people. The configurations we call society and history are a mix of human beings with objects, in which both people and things have some sort of agency and influence each other (Böhme 2006; Boivin 2008; Hicks 2010 for an overview of the debate).

To date, the disciplines of Roman history and archaeology have mainly focused on human agency. They did so even while making objects a central component of their investigations, as in those cases the implicit, underlying research question always was what these objects *represented* in terms of human agency; or, in other words, what they *meant* (Versluys 2014; Van Oyen and Pitts, this volume). However, forms and styles of material culture are able to shape people as effective social entities (Gosden 2005). The 'material and visual ecology' (Wells 2012; Woolf, this volume) of a certain region in a certain period, therefore, matters greatly in the sense that things, through their entanglement with people, become instrumental in shaping *habitus* as well as pathways of change. It is well-known that objects are fundamental to what Pierre Bourdieu (1977) called *habitus* and that they structure human life in an often subconscious way. However, objects are as fundamental to change as they are to continuity. Previously unknown objects, in new styles and made from new materials, often challenge the boundaries of the known, lead to fresh questions and perspectives for the societies they enter, and pave the way for novel practices (van der Leeuw and Torrence 1989; Gosden 2004; Versluys 2017b). For this reason, objects play an important role in the emergence of new cultural configurations and it could even be argued that they 'make up' societies.

It is particularly important that in recognising the role that forms and styles of material culture play in shaping people or (imagined) communities, the present

---
*Faculty of Archaeology, Leiden University.

volume works towards a new, 'truly archaeological' agenda for Roman history and archaeology (Versluys 2014). With that qualification, I do not simply mean to say that objects matter, but rather that objects matter fundamentally 'beyond representation' and beyond being used as mere historical sources.

The difference between these two approaches becomes clear from reading the introduction to the handbook *Writing Material Culture History* (Gerritsen and Riello 2015b), as well as from the papers in this book and the reception of the material turn within Roman studies in general. Providing a critical introduction for students interested in material culture, history and historical methodologies, Gerritsen and Riello mention three ways in which material culture has, in their view, enriched the discipline of history: 1) by complementing other (e.g. written) sources; 2) by making historians ask new questions, and 3) by directing historians towards new themes. All this change is the result of what they characterise as a 'Damascene conversion to material culture': the material turn in history. Laudably taking up and elaborating on the material turn, most contributions to the book do not, however, attempt to rewrite history as a particular relationship between objects and people with things as the *agents provocateurs* of (historical) change. In my view, however, this is the real challenge elicited by the material turn (notable exceptions from the book include Charpy 2015, on how things shaped people through the Industrial Revolution, and Gerritsen and Riello 2015c, on the material landscapes of global history). The 'Damascene conversion to material culture' should not simply be about focusing on objects but about reconceptualising understandings of their impact and agency within societies.

As such, both *Writing Material Culture History* and the present volume show how difficult it is to put the material turn into practice. Scholars have eagerly turned towards objects (again). But they often seem to do so for their own reasons: to acquire new sources, questions and themes; to turn their backs on everything pertaining to post-modern hermeneutics and become empiricists again (for this debate see Hillerdal and Siapkas 2015, who are more positive on neo-empericism than I); and to develop the role of museums beyond issues of heritage and identity alone (see ter Keurs 2014), among others. These aims are, of course, understandable, useful and legitimate. Taking and developing a 'turn' implies looking at it critically, testing it with regard to one's own discipline, and subsequently reworking it. One should indeed not simply 'go with the flow' when there happens to be another theoretical paradigm around (Gardner, this volume). However, the problem remains that the aforementioned perspectives often seem to keep the real challenges at bay. Indeed, it is arguable that they do not use the material turn to its full potential, and nor do they help to develop it conceptually.

Looking at this reticence (or abstention?) with regard to the field of Roman history and archaeology in particular, these perspectives could even be called reductive. Why? In the first place, much critical deconstruction, testing and reworking has already been done. The two most important handbooks of the material turn are probably the *SAGE Handbook of Material Culture* and the *Oxford Handbook of Material Culture Studies*, published in 2006 and 2010, respectively. There was not much Roman archaeology or history in them, nor are they widely used within Roman studies. Moreover, exciting new interpretations are proposed for many periods on the basis of this new paradigm: from the Neolithic (Robb 2013) and the Bronze Age (Vandkilde 2017) to modernity (e.g. Böhme 2006; Goody 2012; Goldhill 2014). Other fascinating debates address the important issues surrounding how things shape the mind (Malafouris 2013), and the extent to which being human depends on particular relationship with objects (Barrett 2014). With a robust foundation to build on, therefore, I propose that we should evaluate the material turn by putting it into practice for Roman archaeology and history (Versluys 2014). The second reason to do so, instead of taking the risk of becoming reductive, is given by the utmost and undeniable relevance of the material turn for our period. As Van Oyen and Pitts assert in their Introduction: 'Archaeologists often remark on the massive and widespread changes in the material environment in the Roman imperial period. There were more "things" around, which impacted on the lives of the many as well as the privileged few. The volume of traded goods increased, networks of circulation expanded, and local production intensified (...). With quantitative increase came qualitative innovation. Objects became ever more differentiated in terms of style and function.' I would argue that the study of every historical period needs a truly material turn, but that the Roman period constitutes a privileged vantage point for such an exercise.

The remainder of my contribution first discusses the three articles of this section against the background of how Roman archaeology and history deals with the material turn. How do the authors position themselves, and what are the strengths and weaknesses of their engagement with the material turn? Second, I briefly explain what I consider to be a fruitful way forward. I argue that in order to understand *how* relationships between people and things are instrumental in shaping the pathways of change, archaeologists should focus on the circulation and impact of classes of objects through their stylistic and material characteristics. For this purpose, I introduce the concept of 'object-scape' as an applied research tool to study these classes of objects and will illustrate its practical application by briefly looking at object-scapes in the Iron Age Levant and the Roman Republic.

Moving beyond representation

In their introduction, Van Oyen and Pitts claim that focusing on what objects *did* provides a more complete theoretical model of how material culture works – a view supported by the rest of the volume. As the articles in this section show, traditional cultural-historical approaches are unsound for a proper understanding of objects, while postcolonial or postmodern approaches, which draw heavily on the notion of identity, are at best only partial approaches – even when identities are understood as complex, overlapping, fragmented, and context-dependent (cf. Pitts 2007). In both strands, 'people' and 'pots' are seen as being related in a representational way. Neither approach is helpful to provide a more complete theoretical model of how material culture works, as they do not move beyond representation. When sketching their more complete theoretical model, Van Oyen and Pitts draw on various notions in their introduction: most prominently, artefact biographies and networks; trajectories, entanglement and globalisation. These should all serve to help focus on what artefacts *were* and what objects *did* in the Roman world.

The articles in this section make use of these notions in different ways and subsequently represent different ways of dealing with the material turn. In her essay, Ellen Swift deals with the relations 'between the physical features of artefacts (their form and material), everyday social practice and experience, and wider cultural traditions of behaviour' and thus illustrates the importance of what I call object-scapes (see below) in order to understand both *habitus* and socio-cultural change. It is interesting to note that she distinguishes form and material as the most important physical features of artefacts, which could also be called style and materiality, respectively. Hence, 'a theoretically informed approach to functional studies', as she calls it, can indeed become important for our understanding of the diversity of social experience within the Roman world. Although Swift's chapter does not deal with the latter aspect specifically, it follows that the more artefacts with these particular physical features are around, the greater the diversity of the social experience. A larger and more diverse object-scape results in increasingly diverse human-thing entanglements – and will therefore also result in a different *habitus*. Her essay also shows how difficult it is to go from the 'physical features of artefacts' to 'wider cultural traditions of behaviour' as instigated by artefacts; and hence to arrive at what Hodder (2011) has characterised as an integrated archaeological perspective. In her careful analyses of seal-rings and dice, Swift often falls back on standard historical narratives, like the survival of pre-Roman cultural practices in Roman Britain and the categories of elite and non-elite, to reconstruct the diversity of social experience. But the question of how objects created these, or other, categories, is yet to be answered. I am not sure whether it is really true that 'by studying ordinary everyday items, such as dice or seal-rings, we can examine the extent to which introduced mental concepts were or were not assimilated into everyday provincial practice', because such a conclusion seemingly considers objects as *representing* a single interpretative concept; and hence singles out just one of many possible affordances.

Swift clearly shows how beneficial it is to try and understand the relationship between objects and social practice by thinking about object agency. The essay by Mol shows this, too, and in addition establishes a convincing connection between *habitus* and social change. In order to achieve this, it is necessary to move away from artefact biographies and their networks proper towards concepts like trajectories, entanglement and globalisation (cf. Boschung, Kreuz and Kienlin 2015), or, in other words, from single objects to classes of objects and the inter-artefactual domain (Gosden 2006). This is because, in Mol's words, some objects *move* us (intentional) but all objects *shape* us (unintentional). Mol defines agency as 'the power that style or objects have to affect human intentions and behaviour'. In her essay, using object agency turns out to be an excellent and effective means to deconstruct cultural taxonomies. Mol is as critical as she is enthusiastic about the potential of the material turn; thus testifying to a serious engagement with its theory and arguing that, through its particular data-sets, Roman archaeology could help to 'soften' the material turn. She usefully reminds us that 'the agency of objects should never be accounted for in isolation, nor should we conceive agency as having only one significance in terms of power and directionality when human-object relationships are concerned.' This leads to the conclusion that 'although society is built up from things, things do not exist without people, they rather co-exist in a complex network of being and becoming'. The notion of being and becoming – the fact that things are not determined by their logical relations within a classification scheme but by their working relations with other things and humans in their environment – is crucial and can significantly contribute to a more complete theoretical model of how material culture works. Mol's case study on 'Aegyptiaca' illustrates both the practical and methodological strength of this model. In practical terms, it demonstrates that, to use an illuminating example, the small marble sphinx-statue found at a canal in the garden of the Casa di Octavius Quartio (II 2,2) in Pompeii was placed there because it was made from marble and because it was a sphinx – and both that subject and that material had a relation to water – *not* because it was Egyptian. Still it has been described as something *representing* Egypt in all scholarly literature thus far. In methodological terms, this allows us to understand how history evolves through the particular relationship between objects and people: the influx of things Egyptian is shown to affect Roman classifications as well as stretch them and, eventually, the influx of things Egyptian also affects the categories of 'Egyptian' and 'Roman' themselves.

The essay by Van Oyen asks how matter came to matter in the Roman empire, and is therefore very much engaged with the similarly fundamental question of 'writing matter into history'. For her analysis of how concrete helped produce an imperial Roman world, she provides us with an Ingoldian account of the organic 'growing' of *opus caementicium*. One way in which Roman concrete can be said to have 'grown', in this sense, is through its physical transformation from a fluid to a solid state. Her analysis beautifully shows how concrete and its constitutive components 'came with specific biographies of material transformation' and how 'concrete as a building material developed along a trajectory of redefinition, categorisation, and differentiation'. '*Caementa* were sorted both in relation to one another (within the layers) and in relation to the structure and its loadbearing requirements'. Hers is certainly not an article about materiality without materials (Ingold 2007). Another important question in understanding how matter matters, is what kind of socio-economic, cultural, or even conceptual changes were brought about in Roman society through, for instance, the use of *opus reticulatum* stones (emphasising 'the unity of concrete as a material over the heterogeneity of its constituent components') in comparison to earlier *opus incertum* or later *opus testaceum* or *latericium* with its terracotta materiality. Were buildings in *opus incertum* perceived differently than those in *opus reticulatum* – even if covered by marble or stucco? What different kind of affordances came with *reticulatum* when compared to *incertum*, and how did those (differing) affordances result in changes in Roman society?

The importance of these questions is underlined by Van Oyen's own analysis of the concrete revolution that took place in the Julio-Claudian period, with Nero's *Domus Aurea* as best-known example. Through concrete and its affordances, a different form of architecture emerged: 'a new world closed in on itself, cut off from surrounding "nature"'. In this way, the unintended consequences of the shift to concrete in Roman architecture changed not only Roman architecture, but also Roman lifestyles and society. The fact that concrete had to be used in vaults – flat concrete ceilings were structurally impossible – set in motion the development of a whole new spatial vocabulary. Thus, concrete's material histories branch out into histories of imperial identities, economic development, control, and citizenship. As Van Oyen concludes: 'The historical footprint of Nero, then, would not have been possible without concrete – without the possibilities of speed and shape it afforded. These possibilities emerged from concrete's much longer material history of transformation and categorisation. Material histories shuffle causality, situating traditional protagonists firmly within their historical entanglements.' In her final analysis, Van Oyen sketches a model that, I think, is similar to Mol's, in viewing material histories as being relational; performative and emergent: 'they have a history and they make history.' The study of Roman artefacts, then, should be about the power of things and the flow of cultural transformations (cf. Saurma-Jeltsch and Eisenbeiss 2010 and Maran and Stockhammer 2012 for historical case studies from this perspective but not from the Roman period).

Object-scapes

One thing that is certainly not desirable when applying the material turn to Roman archaeology and history is more jargon. It could be argued that one of the main conceptual problems is the fact that many debates, in different fields like archaeology, art history, anthropology, and ethnology, are talking about the same problems without awareness of each other's debates and definitions. These and other disciplines can only face the challenges that the material turn poses in tandem (Van Eck, Versluys and ter Keurs 2015). Nevertheless, in my view, it is useful to introduce the term 'object-scape' as a research concept that enables us to move from the stylistic and material properties of artefacts to cultural formation. As demonstrated in the discussion of the three articles above, the link between object-properties and cultural formation is as important as it is difficult to establish. The idea of an object-scape might help here (see Pitts, this volume, and Pitts and Versluys forthcoming for further theoretical background and practical application of this concept).

The influx of new objects leads to new practices, socio-cultural configurations and imaginations. Automobiles, plastics, air-conditioners, computers, and smart phones

13. Discussion. Object-scapes. Towards a material constitution of Romanness?

all have profoundly changed the societies they entered. They did so in practical, technological, and economic terms, but also in social and cultural respects. And so did the influx of iron, glass, marble, terracottas, and bricks in earlier periods. For prehistory, this is abundantly clear. Many Eurasian societies in the second and first millennia BC are characterised as Bronze Age, because in all respects the alloy of bronze is considered as the main 'game changer', with regard to what came before (copper) and after (iron) (Vandkilde 2017, drawing upon earlier work by scholars like Oscar Montelius and Gordon Childe; cf. Van Oyen, this volume). Bronze objects are regarded as literally 'making up' the Bronze Age; and their significance and affordances indeed permeated Bronze Age societies (Kohl 2007). The same is true for historical periods; although, in their case, the fundamental role of objects in shaping human behaviour is often still very much underplayed (Böhme 2006; Goody 2012; Goldhill 2014 are important exceptions and illuminating studies regarding the nineteenth century; as is Appadurai 2013 for the present-day).

Through object-scapes it is possible to identify and investigate (classes of) objects as 'game changers' and look at their impact. I define an object-scape as 'the repertoire(s) of material culture available at a certain site in a certain period in terms of their material and stylistic characteristics'. The concept implies that scholarly interpretation should not focus on what this repertoire represents in terms of human behaviour, but rather on its impact, namely what it does at a certain site in a certain period, and how it moulds human behaviour through its material and stylistic characteristics. The term takes inspiration from Tim Ingold's (1993) *taskscapes* but also from archaeological discussions about the meaning of *landscapes* as constitutive of human history and behaviour (Tilley 2010) and, more specifically, *islandscapes* and *seascapes* (Berg 2007). *Object-scapes* are similar to these and the concept can function, moreover, in relation to what Arjun Appadurai called *ethno-scapes* (Appadurai 1996; cf. Versluys 2015). Charting an object-scape over time will help provide answers to the following interpretative questions: What (classes of) objects were new? Where did they come from? Where, how and why did they innovate? And what were the historical consequences of these changes in the material environment (see Versluys 2017b)?

At this point, I briefly introduce two examples to illustrate what object-scapes are about and how they may help to establish a more integrated archaeological perspective (Hodder 2010), from object to cultural praxis and beyond representation. The first example draws on the important work of Marian H. Feldman on the Bronze and Iron Age Near East (Feldman 2006; 2014). Her recent study on the Iron Age Levant, entitled *Communities of Style* (2014), is concerned with 'the material effects of art objects, particularly that of style, with the human beings who made and used them, proposing the power of their entanglement in creating and structuring communities of inclusion and exclusion' (Feldman 2014, 2). Style is usefully described here as a material effect of objects. Her analysis clearly shows how 'More than simply a guide to attribution, style serves to establish and structure communities through the engagement of human participants with material objects. Style is thus not autochthonous and bound to geography but rather, through its activation of collective memories, constitutive of communities along both spatial and temporal axes' (Feldman 2014, 6). Charting the development of an object-scape of a certain site over a certain period, and focusing on style and material, can provide much insight into how cultural praxes and communities are made up by their material ecology. As Feldman summarises: 'Through the consumption of styles and objects, we can see how art constitutes community identity rather than simply reflects it' (Feldman 2014, 9).

Feldman discusses art where archaeologists would talk about objects or material culture. That difference is not really important, especially not as art might well be a term that simply designates a special form of object agency. I mention her work here deliberately to underline that archaeologists need to engage much more seriously with developments within art history when applying the material turn (Van Eck, Versluys and ter Keurs 2015). One important reason for such a re-orienatation is that more archaeological attention is needed to address the agency of style, as the chapter by Mol underlines (cf. Versluys 2015). Another reason is that art history has a lot of experience with rethinking representation (cf. Belting 2001). Representation is a difficult concept as it constantly plays an important role on many different levels of scholarly interpretation. There is representation involved when an object is excavated or otherwise encountered; when the encounter is experienced there is the representation, in words, of that experience (Gosden 2010). It is thus not only important to rethink Roman artefacts but also to rethink representation, because as much as I endorse the plea to go 'beyond representation' within Roman history and archaeology and apply the material turn, we cannot, I think, do without representation as such.

The second example concerns Republican Italy and the dramatic changes in its object-scape between roughly 200 BC and the turn of the millennium. During this period, substantial and widespread changes occurred in the material environment. Unparalleled amounts of objects, from more different areas and in more different styles, ended up at more different places than ever before in (Mediterranean) history. The Roman conquests of parts of Sicily (211 BC), Greece (168 and 146 BC) and North Africa (146 BC) led to a significant intensification of Mediterranean connectivity and changes in the object-scape, along with it. Moreover, through the conquests of large parts of the Hellenistic East in the first century BC, a direct Roman involvement with the Silk Road was established, which formed a corridor to large parts of middle and eastern Eurasia. The result was an unprecedented influx of new objects, leading to major new practices and configurations. Around 300 BC, the object-scape of Rome contained temple-ornaments, votive objects and grave goods as its major characteristics – while portraits played a minor role (Zanker 2008). The intensification of connectivity resulted in the erection of Greek-style temples, the building of large peristyles and porticoes that displayed large amounts of statues and other objects, the fabrication of new forms and styles of terracotta, and many other things.

One of the consequences of this dramatically altered object-scape was a new culture of collecting and the subsequent emergence of museum and heritage contexts (Rutledge 2012). This development would, among other things, result in the pervasion of Antiquarianism in late Republican Roman society (Schnapp 2013). The circulation, appropriation, collection, and display of non-local artefacts thus shaped Roman society and the city of Rome to a significant degree. This new object-scape would dramatically change Republican lifestyles, across all domains of society. Objects and styles from Greece, from Egypt and Africa and from Asia are most prominent in this respect (Porter 2006; Versluys 2013). Gosden (2005; 2006) has shown the complex range of social effects that was brought about by the changing corpora of objects for proto-historic Britain during this period. Wells (2012) has done the same for parts of temperate Europe, highlighting the dynamics that were brought about by new visual patterns. In Republican Italy, the consumption of new styles and materials likewise constituted new identities and communities that were dependent on the affordances of those foreign objects and their effects. Barrett (2014) recently argued for the existence of a material constitution of humanness. Could there also be a material constitution of Romanness? Or, in other words, were the processes of the formation of the Roman empire and 'becoming Roman' intimately tied up with objects and their agency?

Acknowledgements
This essay was written in April 2016 during a stay in Berlin at the invitation of the excellence cluster TOPOI. I would like to thank TOPOI and in particular Kerstin P. Hofmann for providing me with this stimulating experience. I am grateful to Astrid Van Oyen and Martin Pitts for organising an inspiring and important meeting, and for the feedback they provided on a first draft of this paper. Marike van Aerde kindly corrected the English text.

Part 4

Reflections

Chapter 14

On theory-building in Roman archaeology. The potential for new approaches to materiality and practice

Andrew Gardner[*]

Introduction: debating theory in Roman archaeology

This volume, and the meeting it derives from, represents a refreshing new direction in the engagement between Roman archaeology and archaeological theory. This process of interaction has a complex history, frequently characterised by scepticism from both directions, if not the wilful maintenance of ignorance – by practitioners in both domains – of what the other group has to offer. In this respect, Roman archaeology has traditionally sat alongside other historical sub-disciplines like Medieval archaeology, taking its interpretive cues largely from the textual record, however partial or fragmentary, and regarding insights from other disciplines dealing with human societies with suspicion, and as at best relevant only to prehistory (Frere 1988, 36; cf. Scott 1993a, 6; Gardner 2007, 35–9). It is perhaps no surprise then that 'representational thinking' (Van Oyen and Pitts, this volume) has been prevalent in Roman archaeology, as objects were almost literally illustrative material for text-derived narratives until very recently in the history of the field, and the idea that texts are objects too has not yet had the impact it might (Johnson 1999; Laurence 2001). Another reason for conservatism has been that Roman archaeology is an international field and therefore, like Egyptology or Assyriology, it has straddled a wide range of different national traditions (Andrén 1998). As with the availability of textual evidence, this can of course be a great strength, but as the continental European tradition of Roman archaeology has generally been less engaged with the theoretical debates in Anglophone prehistory since the 1960s, which have come to define 'archaeological theory' in general, this has arguably acted as a further brake on theoretical engagement in the sub-discipline. When this did begin, sporadically

[*] UCL Institute of Archaeology.

from the late 1970s but really taking off in the 1990s, it is no accident that it was primarily in Romano-British archaeology, closer to those prehistoric debates in both scholarly language and in having relatively little in the way of relevant written sources compared to other parts of the empire.

Over the last 25 years, there has been much catching up, and not only has Roman archaeology developed its own trajectory of theoretical innovations (cf. Gardner 2016a), but the debate has increasingly spread further within Roman studies. This is all to the good, but the aim of this chapter is to ask whether Roman archaeology can yet claim a place at the forefront of wider theoretical debate, using the contents of this volume as a springboard. Also – and before tackling that question – I wish to explore how theory-building actually happens in Roman archaeology. Part of the answer to this lies in the dynamics of the contexts in which theoretical discourse takes place, and in the forms which that discourse takes. The annual Theoretical Roman Archaeology Conference (TRAC) has been particularly important for the broadening of theoretical debate, albeit mainly within a British context (both in terms of conference location and audience, and provincial subject-matter) – though there is a long-standing engagement with the Romanist community in the Netherlands and the conference has travelled there and, with the Roman Archaeology Conference, to the USA, Germany and Italy. TRAC is just one conference, though, and while it has undoubtedly nurtured the theoretically-informed work of many of the current generation of Roman archaeologists, including most contributors to this volume, there is a need for other venues and formats. In particular, it is vital that more in-depth theoretical explorations find a home, to enable, both in the interactive space of a meeting and the published space that might result from it, a fuller engagement with what should be profoundly challenging concepts (cf. Gardner 2016a, 10–11). The 'Rethinking Artefacts in Roman Archaology' Laurence Seminar at the University of Cambridge provided just such a venue (with longer papers and more discussion than tends to be possible in bigger conferences) and, in this volume, just such an outcome, and this is to be applauded. Opening up more time and space for discussion is not the only crucial step, though – so too is the hard work of wrestling with concepts that might reveal markedly different goals and principles among practitioners. In the remainder of this brief contribution I try to map out some of the key points of coincidence, and discord, and relate these to the wider archaeological landscape.

Pushing forward with new approaches

The aim of this volume, as I see it, is to explore new ways of comprehending the definitive material transformation that the Roman world presents us with, in particular those inspired by the 'material turn' (from which I would see the 'ontological turn' as a progression; cf. Van Oyen and Pitts, this volume). As the editors state at the outset, the sheer materiality of the Roman period in most parts of the empire is striking, and in terms of explaining or understanding this materiality, self-fulfilling narratives like

'Romanisation' have proven insufficient. The influence of such traditional paradigms on the ways in which artefacts have been excavated, classified and interpreted is profound, and in some ways we need to begin again from the ground up, to rework how we deal with artefacts, both theoretically and methodologically, and in highlighting avenues forward with this project each of the papers has much to offer. How this work generates new higher-order narratives is less immediately clear. Partly this is because such a goal must be seen as a long-term project, only just beginning, if it is going to be possible at all – and how we can go about determining both the length and the viability of such a project as a research community is something I return to below. Partly, also, this may have to do with the nature of the 'material turn' and some of the selectivity of the associated theoretical toolkit, which needs to be evaluated carefully. What is clear is that important new themes are emerging from the work in these papers, which are certainly of theoretical importance, as well as showing that Roman archaeologists are innovating methodologically, and making good use of the high-quality data that they have access to. Earlier 'discussion' contributions in this volume have examined some of these themes in detail, so I have just a few points to add.

In terms of the practice of Roman artefact studies, many of the papers highlight the ways in which getting to grips with the materiality of finds (sometimes literally) opens up new insights, from the role of the capacity and portability of inkwells in writing practices (Eckardt) to the various ways in which the shape and material consistency of dice played a part in gaming (Swift). These point towards the importance of phenomenological engagement with finds as a method, albeit one that raises interesting questions of the universality of embodied experience, which is a recurrent and unresolved dilemma in archaeological theory (cf. Brück 2005; Hamilton and Whitehouse 2006; Lindstrøm 2015). Classification is a related issue which several further papers address, and from a range of different perspectives, but all highlighting aspects of the familiar emic/etic debate (cf. Scott 1993a, 6, 20), as well as the intersection between categories drawn from contextual studies of artefacts and those drawn from written sources (i.e. artefacts with writing on them). Thus, Collins re-examines some of the problems of relating categories of things to categories of people, Mol explores the Roman classification of 'Egyptian' material, and Van Oyen discusses not only the phenomenology of concrete use, but also its variable classification in antiquity. Through the elegant case studies presented in each of the five papers mentioned so far, it is clear that the ways in which people in the Roman period categorised and interacted with objects must underpin future narratives of that period. In a way there is something of a pendulum swing here, in that some of the earliest attempts to classify Roman objects started with things known (or believed to be known) from textual sources, and thus believed to be classifiable in 'Roman' taxonomic terms (e.g. 'samian', Tyers 1996, 6–7). The increased attention in the twentieth century to objects less well-represented in such sources (e.g. coarse pottery) and, latterly, a reaction against textual determinism beginning in the 1970s under the distant influence of the New Archaeology, led to more 'archaeological' classifications, albeit perhaps bypassing some of the important work on the emic/etic problem that had been a key part of the emergence of that paradigm (e.g. Ford 1954; cf. Millett, this volume). Returning to efforts to understand Roman-period categories, but on a firmer multi-evidential basis, is certainly to be welcomed.

The other four main papers in the volume shed equally important light on a further related issue, to do with the variability and standardisation of the Roman material world as, in itself, a crucial characteristic of that specifically 'Roman' world. Pitts, Poblome *et al.*, Murphy, and Jiménez all address the marked standardisation, but also the potential for local variability, in material culture (particularly pottery) across a range of geographical contexts. That a focus on the particular material characteristics of the Roman empire directs us towards such themes is certainly a beneficial consequence of the 'material turn', and one which offers much potential also for methodological innovation in how we chart these phenomena. That each paper uses different concepts to articulate some of the broader narrative significance of their particular cases – such as globalisation, *koine*, provincial networks – is both appealing in highlighting the flexibility of current theoretical work in Roman archaeology, and, I believe, revealing in its implications for some of the limitations of that 'turn', on which I will expand in the next section.

The dynamics of building theory with materials

This volume does indeed move the agenda forward in Roman archaeology with respect to the interlocking questions of the nature of (Roman) things and their articulation with (Roman) narratives. In doing so it also draws into view existing debates around these issues in Roman archaeology and far beyond which bear a little revisiting, in order to illuminate my central concern with how we go about doing theoretical Roman archaeology. The 'material turn' is, for all its concern with 'things', also an interesting case study in the history of ideas and their inter-disciplinary biographies. Partly this is because, like the 'linguistic', 'practice' and other 'turns', this movement is multi-stranded, drawing on different sets of disciplinary experiences and philosophical roots, with sometimes contradictory consequences; in this respect it is (like those other turns) rather intimately associated with post-processualism as an eclectic theoretical disposition (cf. Shanks 2008; Lindstrøm 2015, 209; Thomas 2015, 1287–8). Unlike those other turns, though, the origins of several major approaches within the 'material turn' lie quite close to home, springing from the evolving work of, in particular, Christopher Tilley, Daniel Miller, and Michael Shanks, at the intersection of archaeology and anthropology. Indeed, the former two of these have long worked in the UCL Anthropology department, which has nurtured numerous other key figures developing a 'materiality' approach (Buchli 2002; Miller 2005), while the latter has, with several of his students at Stanford University, been a driving force in the development of 'symmetrical archaeology' (Shanks 2007; Webmoor and Witmore

2008), taken up also in the work of a dispersed network of other scholars (e.g. Olsen 2010). While the 'symmetrical' approach draws considerably on ideas developed in Science and Technology Studies, particularly the work of Bruno Latour (1993; 2005), the 'material turn' has been seen as a project which archaeology can claim leadership in, enfolding also the phenomenological strand pursued by Julian Thomas and others (Jorge and Thomas 2007), a more cognitive-processual strand developing particularly in Cambridge (DeMarrais *et al.* 2004; Malafouris 2013), and other elements including those based upon Gell's art-as-agency approach and Peircean semiotics (Gosden 2005; Knappett 2005).

A couple of interesting points arise out of this potted intellectual history, which necessarily oversimplifies much (cf. Mol; Murphy; Van Oyen; Van Oyen and Pitts this volume; also Gardner 2003 for earlier stages). One is that there is much to be said in favour of a set of approaches which seek to address fundamental issues of the materiality of human existence across time and space, and which have been genuinely influential in other social science fields (Dant 1999; 2005; Attfield 2000; Woodward 2007; Matthewman 2011). The other is that there are also some interesting problems posed by such approaches which generally lead archaeology towards a very anthropological scale and style (in terms of evidential demands) of research, and away from a more sociological one, even as the social structures of the discipline work against the formulation of coherent positions on some of the aforementioned fundamental issues.

By this, I mean that the increasingly fragmented nature of debate in archaeological theory, influenced by a whole host of structural characteristics of the current practice of archaeology (whether at a global scale – see e.g. Mizoguchi 2015; cf. Bintliff 2011; Thomas 2015 – or the smaller scale of the Roman archaeological community – e.g. Gardner 2016a), makes it difficult for individual scholars, or groups of scholars, to develop long-term engagements with an ever-expanding web of ideas and a rapid cycling of priorities. This leads to inconsistencies between rhetoric and practice (Johnson 2006, 125), to terminological and conceptual slippage (e.g. with regard to agency; Gardner 2011b; 2016b; Johannsen 2012; Lindstrøm 2015; Ribeiro 2016), and to curious juxtapositions between what are in many ways incompatible intellectual programmes (e.g. between Darwinian memetics and some materiality approaches, see Gosden 2005, 198; Hodder 2012, 148–57).

All of this, I would argue, further feeds the process of fragmentation. It also creates – perhaps alongside other challenges like increasingly vast databases (Bevan 2015) – new problems of crafting syntheses and narratives. This returns us directly to this volume, where the linkage between new approaches to material culture and new narratives is explicitly on the agenda. I would argue, as others have (Jones 1996; Miettinen 1999; Barrett 2014; Lindstrøm 2015), that for all their novel attention to fundamental aspects of human experience (to retain a degree of anthropocentrism), aspects of some approaches within the 'material turn' positively inhibit developing broader-scale narratives which deliver analytical insights. Thus, for example, the flattening of agencies which is a key part of a symmetrical archaeology diverts us from structures of power (Gardner 2011b, 72–5; 2014; Matthewman 2011, 120–2; cf. Thomas 2015, 1293), while credulity towards alternative ontologies of the 'animated' material world (increasingly referred to as the 'ontological turn'), makes the consideration of the role of ideologies in sustaining social inequalities difficult (Spriggs 2008; Wilkinson 2013; Lindstrøm 2015; cf. Thomas 2015, 1290). Distributing agency can also have troubling moral consequences (Ribeiro 2016). All of these issues of power, inequality and ideology at least need to be up for debate, in part because they are critically important to the role of archaeology in the present day, and strong arguments, which remain compelling, have been made for highlighting them, in the not-too distant past (e.g. from a Marxist perspective, Leone 2005; Leone *et al.* 1987; McGuire 2002; 2008). Crucially for the present volume, it is precisely these kinds of questions and approaches which need to be retained from earlier phases of the development of archaeological theory if a new appreciation of materiality is to be connected also with broader Roman histories. This might require some new ways of working if we are to move forward.

Conclusion: shaping an alternative future for theory-building

In framing this volume around the problem of relating objects and historical narratives, the editors have therefore squarely targeted a key contemporary challenge in archaeological theory. That, in this respect, Roman archaeology might find itself at the cutting edge of theoretical debate is not only to do with the increasing appetite for new approaches among Roman archaeologists, but that this appetite is tempered both with the perspective that catching up on previous trends lends to some of those developments (Scott 1993b, 4), and with the inescapability of the scale of the Roman empire itself, no matter how hard we try to re-imagine it (Barrett 1997). This scale presents its own problems for synthetic narrative, referred to above, but it also furnishes a constant reminder of the need to think not only about the phenomenology of particular clusters of people and things but also major social-structural forces. The case studies provided across the chapters comprising this volume do, as already discussed, furnish some key themes with which to make that articulation work, and demonstrate some of the combinations of different approaches to material culture that the editors pre-figure in their Introduction. As the editors acknowledge, though, and as is inevitable within the constraints of multi-chapter volumes, this marks a beginning, not an end, and there is much still to do. In particular, there is scope for deeper engagement with the purely theoretical issues, to highlight further opportunities for which Roman archaeology is particularly well-suited, but also to overcome some of the contradictions and inconsistencies that we have inherited, and to avoid reinventing old truths or perpetuating old myths. I would have liked to see more of this in some of the chapters collected here, though I am well aware that there is a perpetual problem in theory-building which has to do with the balance between cases and concepts in short-form writing. While a relatively oft-cited critique of media such as TRAC papers (Laurence 1999), I think this is really another symptom of the much wider fragmentation of archaeological debate noted above. In the face of increasingly expansive data resources, and an equally increasingly variegated theoretical landscape, with ever more stuff to think through with ever more ideas, we pursue increasingly individuated and accelerated pathways, partly because that is how one gets (and keeps) a job in the humanities branches of academic archaeology. This situation is unsustainable; it does not serve those who work in archaeology in whatever role, nor does it serve the many wider publics for whom Roman archaeology is an important reference-point. To counter this trend requires collective and collaborative labour, encompassing theory and practice. There are many ways of pursuing this (see Gardner 2016a for some practical suggestions), but the Laurence Seminar in May 2015, and this resulting volume, are exemplary of precisely this kind of labour. Simply put, we need a lot more like them.

Acknowledgements
Many thanks go to the editors for their invitation to participate in the Laurence Seminar in 2015, and this volume, as well as for their forbearance with my fussiness over the terminology of 'material agency'. Thanks also to all of the contributors for the excellent papers which stimulated much of this chapter, other aspects of which have been developed in dialogue with a wide range of colleagues at TRAC and elsewhere over the last couple of years, including Richard Hingley, Matthew Johnson, Lisa Lodwick, and Kathryn Piquette.

Chapter 15

Roman things and Roman people. A cultural ecology of the Roman world

*Greg Woolf**

The book you are reading is an artefact. It is not quite a record of those conversations that took place in Cambridge in May 2015, in and around the formal conference session. It is not an exact record because the editors/organisers have worked hard – thanks are due to both – and also because many contributors, thinking back a year to the actual presentations and comparing them to the papers gathered here, have had second thoughts, strengthened some arguments, withdrawn others, expressed themselves with more nuance or determination, and in some cases have responded (as I do now) to both written versions and their own memories of the talks they heard on those two days. Conventionally we write about Conference Proceedings or Acts; but for a discussion in which agency loomed so large we should perhaps be up front about the fact that the proceedings have moved on, and our agency today is already producing different *acta* to those produced on the day. This artefact is not, of course, the only product of those discussions (even if is the most measurable output). Those of us who attended are also products, because in little ways and perhaps some large ones we exercise our agency (in writing, speaking, teaching, engaging in peer review etc.) in slightly different ways because of our co-presence at that meeting. The Laurence Seminar was a node, a moment in time at which our trajectories intersected, and what came out the other end – people and papers – were transformed by the encounter. All good conferences should do this, but not all are as successful as this meeting was.

My opening is not intended as a modish exercise in reflectivity, but to introduce my main theme, the relationship between the experience of people and that of things over time. Our focus was on artefacts, and several papers allude to the 'material turn': but people lurked constantly in the wings. Even the commitment to go beyond instrumentalism and representation evokes those who used objects as instruments, and that special form of instrumentality in which objects were used by one person

---

*Institute of Classical Studies, University of London.

(maker, user, giver) to represent one immaterial thing to another person (recipient, user or viewer). No paper spends much time on objects circulating in unpeopled worlds, despite the fact that most archaeologically preserved objects have in fact spent part of their cultural biography out of touch with society. Our material turn gives us a different way into conversations about people and things: it does not take us away from people.

The term 'representation' is used in this volume in a range of ways but essentially it deals with two families of relationships. The first family is located firmly in the past, evoked in discussions of how artefacts were used, both deliberately and with less conscious intent, to mediate relations between different human actors. Sometimes a gift of an object materially changed a relationship, as in the presentation of an auxiliary *diploma* to mark the grant of citizenship, or the dedication of a childhood doll to mark the transition to womanhood. This is a clear instrumental use of specific items of material culture, a use of things to change people. A vast ethnography and a mass of archaeological theory informs our understanding of this species of deliberate and customary artefact-use, and it has been incorporated into Roman studies for a long time. More often we have been discussing how the use of a particular item of clothing or tableware *signified* adherence to a particular set of social values. Mingled with these issues are questions of intent and self-consciousness about the use of artefacts: what was going through the mind of an adult Roman subject when he put on a toga for a particular occasion? That sort of question is in the end unanswerable, but several papers here make use of ideas like Bourdieu's *habitus* to describe the problem. These questions also have a long currency in archaeological theory, especially in the debate over the communicative functions of style, as well as in relation to a proposed 'ontological turn'.

The second family of representational relationships are those between modern researchers and relics of the Roman past. Specifically, these papers discuss the way we are accustomed to use a particular set of artefacts as proxies for particular identities (Roman, British, military statues etc.) or else as indicators of phenomena such as literacy. As the editors make clear, there can be no real objection to this general procedure. Natural scientists resort to proxy data all the time, as when exoplanets are detected by their effects on the light coming from the stars they orbit or when the pace of global warming is inferred from directly measurable phenomena such as changes in sea levels or the retreat of glaciers. Some applications have turned out to be misleading, like the culture-historical equation of particular kinds of material culture with particular ethnic groups. But there is nothing wrong in principle with asking what particular artefact classes (or their use patterns) represent. Ceramic studies naturally loom large, but other artefact types are brought into the debate. The questions posed are related to larger ones about inference and what might constitute an interpretative archaeology.

What is common to the analysis of both these families of relationships, is that artefacts are treated as secondary to humans, as passive objects in the control of humans, rather than as subjects possessing their own agency. Most of the contributors to this volume are engaged to some degree or another in a critique of such views. Most are agreed, I think, that artefacts do have some degree of agency, that they have effects beyond those intended or programmed by their human makers and users, and that the properties of artefacts include affordances that elicit, facilitate or stimulate particular responses on the part of humans who encounter them.

That agency in the Roman case turns out to be both more various, and less predictable than is sometimes emphasised. The centuries before and after the turn of the millennium saw the production of many new kinds of artefact, and also some new kinds of material. Just as in the industrialised world an explosion of new materials made possible much more than their inventors could have intended. The history of early imperial architecture is very largely a working out of the new possibilities created by access to new materials. A number of papers take care to assert that representational approaches of one kind or another still have some utility. Historians of Roman art are still trying to assimilate the impact of arguments about the agency exercised by works of art, and the boundary between a work of art and an artefact is a difficult one to establish. Many things we would not consider artworks clearly played a representational role. But then as now objects impacted on people in many other ways. Put bluntly, there is more to Roman things than what they meant or even what they were meant to mean.

What follows if all this is correct? That question returns us again to the practice of archaeology. It makes a difference whether one is curating or studying a single object, considering a category of artefacts (and several contributors have much to say about categories and taxonomies), or whether one is trying to write history from artefacts, as the editors encouraged us to do. The remainder of my comments relate to this last topic, since it is very much of the moment.

Several suggestions have been made about how we might envisage the big picture, and generate macro-scale narratives about ancient Rome that do not begin and end with human agency. One of these ideas is the notion of a 'consumer revolution', perhaps beginning in the second and last centuries BC, and attested by the proxy data of a vast expansion in the quantity of Roman-style manufactures, most produced first in central Italy, and then in other Italian and provincial locations. Some of us have found this an attractive formulation, one originally borrowed from studies of early modern Europe (Woolf 1998; Wallace-Hadrill 2008). But it is of course a perfect example of an account in which human agency does all the work, from stimulating the demand in the first place to developing a series of production and distribution systems to satisfy it. If that approach is to be saved, we need to ask what certain kinds of artefacts did to make human agents desire them. What were the 'technologies of enchantment' (Garrow and Gosden 2012) possessed by some Roman-style goods? Gosden (2001) developed the idea of a *sensorium*, a material environment which elicits particular desires and habits of behaviour: it draws on the work of the art historian W.J. Mitchell (1996) and the anthropologist Alfred Gell (1998) and coheres well with ideas about the extended mind, symbolic storage and attempts by Giddens and Bourdieu to reconcile individual agency with the predictability of human behaviour *en masse*. The relationship between human and material agencies is recursive and dialectical. 'We build the house and the house builds us', as it is sometimes put. Miguel John Versluys proposes in this volume the idea of an 'object-scape' to describe a dispersed class of objects that brings with it a series of human-thing entanglements. Martin Pitts road tests this idea in relation to Gallo-Belgic pottery, with thought-provoking results.

The potential of many of these ideas remains to be worked through, but it is possible to imagine at least one objection to all of them. Implicit in all these formulations (and others such as entanglement theory) is the sharp dichotomy drawn between people and things. Perhaps the best way to approach this is through examining the category 'artefact'. Romanists rarely have difficulty identifying artefacts since most of their characteristics are the results of processes of manufacture that completely transform the raw material. Objects made of iron, glass, concrete or ceramic could not have come about without transformations that only humans could organise. Even materials that were not physically transformed to a significant degree, such as granites, basalt and marbles, are usually found as parts of complex objects which have no possible natural origin. For what it is worth both Renaissance and ancient ideas about manufacture stressed the transformative power of human agency. But the question of what an artefact is, is not always so clear. Archaeologists often speak of biofacts or ecofacts, meaning organic finds in archaeological assemblages that have not been converted into tools or furniture, yet are relics of human collection, agriculture or digestion. Primate archaeology raises even more sharply the question of when a stick or stone used as a tool becomes an artefact. And once we populate the Roman sensorium or object-scape with plants and animals, where will we draw the line? Does stock-breeding turn an animal into an artefact, or must that wait for butchery? Gardens are arguably as complex artefacts as *atria*. If a cultivated landscape is an artefact, is an orchard an object-scape?

Perhaps most crucial is our habitual reluctance to treat human bodies as artefacts. Yet when one of Rome's subjects begins to depilate or shave, to grow or cut hair into a particular style, to abandon ancestral practices of tattooing, or when a Roman brands his or her slave, is there really such a difference from transforming other biofacts into artefacts? It would be convenient too if this stopped with the materiality of the body, or with its external surfaces and organs. But it is common enough now to discuss self-fashioning (in Greenblatt's phrase) or *le souci de soi*, Foucault's 'care of the self'. And if we, and our animals and plants and homes and dreams and ambitions are all artefacts, how can we justify a distinction between human and material agency? The material turn, in other words, risks perpetuating Romantic and anthropocentric ideals about the separation of man from nature, and perhaps also a sense that the essence of being human is an immaterial thing, whether we call it soul or self. Yet our bodies' material components have affordances as well, and they have an agency that is not entirely under our conscious or deliberate control.

Much of this has little special applicability to the Roman world. But the huge geographical and chronological extent of that world, and the fact we know its people and other artefacts so well, makes it an excellent place to try out some of these ideas. And it does have its peculiarities. As several essays suggest, one of these peculiarities is the appearance over the last centuries BC of relatively high levels of standardisation in many categories of object. There are many early precedents for this sort of phenomenon from the Uruk phenomenon of fourth millennium BC Mesopotamia to the spread of *Linearbandkeramik* in the early European Neolithic. But Roman standardisation is more comprehensive – more materials and artefact types were involved – and easier to contextualise. At a stylistic level that standardisation diminishes gradually over the first centuries AD but in many media – tableware for instance, and domesticated animals – there remained recognisable family resemblances well into the middle ages. It is as if across the vast area controlled by Rome patterns of resonance began to intensify over the last centuries BC, and then to diminish into more regionally fragmented patterns.

Patterning like this is observable because we can study manufactures *en masse* in a way that is rarely possible. But we lack good analytical tools for examining the phenomenon. Wengrow's (2014) interest in the implications of mechanical reproduction might contribute to this picture, but most approaches are more easily applied to single objects or classes of complex artefacts with few members. I am thinking of Gell's approach to style, in which an artefact category becomes an 'object' and particular artefacts 'indices' of it, and Kopytoff's (1986) notion of cultural biographies which allow us to describe the changing social valences of particular artefacts from their creation to their deposition. These approaches seem better suited to studying artefact categories such as archaic Greek temples or 'Celtic' metalwork than to Roman period brooches or tableware.

If we are to examine agency in such a way to include humans and animals and plants within our super-category of Roman period artefacts – in what some might call a symmetrical archaeology (Witmore 2007) – we do not need a cultural biography or artefact biographies so much as a cultural *ecology*. We might imagine the Roman world as a vast ecosystem in which different categories of actors play the role of species, each with its own agency. The key questions then become, as in the study of any ecosystem, how are its components related, how do the dynamics of competition, predation, symbiosis, and reproduction intersect to sustain or transform the order of the system?

Put this way, it is immediately apparent that the material world of the Roman period was a relatively stable system. The main species of artefact, of animal and plant and human hardly changed between the second century BC and the sixth AD or even later. There were some technological innovations of course. But they hardly disrupted the cultural ecology in the way that earlier innovations had done, innovations such as the domestication of the horse, the generalisation of iron working, or maritime transport. When the Arab armies of conquest took over half the Mediterranean basin in the seventh century they found more or less the same techniques of agriculture, building materials, industrial techniques, and domesticated species as those that the Romans had found in their own period of expansion around a millennium before. Compared to the thousand years before that expansion (from 1300–300 BC, say) or to the thousand years after (700–1700 AD), the Roman millennium was relatively stable. Stability is not necessarily a good thing of course, and nor was the standardisation which several essays discuss. In ecological terms standardisation represents a loss of diversity, a thinning of reproductive options, a narrowing of the range of affordances. So, in a different way does the solidification of stylistic canons, the classicisation of particular literary and aesthetic motifs, the entrenchment of the power of particular interest groups. Low diversity systems can endure for long periods, but they are not particularly resilient.

Conventional accounts of the endurance of the Roman order and of its collapse still focus on human agency, that of individuals and that of institutions. Most narratives of decline and fall assume that survival and disaster alike are to be attributed to the conduct of the political, fiscal, and military elite. Changes in Roman material culture are most often seen as consequential to political change, rather than as bound up in it. Once again people are attributed agency, and neither the agency nor the affordances of material culture play much of a part in the story. Yet in many ecosystems those species at the top of the food chain are the most vulnerable to change, and disruption rarely comes from the top. Perhaps we might understand long term trajectories of growth, stability, and decline better if we began from lower down, from Roman things rather than Roman people. Were the standardised forms that emerged and were so widely disseminated in the last centuries BC in some way implicated in the stability of the period that followed? Did they establish a *sensorium* that elicited a particularly limited range of responses from human agents? Giddens explored the contribution of spaces to the routinisation of behaviour. Might the agency of Roman things have been the very opposite of dynamic? Change happened, of course, but it was slow and it was incremental rather than discontinuous and rapid. What role did the stability of Roman artefacts have in the stability of Roman society?

As we move beyond representation and instrumentality we take a great weight of responsibility off the shoulders of Roman actors. Humans are no longer the sole drivers of Roman success and Roman failure. Romans put human virtue and customs at the heart of their historical causation, but we do not need to do the same. Neither expansion nor collapse is to be explained primarily in terms of human values, ideologies, beliefs or motivations. And in fact, some of the political and military failures seem less cataclysmic when we consider how much of the Roman material order persisted under new management. Taking things seriously allows us to put people in perspective.

Bibliography

'Amr, K. (1991) Preliminary report on the 1991 Season at Zurrabah. *Annual of the Department of Antiquities of Jordan* 35, 313–22.

'Amr, K. and A. Al-Momani (1999) The discovery of two additional pottery kilns at Az-Zurraba/Wadi Musa. *Annual of the Department of Antiquities of Jordan* 43, 175–94.

Adam, J.-P. (1984) *La construction romaine. Matériaux et techniques*. Paris, Picard.

Agnew, J.A. (2013) Arguing with regions. *Regional Studies* 47.1, 6–17.

Aldhouse-Green, M. and P. Webster (eds) (2002) *Artefacts and Archaeology. Aspects of the Celtic and Roman World*. Cardiff, University of Wales Press.

Alexandridis, A. (2010) Neutral bodies? Female portrait statue types from the late republic to the second century CE. In S. Hales and T. Hodos (eds) *Material Culture and Social Identities in the Ancient World*, 252–79. Cambridge, Cambridge University Press.

Allason-Jones, L. (ed.) (2011) *Artefacts in Roman Britain. Their Purpose and Use*. Cambridge, Cambridge University Press.

Allen, J. (2003) *Lost Geographies of Power*. Oxford, Blackwell.

Allen, J. (2004) The whereabouts of power: politics, government and space. *Geografiska Annaler B* 86, 19–32.

Allen, J. (2016) *Topologies of Power. Beyond Territory and Networks*. London, Routledge.

Allen, J. and A. Cochrane (2007) Beyond the territorial fix: regional assemblages, politics and power. *Regional Studies* 41.9, 1161–75.

Andrén, A. (1998) *Between Artifacts and Texts. Historical Archaeology in Global Perspective*. Transl. A. Crozier. New York, Plenum.

Andrews, C. (2013) Are Roman seal boxes evidence for literacy? *Journal of Roman Archaeology* 26, 423–38.

Apel, J. (2008) Knowledge, know-how and raw material: the production of late Neolithic flint daggers in Scandinavia. *Journal of Archaeological Method and Theory* 15.1, 91–111.

Appadurai, A. (1996) *Modernity at Large. Cultural dimensions of Globalisation*. Minneapolis (MN), University of Minnesota Press.

Appadurai, A. (2013) *The Future as Cultural Fact. Essays on the Global Condition*. London, Verso.

Attfield, J. (2000) *Wild Things. The Material Culture of Everyday Life*. Oxford, Berg.

Austin, J. (2010) Writers and Writing in the Roman Army at Dura Europos. Unpublished PhD thesis, University of Birmingham.

Bagnall, R.S. (2011) *Everyday Writing in the Graeco-Roman East*. Berkeley (CA), University of California Press.

Bagnall, R.S. and R. Cribiore (2006) *Women's Letters from Ancient Egypt. 300 BC – 800 AD*. Ann Arbor (MI), University of Michigan Press.

Bailey, D.M. (1997) Roman pottery lamps. In I. Freestone and D. Gaimster (eds) *Pottery in the Making. Ceramic Traditions*, 164–9. Washington D.C., Smithsonian Institution Press.

Bailey, G. (2007) Time perspectives, palimpsests and the archaeology of time. *Journal of Anthropological Archaeology* 26, 198–223.

Baird Callicot, J. (1996) Traditional American Indian and western European attitudes toward nature. In M. Oelschlaeger (ed.) *Postmodern Environmental Ethics*, 192–220. Albany (NY), State of New York University Press.

Ball, L.F. (2003) *The Domus Aurea and the Roman Architectural Revolution*. Cambridge, Cambridge University Press.
Ballet, P., F. Béguin, T. Herbich, G. Lecuyot and A. Schmitt (2007) Recherches sur les ateliers hellénistiques et romains de Bouto (Delta). In J.-C. Goyon and C. Cardin (eds) *Actes du neuvième congrès international des égyptologues, Grenoble, 6-12 Septembre 2004. Orientalia Lovaniensia Analecta 150*, 133–43. Leuven, Peeters.
Barad, K. (2003) Posthumanist performativity: toward an understanding of how matter comes to matter. *Signs* 28.3, 801–31.
Barad, K. (2007) *Meeting the Universe Halfway. Quantum Physics and the Entanglement of Matter and Meaning*. Durham (NC), Duke University Press.
Barber, B. and D. Bowsher (2000) *The Eastern Cemetery of Roman London. Excavations 1983-1990*. MoLAS Monograph 4. London, Museum of London.
Barrett, J.C. (1997) Romanization: a critical comment. In D. Mattingly (ed.) *Dialogues in Roman Imperialism*, 51–64. Portsmouth, Journal of Roman Archaeology Supplementary Series 23.
Barrett, J C. (2014) The material constitution of humanness. *Archaeological Dialogues* 21.1, 65–74.
Barsalou, L.W. (1992) Frames, concepts, and conceptual fields. In E. Kittay and A. Lehrer (eds) *Frames, Fields and Contrasts. New essays in Semantic and Lexical Organization*, 21–74. Hillsdale (NJ), Lawrence Erlbaum.
Bartman, E. (1992) *Ancient Sculptural Copies in Miniature*. Leiden, Brill.
Bechert, T. (1974) *Asciburgium - Ausgrabungen in einem römischen Kastell am Niederrhein*. Duisburg, Walter Braun.
Belting, H. (2001) *Bild-Anthropologie. Entwürfe für eine Bildwissenschaft*. Munich, W. Fink.
Bennett, J. (2010) *Vibrant Matter*. Durham (NC), Duke University Press.
Berg, I. (2007) Aegean Bronze Age seascapes – a case study in maritime movement, contact and interaction. In S. Antoniadou and A. Pace (eds) *Mediterranean Crossroads*, 387–415. Athens, Pierides Foundation.
Bes, P. (2015a) Roman-period finds from the Cide region. In K. Winther-Jacobsen and L. Summerer (eds) *Landscape Dynamics and Settlement Patterns in Northern Anatolia during the Roman and Byzantine Period*. Geographica Historica 32, 23–42. Stuttgart, Franz Steiner.
Bes, P. (2015b) *Once Upon a Time in the East. The Chronological and Geographical Distribution of Terra Sigillata and Red Slip Ware in the Roman East*. Roman and Late Antique Mediterranean Pottery 6. Oxford, Archaeopress.
Bes, P. and J. Poblome (2008) (Not) see the wood for the trees? 19,700+ sherds of tableware and what we can do with them. *Rei Cretariae Romanae Fautorum Acta* 40, 505–14.
Bes, P. and J. Poblome (in press) Urban Thespiai: the Late Hellenistic to Late Roman Pottery. In J. Bintliff and A. Snodgrass (eds) *The Urban Survey of the City of Thespiai (1985-1986)*. Cambridge, McDonald Institute.
Bevan, A. (2014) Mediterranean containerization. *Current Anthropology* 55.4, 387–418.
Bevan, A. (2015) The data deluge. *Antiquity* 89.348, 1473–84.
Bianchi, E. (2004) Produzioni laterizie e cantieri edilizii traianei. In E. De Sena and H. Dessales (eds) *Metodi e approci archaeologici. L'industria ed il commercio nell'Italia antica*. BAR International Series 1262, 268–90. Oxford, Archaeopress.
Bianchi, E., P. Brune, M. Jackson, F. Marra and R. Meneghini (2011) Archaeological, structural, and compositional observations of the concrete architecture of the Basilica Ulpia and Trajan's Forum. *Comm. Humm. Litt.* 128, 73–95.
Bianchi Bandinelli, R. (1970) *Rome. The Center of Power*. Transl. P. Green. New York, G. Braziller.
Biddulph, E. (2013) The blind potter: the evolution of samian ware and its imitations. In M. Fulford and E. Durham (eds) *Seeing Red. New Economic and Social Perspectives on Gallo-Roman Terra Sigillata*, 368–80. London, Institute of Classical Studies.

Bidwell, P. (1999) A survey of pottery production and supply at Colchester. In R. Symonds and S. Wade (eds) *Roman Pottery from Excavations in Colchester, 1971-86*, 488–99. Colchester, Colchester Archaeological Reports 10.
Bilkei, I. (1980) Römische Schreibgeräte aus Pannonien. *Alba Regia* 18, 61–90.
Bintliff, J. (2011) The death of archaeological theory? In J. Bintliff and M. Pearce (eds) *The Death of Archaeological Theory?*, 7–22. Oxford, Oxbow Books.
Blake, M.E. and E.B. Van Deman (1947) *Ancient Roman Construction in Italy from the Prehistoric Period to Augustus*. Washington D.C., Carnegie Institution.
Blake, M.E. (1959) *Roman Construction in Italy from Tiberius through the Flavians*. Washington D.C., Carnegie Institution.
Bleed, P. (2008) Skill matters. *Journal of Archaeological Method and Theory* 15, 154–66.
Böhme, H. (1974) *Germanische Grabfunde des 4. und 5. Jahrhunderts zwischen unterer Elbe und Loire. Studien zur Chronologie und Bevölkerungsgeschichte*. Munich, Beck.
Böhme, H. (2006) *Fetischismus und Kultur. Eine andere Theorie der Moderne*. Hamburg, Rowohlt Taschenbuch.
Böhner, K. (1963) Zur historischen Interpretation der sogenannten Laetengräber. *Jahrbuch des Römisch-Germanischen Zentralmuseums* 10, 139–67.
Boivin, N. (2008) *Material Cultures, Material Minds. The Impact of Things on Human Thought, Society, and Culture*. Oxford, Oxford University Press.
Bonifay, M. (2004) *Etudes sur la céramique romaine tardive d'Afrique*. BAR International Series 1301. Oxford, Archaeopress.
Booth, P. (2014) A late Roman military burial from the Dyke Hills, Dorchester on Thames, Oxfordshire. *Britannia* 45, 243–73.
Booth, P., A. Simmonds, A. Boyle, S. Clough, H. Cool and D. Poore (2010) *The Late Roman Cemetery at Lankhills, Winchester. Excavations 2000-2005*. Oxford, Oxford Archaeology.
Boschung, D., P.-A. Kreuz and T. Kienlin (eds) (2015) *Biography of Objects. Aspekte eines kulturhistorischen Konzepts*. Paderborn, Wilhelm Fink.
Bourdieu, P. (1977) *Outline of a Theory of Practice*. Transl. R. Nice. Cambridge, Cambridge University Press.
Bowman, A.K. (2003) *Life and Letters on the Roman Frontier*. London, British Museum Press.
Bowman, A.K. and A. Wilson (2009) Quantifying the Roman economy: integration, growth, decline? In A.K. Bowman and A. Wilson (eds) *Quantifying the Roman Economy. Methods and Problems*, 3–84. Oxford, Oxford University Press.
Bowman, A.K. and G. Woolf (eds) (1994) *Literacy and Power in the Ancient World*. Cambridge, Cambridge University Press.
Boyle, A.J. and W.J. Dominik (eds) (2003) *Flavian Rome. Culture, Image, Text*. Leiden, Brill.
Božič, D. (2001a) Zum Schreibgerät aus dem Grab einer Ärztin aus Vindonissa. *Intrumentum* 14, 30–2.
Božič, D. (2001b) Les couvercles des encriers en bronze de type Biebrich. *Instrumentum* 14, 33–4.
Božič, D. and M. Feugère (2004) Les instruments de l'écriture. *Gallia* 61, 21–41.
Brather, S. (2005) Acculturation and ethnogenesis along the frontier: Rome and the ancient Germans in an archaeological perspective. In F. Curta (ed.) *Borders, Barriers, and Ethnogenesis. Frontiers in Late Antiquity and the Middle Ages*, 139–71. Turnhout, Brepols.
Braudel, F. (1972) *The Mediterranean and the Mediterranean World in the Age of Philip II*. Berkeley (CA), University of California Press.
Brenner, N. (2001) The limits to scale? Methodological reflections on scalar structuration. *Progress in Human Geography* 25.4, 591–614.
Broekaert, W. (2015) Recycling networks: the structure of the Italian business community on Delos. In P. Erdkamp and K. Verboven (eds) *Structure and Performance in the Roman Economy. Models, Methods and Case Studies*. Collection Latomus 350, 143–82. Brussels, Latomus.

Brown, D. (1975) A fifth-century burial at Kingsholm. *Antiquaries Journal* 55, 290–4.
Brubaker, R. and F. Cooper (2000) Beyond 'identity'. *Theory and Society* 29, 1–47.
Brück, J. (2001) Monuments, power and personhood in the British Neolithic. *Journal of the Royal Anthropological Institute* 7.4, 649–67.
Brück, J. (2005) Experiencing the past? The development of a phenomenological archaeology in British prehistory. *Archaeological Dialogues* 12.1, 45–72
Brughmans, T. (2013) Thinking through networks: a review of formal network methods in archaeology. *Journal of Archaeological Method and Theory* 20, 623–62.
Brughmans, T. and J. Poblome (2016a) MERCURY: an agent-based model of tableware trade in the Roman East. *Journal of Artificial Societies and Social Simulation* 19.1.3, DOI: 10.18564/jasss.2953.
Brughmans, T. and J. Poblome (2016b) Roman bazaar or market economy? Explaining tableware distributions in the Roman East through computational modelling. *Antiquity*, 90.350, 393–408.
Brulet, R., F. Vilvorder and R. Delage (2010) *La céramique romaine en Gaule du nord. Dictionnaire des céramiques: la vaisselle à large diffusion*. Turnhout, Brepols.
Bubenik, V. (2010) The rise of koine. In A.-F. Christidis (ed.) *A History of Ancient Greek. From the Beginnings to Late Antiquity*, 342–345. Cambridge, Cambridge University Press.
Buchli, V. (1995) Interpreting material culture: the trouble with text. In I. Hodder, M. Shanks, A. Alexandri, V. Buchli, J. Carman, J. Last and G. Lucas (eds) *Interpreting Archaeology. Finding Meaning in the Past*, 182–93. London, Routledge.
Buchli, V. (ed.) (2002) *The Material Culture Reader*. Oxford, Berg.
Butzer, K.W. (1982) *Archaeology as Human Ecology. Method and Theory for a Contextual Approach*. Cambridge, Cambridge University Press.
Calvi, M.C. (2005) *Le ambre romane di Aquileia*. Aquileia, Associazione Nazionale per Aquileia.
Carbone, G. (2005) *Tabliope. Ricerche su gioco e letteratura nel mondo greco-romano*. Napoli, Dipartimento di Filologia Classica dell'Università degli Studi di Napoli Federico II.
Carettoni G.P. (1983) La decorazione pittorica nella Casa di Augusto sul Palatino, *Mitteilungen des Deutschen Archäologischen Instituts, Römische Abteilung* 90, 373–419.
Carratelli, G.P. (ed.) (1990–2003) *Pompei, Pitture e Mosaici*, Rome, Istituto dell' Enciclopedia italiana
Casella, E.C. and C. Fowler (eds) (2004) *The Archaeology of Plural and Changing Identities. Beyond Identification*. New York, Springer.
Chadour, A.B. (1994) *Rings. The Alice and Louis Koch Collection, Forty Centuries seen by Four Generations*. Leeds, Maney.
Chadour, A.B. and R. Joppien (1985) *Schmuck II. Fingerringe*. Cologne, Kunstgewerbemuseum der stadt Köln.
Charpy, M. (2015) How things shape us: material culture and identity in the Industrial Age. In A. Gerritsen and G. Riello (eds) *Writing Material Culture History*, 199–221. London, Bloomsbury.
Christidis, A.-F. (2010) The nature of language. In A.-F. Christidis (ed.) *A History of Ancient Greek. From the Beginnings to Late Antiquity*, 27–64. Cambridge, Cambridge University Press.
Clark, A. (2008) Where brain, body and world collide. In C. Knappett and L. Malafouris (eds) *Material Agency. Towards a Non-Anthropocentric Approach*, 1–18. New York, Springer.
Clarke, G. (1979) *Winchester Studies 3. Pre- and post-Roman Winchester, part II. The Roman cemetery at Lankhills*. Oxford, Clarendon.
Coarelli, F. (1977) Public building in Rome between the Second Punic War and Sulla. *Papers of the British School at Rome* 45, 1–23.
Cockle, H. (1981) Pottery manufacture in Roman Egypt: a new papyrus. *Journal of Roman Studies* 71, 87–97.
Colla, E. (2007) *Conflicted Antiquities, Egyptology, Egyptomania, Egyptian modernity*. Durham (NC), Duke University Press.
Collinge, C. (2006) Flat ontology and the deconstruction of scale: a response to Marston, Jones and Woodward. *Transactions of the Institute of British Geographers* 31.2, 244–51.

Collins, R. (2006) Late Roman frontier communities in north Britain: a theoretical context for the 'end' of Hadrian's Wall. In B. Croxford, H. Goodchild, J. Lucas and N. Ray (eds) *TRAC 2005. Proceedings of the Fifteenth Annual Theoretical Roman Archaeology Conference, Birmingham 2005*, 1–11. Oxford, Oxbow Books.

Collins, R. (2012) Social spaces at the end of empire: the *limitanei* of Hadrian's Wall. In D. Totten and K. Lafrenze Samuels (eds) *Making Roman Places, Past and Present*, 65–80. Portsmouth, Journal of Roman Archaeology Supplementary Series 89.

Collins, R. (2015) After the auxiliaries: veterans in 4th century Britain. In L. Vagalinski and N. Sharankov (eds) *Proceedings of the 22nd International Congress of Roman Frontier Studies*, 471–5. Sofia, National Archaeological Institute.

Combes, P.-P. and L. Gobillon (2014) The empirics of agglomeration economies. *IZA Discussion Papers* 8508.

Cool, H.E.M. (2006) *Eating and Drinking in Roman Britain*. Cambridge, Cambridge University Press.

Cool, H.E.M. (2010) Objects of glass, shale, bone and metal (except nails). In P. Booth, A. Simmonds, A. Boyle, S. Clough, H.E.M. Cool and D. Poore (eds) *The Late Roman Cemetery at Lankhills, Winchester. Excavations 2000-2005*, 267–309. Oxford, Oxford Archaeology.

Cool, H.E.M. and J. Price (1995) *Roman Vessel Glass from Excavations in Colchester, 1971-85*. Colchester, Colchester Archaeological Trust.

Cooley, A.E. (ed.) (2002) *Becoming Roman, Writing Latin? Literacy and Epigraphy in the Roman West*. Portsmouth, Journal of Roman Archaeology Supplementary Series 48.

Corbier, M. (2006) *Donner à voir, donner à lire. Mémoire et communication dans la Rome ancienne*. Paris, CNRS.

Cordie-Hackenberg, R. and A. Haffner (1991) *Das Keltisch-römische Gräberfeld von Wederath-Belginum 4*. Mainz, Philipp Von Zabern.

Cordie-Hackenberg, R. and A. Haffner (1997) *Das Keltisch-römische Gräberfeld von Wederath-Belginum 5*. Mainz, Philipp Von Zabern.

Cornell, T.J. (1995) *The Beginnings of Rome. Italy and Rome from the Bronze Age to the Punic Wars (c.1000-264 BC)*. London, Routledge.

Costin, C. and R. Wright (1998) *Craft and Social Identity*. Arlington (VA), American Anthropological Association.

Coulston, J. (2010) Military equipment of the 'long' fourth century on Hadrian's Wall. In R. Collins and L. Allason-Jones (eds) *Finds from the Frontier. Material Culture in the 4th-5th centuries*, 50–63. York, Council for British Archaeology.

Cowie, R., A. Wardle and A. Thorp (2013) *Roman Roadside Settlement and Rural Landscape at Brentford. Archaeological Investigations at Hilton London Syon Park Hotel, 2004-10*. London, Museum of London Archaeology.

Crawford, M. (1983) Numismatics. In M. Crawford (ed.) *Sources for Ancient History*, 185–233. Cambridge, Cambridge University Press.

Cribiore, R. (2001) *Gymnastics of the Mind. Greek Education in Hellenistic and Roman Egypt*. Princeton (NJ), Princeton University Press.

Cristofani, M. (1979) Recent advances in Etruscan epigraphy and language. In D. Ridgway and F.R. Ridgway (eds) *Italy before the Romans. The Iron Age, Orientalizing and Etruscan Periods*. London, Academic Press.

Cristofani, M. (1990) *La grande Roma dei Tarquini*. Rome, Bretschneider.

Crummy, N. (1983) *The Roman Small Finds from Excavations in Colchester 1971-79*. Colchester, Colchester Archaeological Reports 2.

Cunliffe, B. (1988) *Greeks, Romans and Barbarians. Spheres of Interaction*. London, Guild.

Curran, B.A., A. Grafton, P.O. Long and B. Weiss (2009) *Obelisk. A History*. Cambridge (MA), Burndy Library.

Dalaison, J. (2014) Civic pride and local identities: the Pontic cities and their coinage in the Roman period. In T. Bekker-Nielsen (ed.) *Space, Place and Identity in Northern Anatolia*. Geographica Historica 29, 125–55. Stuttgart, Franz Steiner.

Dalton, O.M. (1901) *Catalogue of Early Christian Antiquities and Objects from the Christian East in the Department of British and Medieval Antiquities and Ethnography of the British Museum*. London, British Museum.

Dalton, O.M. (1912) *Franks Bequest Catalogue of the Finger Rings, Early Christian, Byzantine, Teutonic, Medieval and Later*. London, British Museum Press.

Dant, T. (1999) *Material Culture in the Social World*. Buckingham, Open University Press.

Dant, T. (2005) *Materiality and Society*. Maidenhead, Open University Press.

David, F. (1962) *Games, Gods and Gambling. The Origin and History of Probability and Statistical Ideas from the Earliest Times to the Newtonian Era*. London, Griffin and co.

de Boüard, M. (1966) Haute et Basse Normandie. *Gallia* 24, 257–73.

De Caro, S. (2006) *Egittomania, Iside e il mistero*. Milan, Electa.

De Laet, S., J. Dhondt and J. Nenquin (1952) Les Laeti du Namurois et l'origine de la civilisation mérovingienne. *Études d'histoire et d'archéologie dédiées à Ferdinand Courtoy*, 149–72.

De Landa M. (2002) *Intensive Science and Virtual Philosophy*. London, Continuum.

de Vos, M. (1980) *L'egittomania in pitture e mosaici romano-campani della prima età imperiale*. Leiden, Brill.

Degeest, R. (2000) *The Common Wares of Sagalassos. Studies in Eastern Mediterranean Archaeology III*. Turnhout, Brepols.

Degryse, P. (ed.) (2014) *Glass Making in the Greco-Roman World. Results of the ARCHGLASS Project*. Studies in Archaeological Sciences 4. Leuven, Leuven University Press.

Degryse, P. and J. Poblome (2008) Clays for mass production of table and common wares, amphorae and architectural ceramics at Sagalassos. In P. Degryse and M. Waelkens (eds) *Sagalassos VI. Geo- and Bio-archaeology at Sagalassos and in Its Territory*, 231–54. Leuven, Leuven University Press.

Degryse, P., J. Poblome, W. Viaene, H. Kucha, R. Ottenburgs, M. Waelkens and J. Naud (2008) Provenancing the slip of Sagalassos Red Slip Ware. In P. Degryse and M. Waelkens (eds) *Sagalassos VI. Geo- and Bio-archaeology at Sagalassos and in its Territory*, 255–60. Leuven, Leuven University Press.

DeLaine, J. (1997) *The Baths of Caracalla. A Study in the Design, Construction, and Economics of Large-Scale Building Projects in Imperial Rome*. Portsmouth, Journal of Roman Archaeology Supplementary Series 25.

DeLaine, J. (2000) Building the Eternal City: the building industry of imperial Rome. In J. Coulston and H. Dodge (eds) *Ancient Rome. The Archaeology of the Eternal City*, 119–41. Oxford, Oxford School of Archaeology.

DeLaine, J. (2006) The cost of creation: technology at the service of construction. In E. Lo Cascio (ed.) *Innovazione tecnica e progresso economico nel mondo romano*, 237–52. Bari, Edipuglia.

Deleuze, G. and F. Guattari (2012) [1987] *A Thousand Plateaus. Capitalism and Schizophrenia*. Transl. B. Massumi. London, Bloomsbury.

Della Corte, M. (1932) Una famiglia di Sacerdote d'Iside. I MM, Lorei Tiburtini di Pompei, Tivoli. *Atti e memorie della Società tiburtina di storia e d'arte* 11–12, 182–216.

DeMarrais, E., C. Gosden and C. Renfrew (eds) (2004) *Rethinking Materiality. The Engagement of Mind with the Material World*. Cambridge, McDonald Institute.

Deru, X. (1996) *La céramique belge dans le nord de la Gaule*. Louvain-la-Neuve, Département d'archéologie et d'histoire de l'art.

Derudder, B. and P. Taylor (2005) The cliquishness of world cities. *Global Networks* 5.1, 71–91.

Derudder, B., F. Witlox and G. Catalano (2003) Hierarchical tendencies and regional patterns in the world city network: a global urban analysis of 234 cities. *Regional Studies* 37.9, 875–86.

Descola, P. 2013. *Beyond Nature and Culture*. Chicago, University of Chicago Press.

Díaz-Andreu, M., S. Lucy, S. Babić and D.E. Edwards (eds) (2005) *The Archaeology of Identity. Approaches to Gender, Age, Status, Ethnicity and Religion*, 1–12. London, Routledge.

Dietler, M. (2010) *Archaeologies of Colonialism. Consumption, Entanglement, and Violence in Ancient Mediterranean France*. Los Angeles (CA), University of California Press.
Diez, E. (1953) Librarii auf norischen Grabsteinen. *Schild von Steier* 2, 123–34.
Dobres, M.-A. (2000) *Technology and Social Agency. Outlining a Practice Framework for Archaeology*. Oxford, Blackwell.
Dobres, M.-A. and J.E. Robb (2005) "Doing" agency: introductory remarks on methodology. *Journal of Archaeological Method and Theory* 12, 159–66.
Dornan, J.L. (2002) Agency and archaeology: past, present, and future directions. *Journal of Archaeological Theory and Method* 9, 303–29.
Dörtlük, K., B. Varkıvanç, T. Kahya, J. des Courtils, D. Alparslan and R. Boyraz (eds) (2006) *The IIIrd Symposium on Lycia*. Antalya, Zero Prodüksiyon.
Dunnell, R. (1986) Methodological issues in Americanist artifact classification. In M.B. Schiffer (ed.) *Advances in Archaeological Method and Theory* 9, 149–207. Orlando (FL), Academic Press.
Dunnell, R. (2001) Foreword. In T.D. Hurt and G.F.M. Rakita (eds) *Style and Function. Conceptual Issues in Evolutionary Archaeology*, xiii–xxiv. Westport (CT), Bergin and Garvey.
Duranton, G. and D. Puga (2004) Micro-foundations of urban agglomeration economies. In J.V. Henderson and J.-F. Thisse (eds) *Handbook of Regional and Urban Economics* 4, 2063–117. Amsterdam, Elsevier.
Dzierzykray-Rogalski, T. and C. Gezeszyk (1991) Les dermatoglyphes: empreintes des lignes papillaires relevés sur les lampes de Kôm el-Dikka (Alexandrie). *Cahiers de la Céramique Egyptienne* 2, 14–21.
Eckardt, H. (2002) *Illuminating Roman Britain*. Montagnac, Éditions Monique Mergoil.
Eckardt, H. (2005) The social distribution of Roman artefacts: the case of nail-cleaners and brooches in Britain. *Journal of Roman Archaeology* 18, 139–60.
Eckardt, H. (2014) *Objects and Identities. Roman Britain and the North-West Provinces*. Oxford, Oxford University Press.
Eckardt, H. (forthcoming) *Writing power in the Roman world. Literacies and Material Culture*. Cambridge, Cambridge University Press.
Eckardt, H., G. Müldner and G. Speed (2015) The late Roman field army in northern Britain? Mobility, material culture and multi-isotope analysis at Scorton (N Yorks.). *Britannia* 46, 191–223.
Elden, S. (2007) Governmentality, calculation, territory. *Environment and Planning. Society and Space* 25, 562–80.
Elsner, J. (2003) Style. In R.S. Nelson and R. Shiff (eds) *Critical Terms for Art History*, 98–109. Chicago (IL), The University of Chicago Press.
Eogan, G. (1974) Report on the excavation of some passage graves, unprotected inhumation burials and a settlement site at Knowth, County Meath. *Proceedings of the Royal Irish Academy Section. Archaeology, Celtic Studies, History* 74, 111–2.
Ettlinger, E., B. Hedinger, B. Hoffmann, P. Kenrick, G. Pucci, K. Roth-Rubi, G. Schneider, S. Von Schnurbein, C.M. Wells and S. Zabehlicky-Scheffenegger (1990) *Conspectus formarum terrae sigillatae italico modo confectae*. Bonn, Rudolph Habelt.
Evans, J. (2016) Forms of knowledge: changing technologies of Romano-British pottery. In M. Millett, L. Revell and A. Moore (eds) *The Oxford Handbook of Roman Britain*, 508–29. Oxford, Oxford University Press.
Evans, J., C.A. Chenery and J. Montgomery (2012) A summary of strontium and oxygen isotope variation in archaeological human tooth enamel excavated from Britain. *Journal of Analytical Atomic Spectrometry* 27, 754–64.
Feeney, D. (2016) *Beyond Greek. The Beginnings of Latin Literature*. Cambridge (MA), Harvard University Press.
Feldman, M.H. (2006) *Diplomacy by Design. Luxury Arts and an 'International Style' in the Ancient Near East, 1400-1200 BCE*. Chicago (IL), University of Chicago Press.

Feldman, M.H. (2014) *Communities of Style. Portable Luxury Arts, Identity, and Collective Memory in the Iron Age Levant*. Chicago (IL), University of Chicago Press.

Ferris, I. (2012) *Roman Britain through its Objects*. Stroud, Amberley.

Feugère, M. and C. Picod (2014) Reconstitution de dés en matière dure animale, antiques et médiévaux. *Instrumentum* 39, 37–42.

Fewster, K. (2014) On practice. In A. Gardner, M. Lake and U. Sommer (eds) *The Oxford Handbook of Archaeological Theory*. Oxford, Oxford University Press.

Flad, R.K. and Z.X. Hruby (2007) "Specialized" production in archaeological contexts: rethinking specialization, the social value of products, and the practice of production. *Archaeological Papers of the American Anthropological Association* 17.1, 1–19.

Flemming, R. (2007) Women, writing and medicine in the classical world. *Classical Quarterly* 57.1, 257–79.

Ford, J.A. (1954) Comment on A.C. Spaulding, 'Statistical techniques for the discovery of artifact types'. *American Antiquity* 19.4, 390–1.

Foster, R.J. (2006) Tracking globalization: commodities and value in motion. In C. Tilley, W. Keane, S. Küchler, M. Rowlands and P. Spyer (eds) *Handbook of Material Culture*, 285–302. London, Sage.

Foucault, M. (1975) *Surveiller et punir. Naissance de la prison*. Paris, Gallimard.

Fowler, C. (2004) *The Archaeology of Personhood. An Anthropological Approach*. London, Routledge.

Fowler, C. (2013) *The Emergent Past. A Relational Realist Archaeology of Early Bronze Age Mortuary Practices*. Oxford, Oxford University Press.

Fowler, C. and O.J.T. Harris (2015) Enduring relations: exploring a paradox of new materialism, *Journal of Material Culture* 20.2, 127–48.

Frere, S. (1988) Roman Britain since Haverfield and Richmond. *History and Archaeology Review* 3, 31–6.

Fujita, M. and J. Thisse (2002) *Economics of Agglomeration, Cities, Industrial Location and Regional Growth*. Cambridge, Cambridge University Press.

Fulford, M. (2009) Approaches to quantifying Roman trade: a response. In A. Bowman and A. Wilson (eds) *Quantifying the Roman Economy. Methods and Problems*, 250–8. Oxford, Oxford University Press.

Fünfschilling, S. (2012) Schreibgeräte und Schreibzubehör aus Augusta Raurica. *Jahresberichte aus Augst und Kaiseraugst* 33, 163–236.

Galanakis, Y. (2009) What's in a word? The manifold character of the term koiné and its uses in the archaeology of Bronze Age Aegean. In G. Deligiannakis and Y. Galanakis (eds) *The Aegean and its Cultures*. BAR International Series 1975, 5–11. Oxford, Archaeopress.

Galimberti, A. (2016) Emperor Domitian. In A. Zissos (ed.) *A Companion to the Flavian Age of Imperial Rome*, 92–108. Chichester, Wiley-Blackwell.

Gallia, A.B. (2016) Remaking Rome. In A. Zissos (ed.) *A Companion to the Flavian Age of Imperial Rome*, 148–65. Chichester, Wiley-Blackwell.

Gardner, A. (2003) Seeking a material turn: the artefactuality of the Roman empire. In G. Carr, E. Swift and J. Weekes (eds) *TRAC 2002. Proceedings of the 12th Annual Theoretical Roman Archaeology Conference*, 1–13. Oxford, Oxbow Books.

Gardner, A. (2004) *Agency Uncovered. Archaeological Perspectives on Social Agency, Power and Being Human*. London, UCL Press.

Gardner, A. (2007) *An Archaeology of Identity. Soldiers and Society in Late Roman Britain*. Walnut Creek (CA), Left Coast Press.

Gardner, A. (2011a) Paradox and praxis in the archaeology of identity. In L. Amundsen-Meyer, N. Engel and S. Pickering (eds) *Identity Crisis. Archaeological Perspectives on Social Identity. Proceedings of the 42nd (2009) Chacmool Conference*, 11–26. Calgary, Chacmool Archaeology Association.

Gardner, A. (2011b) Action and structure in interpretive archaeologies. In E.E. Cochrane and A. Gardner (eds) *Evolutionary and Interpretive Archaeologies. A Dialogue*, 63–82. Walnut Creek (CA), Left Coast Press.

Gardner, A. (2016a) Debating Roman imperialism: critique, construct, repeat? In M.J. Mandich, T.J. Derrick, S. González Sánchez, G. Savani and E. Zampieri (eds) *TRAC 2015. Proceedings of the 25th Annual Theoretical Roman Archaeology Conference*, 1–14. Oxford, Oxbow Books.

Gardner, A. (2016b) Changing materialities. In M. Millett, A. Moore and L. Revell (eds) *The Oxford Handbook to Roman Britain*, 481–509. Oxford, Oxford University Press.

Garrow, D. and C. Gosden (2012) *Technologies of Enchantment? Exploring Celtic Art. 400 BC to AD 100*. Oxford, Oxford University Press.

Gell, A. (1998) *Art and Agency. An Anthropological Theory*. Oxford, Clarendon.

Genin, M. (2007) *La Graufesenque (Millau, Aveyron). Volume II. Sigillées lisses et autres productions*. Pessac, Éditions de la Fédération Aquitania.

Gerritsen, A. and S. MacDowall (2012) Material culture and the Other: European encounters with Chinese porcelain, ca. 1650–1800. *Journal of World History* 23.1, 87–113.

Gerritsen, A. and G. Riello (2015a) *Writing Material Culture History*. London, Bloomsbury.

Gerritsen, A. and G. Riello (2015b) Introduction: writing material culture history. In A. Gerritsen and G. Riello (eds) *Writing Material Culture History*, 1–13. London, Bloomsbury.

Gerritsen, A. and G. Riello (2015c) Spaces of global interactions: the material landscapes of global history. In A. Gerritsen and G. Riello (eds) *Writing Material Culture History*, 111–34. London, Bloomsbury.

Gibbon, E. (1909) *The History of the Decline and Fall of the Roman Empire*. Ed. J.B. Bury. London, Methuen.

Gibson, J.J. (1979) *The Ecological Approach to Visual Perception*. Boston (MA), Houghton Mifflin.

Giddens, A. (1984) *The Constitution of Society. Outline of the Theory of Structuration*. Cambridge, Polity.

Gillam, J. and C. Daniels (1961) The Roman mausoleum at Shorden Brae, Beaufront, Corbridge, Northumberland. *Archaeologia Aeliana* 39 (4th series), 37–61.

Giuliani, A. (2007) Innovationen im Beleuchtungswesen in Kleinasien. In M. Meyer (ed.) *Neue Zeiten – Neue Sitten. Zu Rezeption und Integration römischen und italischen Kulturguts in Kleinasien*, 171–80. Vienna, Phoibos.

Goldhill, S. (2014) *The Buried Life of Things. How Objects Made History in Nineteenth-Century Britain*. Cambridge, Cambridge University Press.

Goody, J. (2012) *Metals, Culture and Capitalism. An Essay on the Origins of the Modern World*. Cambridge, Cambridge University Press.

Gosden, C. (2001) Making sense: archaeology and aesthetics. *World Archaeology*, 33.2, 163–7.

Gosden, C. (2004) *Archaeology and Colonialism. Culture Contact from 5000 BC to the Present*. Cambridge, Cambridge University Press.

Gosden, C. (2005) What do objects want? *Journal of Archaeological Method and Theory* 12.3, 193–211.

Gosden, C. (2006) Material culture and long-term change. In C. Tilley, W. Keane, S. Küchler, M. Rowlands and P. Spyer (eds) *Handbook of Material Culture*, 425–42. London, Sage.

Gosden, C. (2010) Words and things: thick description in archaeology and anthropology. In D. Garrow and T. Yarrow (eds) *Archaeology and Anthropology. Understanding Similarity, Exploring Difference*, 110–16. Oxford, Oxbow Books.

Graf, F. (2005) Rolling the dice for an answer. In S. Iles-Johnston and P. Struck (eds) *Mantikê. Studies in Ancient Divination*, 51–97. Leiden, Brill.

Graham, E.-J. (2009) Becoming persons, becoming ancestors: personhood, memory and the corpse in Roman rituals of social remembrance. *Archaeological Dialogues* 16.1, 51–74.

Graham, S. and S. Marvin (2001) *Splintering Urbanism. Networked Infrastructures, Technological Mobilities and the Urban Condition*. London, Psychology Press.

Graham, S. and C. McFarlane (eds) (2015) *Infrastructural Lives. Urban Infrastructure in Context*. London, Routledge.

Graves-Brown, P. (2013) Review of 'In Defense of Things'. *Journal of the Royal Anthropology Institute* 19, 23–41.

Greene, K. (2005) Roman pottery: models, proxies and economic interpretation, *Journal of Roman Archaeology* 18, 34–56.
Greene, K. (2008) Learning to consume: consumption and consumerism in the Roman empire. *Journal of Roman Archaeology* 21, 64–82.
Greep, S. (1983) Objects of Animal Bone, Antler, Ivory and Teeth from Roman Britain. Unpublished PhD thesis, University of Wales.
Haas, C. (1996) *Writing Technology. Studies in the Materiality of Literature*. Mahwah, Lawrence Erlbaum.
Haffner, A. (1971) *Das Keltisch-römische Gräberfeld von Wederath-Belginum 1*. Mainz, Philipp Von Zabern.
Haffner, A. (1974) *Das Keltisch-römische Gräberfeld von Wederath-Belginum 2*. Mainz, Philipp Von Zabern.
Haffner, A. (1978) *Das Keltisch-römische Gräberfeld von Wederath-Belginum 3*. Mainz, Philipp Von Zabern.
Hahn, H.P and H. Weiss (eds) (2013a) *Mobility, Meaning and Transformations of Things*. Oxford, Oxbow Books.
Hahn, H.P and H. Weiss (2013b) Introduction: biographies, travels and itineraries of things. In H.P. Hahn and H. Weiss (eds) *Mobility, Meaning and Transformations of Things*, 1–14. Oxford, Oxbow Books.
Haines-Eitzen, K. (1998) 'Girls trained in beautiful writing': female scribes in Roman Antiquity and Early Christianity. *Journal of Early Christian Studies* 6.4, 629–46.
Hales, S. (2010) Tricks with mirrors: remembering the dead of Noricum. In S. Hales and T. Hodos (eds) *Material Culture and Social Identities in the Ancient World*, 227–51. Cambridge, Cambridge University Press.
Hall, M.A. and K. Forsyth (2011) Roman rules? The introduction of board games to Britain and Ireland. *Antiquity* 85.330, 1325–38.
Halsall, G. (1992) The origins of the *Reihengräberzivilisation*: forty years on. In J. Drinkwater and H. Elton (eds) *Fifth-Century Gaul. A Crisis of Identity*, 196–207. Cambridge, Cambridge University Press.
Halsall, G. (2000) Archaeology and the late Roman frontier in northern Gaul: the so-called 'Föderatengräber' reconsidered. In W. Pohl and H. Reimitz (eds) *Grenze und Differenz in frühen Mittelalter*, 167–180. Vienna, Forschungen zur Geschichte des Mittelalters 1.
Hamilton, S. and R. Whitehouse (2006) Phenomenology in practice: towards a methodology for a 'subjective' approach. *European Journal of Archaeology* 9, 31–71.
Harloe, K. (2013) *Winckelmann and the Invention of Antiquity. History and Aesthetics in the Age of Altertumswissenschaft*. Oxford, Oxford University Press.
Harman, G. (2015) Materialism is not the solution on matter, form and mimesis. *Nordic Journal of Aesthetics* 47, 94–110
Harper, P.O. (1992) Evidence for the existence of state controls in the production of Sassanian silver vessels. In S.A. Boyd and M.M. Mango (eds) *Ecclesiastical Silver Plate in Sixth-Century Byzantium. Papers of the Symposium held May 16-18, 1986, at the Walters Art Gallery, Baltimore, and Dumbarton Oaks, Washington, D.C.*, 147–54. Washington D.C., Dumbarton Oaks.
Harris, L.M. and S. Alatout (2010) Negotiating hydro-scales, forging states: comparison of the upper Tigris/Euphrates and Jordan River basins. *Political Geography* 29.3, 148–56.
Harris, W.V. (1989) *Ancient Literacy*. Cambridge (MA), Harvard University Press.
Harris, W.V. (2015) Prolegomena to a study of the economics of Roman art. *American Journal of Archaeology* 119.3, 395–417.
Haselgrove, C. (1982) Wealth, power and prestige: the dynamics of late Iron Age political centralisation in south-east England. In C. Renfrew and S. Shennan (eds) *Ranking, Resource and Exchange*, 79–88. Cambridge, Cambridge University Press.
Hawkes, C.F.C. and M.R. Hull (1947) *Camulodunum. First report on the Excavations at Colchester 1930-1939*. Oxford, Society of Antiquaries.
Hawkes, S. and G. Dunning (1961) Soldiers and settlers in Britain, fourth to fifth century. *Medieval Archaeology* 61, 1–70.

Hawthorne, J. (1997) Post processual economics: the role of African red slip ware vessel volume in Mediterranean demography. In K. Meadows, C. Lemke and J. Heron (eds) *TRAC 96. Proceedings of the Sixth Annual Theoretical Roman Archaeology Conference Sheffield 1996*, 29–37. Oxford, Oxbow Books.

Hawthorne, J. (2000) Vessel volume as a factor in ceramic quantification: the case of African Red Slip ware. In K. Lockyear, T.J.T. Sly and V. Mihăilescu-Bîrliba (eds) *CAA 96. Computer Applications and Quantitative Methods in Archaeology*, 19–24. Oxford, Archaeopress.

Hayes, J.W. (1997) *Handbook of Mediterranean Roman Pottery*. Norman (OK), University of Oklahoma Press.

Hemelrijk, E. (2004) *Matrona Docta. Educated Women in the Roman Elite from Cornelia to Julia Domna*. London, Routledge.

Henare, A., M. Holbraad and S. Wastell (2007) Introduction: thinking through things. In A. Henare, M. Holbraad and S. Wastell (eds) *Thinking Through Things. Theorizing Artefacts Ethnographically*, 1–31. London, Routledge.

Henkel, F. (1913) *Die römischen Fingerringe der Rheinlande und der benachbarten Gebiete. Mit Unterstützung der Römisch-germanischen Kommission des Kaiserlich Archäologischen Instituts*. Berlin, Georg Riemer.

Herzfeld, M. (2003) *The Body Impolitic. Artisans and Artifice in the Global Hierarchy of Value*. Chicago (IL), University of Chicago Press.

Heywood, P. (2012) Anthropology and what there is: reflections on 'ontology'. *Cambridge Anthropology* 30.1, 143–51.

Hicks, D. (2010) The material-culture turn: event and effect. In D. Hicks and M.-C. Beaudry (eds) *The Oxford Handbook of Material Culture Studies*, 25–98. Oxford, Oxford University Press.

Hill, J.D. (2001) Romanisation, gender and class: recent approaches to identity in Britain and their possible consequences. In S. James and M. Millett (eds) *Britons and Romans. Advancing an Archaeological Agenda*, 12–18. York, Council for British Archaeology.

Hillerdal, C. and J. Siapkas (eds) (2015) *Debating Archaeological Empiricism. The Ambiguity of Material Evidence*. New York, Routledge.

Hingley, R. (2005) *Globalizing Roman Culture*. London, Routledge.

Hingley, R. and S. Willis (eds) (2007) *Roman Finds. Context and Theory*. Oxford, Oxbow Books.

Hintermann, D. (2000) *Der Südfriedhof von Vindonissa. Archäologische und naturwissenschaftliche Untersuchungen im römerzeitlichen Gräberfeld Windisch-Dägerli*. Brugg, Gesellschaft pro Vindonissa.

Hintermann, D. (2012) *Vindonissa-Museum Brugg. Ein Ausstellungsführer*. Brugg, Kantonsarchäologie Aargau.

Hjørland, B. (2009) Concept theory. *Journal of the American Society for Information Science and Technology* 60.8, 1519–36.

Hodder, I. (1979) Pottery distributions: service and tribal areas. In M. Millett (ed.) *Pottery and the Archaeologist*, 7–24. London, Institute of Archaeology.

Hodder, I. (1995) *Theory and Practice in Archaeology*. London, Routledge.

Hodder, I. (2011) Human-thing entanglement: towards an integrated archaeological perspective. *Journal of the Royal Anthropological Institute* n.s. 17, 154–77.

Hodder, I. (2012) *Entangled. An Archaeology of the Relationships between Humans and Things*. Oxford, Wiley-Blackwell.

Hodder, I. and S. Hutson (2005) *Reading the Past. Current Approaches to Interpretation in Archaeology*. Cambridge, Cambridge University Press.

Hodder, I. and R. Preucel (1996) Nature and culture. In I. Hodder and R. Preucel (eds) *Contemporary Archaeological Theory. A Reader*, 23–38. Oxford, Blackwell.

Hodos, T. (2010) Local and global perspectives in the study of social and cultural identities. In S. Hales and T. Hodos (eds) *Material Culture and Social Identities in the Ancient World*, 3–31. Cambridge, Cambridge University Press.

Hodos, T., A. Geurds, P. Lane, I. Lilley, M. Pitts, G. Shelach, M. Stark and M.J. Versluys (eds) (2017) *The Handbook of Archaeology and Globalisation*. London, Routledge.

Hohlfelder, R.L. and J.P. Oleson (2014) Roman maritime concrete technology in its Mediterranean context. In J.P. Oleson (ed.) *Building for Eternity. The History and Technology of Roman Concrete Engineering in the Sea*, 223–35. Oxford, Oxbow Books.

Holbraad, M. (2007) The power of powder: multiplicity and motion in the divinatory cosmology of Cuban Ifà (or *mana*, again). In A. Henare, M. Holbraad and S. Wastell (eds) *Thinking Through Things. Theorizing Artefacts Ethnographically*, 189–225. London, Routledge.

Holloway, R.R. (1994) *The Archaeology of Early Rome and Latium*. London, Routledge.

Howgego, C. (1994) Coin circulation and the integration of the Roman economy, *Journal of Roman Archaeology* 7, 5–21.

Hudson, N. (2006) *Dining in the Late Roman East*. Unpublished PhD thesis, University of Minnesota.

Humphrey, J. (ed.) (1991) *Literacy in the Roman World*. Portsmouth, Journal of Roman Archaeology Supplementary Series 3.

Hurt, T.D. and G.F.M. Rakita (eds) (2001) *Style and Function. Conceptual Issues in Evolutionary Archaeology*. London, Bergin and Garvey.

Iacomi, V. (2010) Some notes on Late-Antique oil and wine production in Rough Cilicia (Isauria) on the light of epigraphic sources: funerary inscriptions from Korykos, LR 1 amphorae production in Elaiussa Sebaste and the Abydos Tariff. In Ü. Aydınoğlu and A.K. Senol (eds) *Olive Oil and Wine Production in Anatolia during Antiquity/ Antikçagda Anadolu'da Zeytinyagi ve Sarap Üretimi*, 19–32. Istanbul, Ege Yayınları.

Ingold, T. (1988) Tools, minds and machines: an excursion in the philosophy of technology. *Techniques et Culture* 12, 294–311.

Ingold, T. (1993) The temporality of landscape. *World Archaeology* 25, 152–74.

Ingold, T. (2000) *The Perception of the Environment. Essays in Livelihood, Dwelling and Skill*. London, Routledge.

Ingold, T. (2007) Materials against materiality. *Archaeological Dialogues* 14.1, 1–16.

Ingold, T. (2010) The textility of making. *Cambridge Journal of Economics* 34, 91–102.

Ingold, T. (2012) Toward an ecology of materials. *Annual Review of Anthropology* 41, 427–42.

Insoll, T. (2007) Introduction: configuring identities in archaeology. In T. Insoll (ed.) *The Archaeology of Identities. A Reader*, 1–18. London, Routledge.

Isings, C. (1980) Glass from the *canabae legionis* at Nijmegen. *Berichten van de Rijksdienst voor het Oudheidkundig Bodemonderzoek* 30, 283–346.

Jackson, M.D. (2014) Sea-water concretes and their material characteristics. In J.P. Oleson (ed.) *Building for Eternity. The History and Technology of Roman Concrete Engineering in the Sea*, 141–87. Oxford, Oxbow Books.

Jackson, M.D. and C.D. Kosso (2013) *Scientia* in Republican era stone and concrete masonry. In J. DeRose Evans (ed.) *A Companion to the Archaeology of the Roman Republic*, 268–84. Chichester, Wiley-Blackwell.

Jackson, M., M. Zelle, L. Vandeput and V. Köse (2012) Primary evidence for Late Roman D Ware production in southern Asia Minor: a challenge to 'Cypriot Red Slip Ware'. *Anatolian Studies* 62, 89–114.

Jackson, R. (1988) *Doctors and Diseases in the Roman Empire*. London, British Museum Press.

James, S. (2001) Romanization and the peoples of Britain. In N. Terrenato and S. Keay (eds) *Italy and the West. Comparative Issues in Romanization*, 187–209. Oxford, Oxbow Books.

Jennings, J. (2011) *Globalizations and the Ancient World*. Cambridge, Cambridge University Press.

Jiménez, A. (2010) Reproducing difference: mimesis and colonialism in Roman Hispania. In B. Knapp and P. van Dommelen (eds) *Material Connections. Mobility, Materiality and Mediterranean Identities*, 38–63. London, Routledge.

Jiménez, A. (2011) Changing to remain the same: the south of the Iberian Peninsula between the third and the first centuries BC. In T. Moore and L. Armada (eds) *Atlantic Europe in the First Millennium BC. Crossing the Divide*, 506–18. Oxford, Oxford University Press.

Johannsen, N. (2012) Archaeology and the inanimate agency proposition: a critique and a suggestion. In N. Johannsen, M.D. Jessen and H.J. Jensen (eds) *Excavating the Mind. Cross-sections through Culture, Cognition and Materiality*, 305–47. Aarhus, Aarhus University Press.

Johns, C. (1996) *The Jewellery of Roman Britain. Celtic and Classical Traditions*. London, University College London Press.

Johnson, M.H. (1999) Rethinking historical archaeology. In P.P.A. Funari, M. Hall and S. Jones (eds) *Historical Archaeology. Back from the Edge*, 23–36. London, Routledge.

Johnson, M.H. (2006) On the nature of theoretical archaeology and archaeological theory. *Archaeological Dialogues* 13.2, 117–82.

Jones, M.P. (1996) Posthuman agency: between theoretical traditions. *Sociological Theory* 14.3, 290–309.

Jorge, V.O. and J. Thomas (eds) (2007) *Overcoming the Modern Invention of Material Culture. Journal of Iberian Archaeology*. Special edition 9/10. Porto: ADECAP.

Jundi, S. and J.D. Hill (1998) Brooches and identities in first century A.D. Britain: more than meets the eye? In C. Forcey, J. Hawthorne and R. Witcher (eds) *TRAC 97. Proceedings of the Seventh Annual Theoretical Roman Archaeology Conference, Nottingham 1997*, 125–37. Oxford, Oxbow Books.

Winther-Jacobsen, K. and L. Summerer (eds) (2015) *Landscape Dynamics and Settlement Patterns in Northern Anatolia during the Roman and Byzantine Period*. Geographica Historica 32. Stuttgart, Franz Steiner.

Keay, S. (2001) Romanization and the Hispaniae. In N. Terrenato and S. Keay (eds) *Italy and the West. Comparative Issues in Romanization*, 117–44. Oxford, Oxbow Books.

Khoo, C.S.G. and J.C. Na (2006) Semantic relations in information science. *Annual Review of Information Science and Technology* 40, 157–228

Kirk, J. and E. Leeds (1954) Three Early Saxon graves from Dorchester, Oxon. *Oxeniensia* 17/18, 63–76.

Kirsh, D. (2010) Explaining artefact evolution. In L. Malafouris and C. Renfrew (eds) *The Cognitive Life of Things. Recasting the Boundaries of the Mind*, 121–44. Cambridge, McDonald Institute.

Klaus, G. (1973) *Modern Logics*. Berlin, Deutscher Verlag der Wissenschaften.

Klingshorn, W. (2002) Defining the *Sortes Sanctorum*: Gibbon, Du Cange, and early Christian lot divination. *Journal of Early Christian Studies* 10, 77–130.

Klingshorn, W. (2005) Christian divination in late Roman Gaul: the *Sortes Sangallenses*. In S. Iles-Johnson and P. Struck (eds) *Mantikê: Studies in Ancient Divination*, 99–128. Leiden, Brill.

Knappett, C. (2002) Photographs, skeuomorphs and marionettes: some thoughts on mind, agency and object. *Journal of Material Culture* 7.1, 97–117.

Knappett, C. (2004) The affordances of things: a post-Gibsonian perspective on the relationality of mind and matter. In E. Demarrais, C. Gosden and C. Renfrew (eds) *Rethinking Materiality. The Engagement of Mind with the Material World*, 43–51. Cambridge, McDonald Institute.

Knappett, C. (2005) *Thinking through Material Culture. An Interdisciplinary Perspective*. Philadelphia (PA), University of Pennsylvania Press.

Knappett, C. (2011) *An Archaeology of Interaction, Network Perspectives on Material Culture and Society*. Oxford, Oxford University Press.

Knappett, C. (ed.) (2013) *Network Analysis in Archaeology. New Approaches to Regional Interaction*. Oxford, Oxford University Press.

Knox, H., M. Savage and P. Harvey (2006) Social networks and the study of relations: networks as method, metaphor and form. *Economy and Society* 35.1, 113–40.

Kohl, P.L. (2007) *The Making of Bronze Age Eurasia*. Cambridge, Cambridge University Press.

Kopytoff, I. (1986) The cultural biography of things: commoditization as process. In A. Appadurai (ed.) *The Social Life of Things. Commodities in Cultural Perspective*, 64–91. Cambridge, Cambridge University Press.

Koster, A. (2013) *The Cemetery of Noviomagus and the Wealthy Burials of the Municipal Elite*. Nijmegen, Museum Het Valkhof.

Künzl, E. (2002) *Medizin in der Antike. Aus einer Welt ohne Narkose und Aspirin*. Stuttgart, Theiss.

Künzl, E. and H. Engelmann (1997) Römische Ärztinnen und Chirurginnen: Beiträge zu einem antiken Frauenberufsbild. *Antike Welt* 28.5, 375–79.

Laes, C. and J. Strubbe (2014) *Youth in the Roman Empire. The Young and the Restless Years?* Cambridge, Cambridge University Press.

Lake, M. (1998) Digging for memes: the role of material objects in cultural evolution. In C. Renfrew and C. Scarre (eds) *Cognition and Material Culture. The Archaeology of Symbolic Storage*, 77–88. Cambridge, McDonald Institute.

Lancaster, L. (2005) *Concrete Vaulted Construction in Imperial Rome. Innovations in Context*. Cambridge, Cambridge University Press.

Lancaster, L. (2015) *Innovative Vaulting in the Architecture of the Roman Empire. 1st to 4th Centuries CE*. Cambridge, Cambridge University Press.

Lancaster, L. and R.B. Ulrich (2014) Materials and techniques. In R.B. Ulrich and C.K. Quenemoen (eds) *A Companion to Roman Architecture*, 157–92. Malden, Wiley-Blackwell.

Lancaster, L., G. Sottili, F. Marra and G. Ventura (2010) Provenancing of lightweight volcanic stones used in ancient Roman concrete vaulting: evidence from Turkey and Tunisia. *Archaeometry* 52.6, 949–69.

Lancaster, L., G. Sottili, F. Marra and G. Ventura (2011) Provenancing of lightweight volcanic stones used in ancient Roman concrete vaulting: evidence from Rome. *Archaeometry* 53.4, 707–27.

Latour, B. (1993) *We Have Never Been Modern*. Cambridge (MA), Harvard University Press.

Latour, B. (1999) *Pandora's Hope. Essays on the Reality of Science Studies*. Cambridge (MA), Harvard University Press.

Latour, B. (2005) *Reassembling the Social. An Introduction to Actor-Network-Theory*. Oxford, Oxford University Press.

Laurence, R. (1999) Theoretical Roman archaeology. *Britannia* 30, 387–90.

Laurence, R. (2001) Roman narratives: the writing of archaeological discourse – a view from Britain? *Archaeological Dialogues* 8.2, 90–122.

Laurence, R. and F. Trifilò (2015) The global and the local in the Roman empire: connectivity and mobility from an urban perspective. In M. Pitts and M.J. Versluys (eds) *Globalisation and the Roman empire*, 99–122. Cambridge, Cambridge University Press.

Leader-Newby, R.E. (2004) *Silver and Society in Late Antiquity. Functions and Meanings of Silver Plate in the Fourth to Seventh Centuries*. Aldershot, Ashgate.

Lechtman, H. (1977) Style in technology - some early thoughts. In H. Lechtman and R. Merrill (eds) *Material Culture. Styles, Organisation, and Dynamics of Technology*, 3–20. St. Paul, West Publishing.

Lechtman, H. and A. Steinberg (1979) The history of technology: an anthropological point of view. In G. Bugliarello and B. Doner (eds) *The History and Philosophy of Technology*, 135–60. Chicago (IL), University of Illinois Press.

Lechtman, H. and L.W. Hobbs (1986) Roman concrete and the Roman architectural revolution. In W.D. Kingery (ed.) *High-Technology Ceramics. Past, Present, and Future. The Nature of Innovation and Change in Ceramic Technology*. Ceramics and Civilization 3, 81–128. Westville (OH), The American Ceramic Society.

Leidwanger, J. (2014) Maritime networks and economic regionalism in the Roman Eastern Mediterranean. *Les Nouvelles de l'Archéologie* 135, 32–8.

Lembke, K. (1994) *Das Iseum Campense in Rom. Studie über den Isiskult unter Domitian*. Heidelberg, Verlag Archäologie und Geschichte.
Lemonnier, P. (1986) The study of material culture today: toward an anthropology of technical systems. *Journal of Anthropological Archaeology* 5, 147–86.
Lemonnier, P. (1992) *Elements for an Anthropology of Technology*. Ann Arbor (MI), University of Michigan Press.
Leone, M.P. (2005) *The Archaeology of Liberty in an American Capital*. Berkeley (CA), University of California Press.
Leone, M.P., P.B. Potter Jr. and P.A. Shackel (1987) Towards a critical archaeology. *Current Anthropology* 28.3, 283–302.
Leroi-Gourhan, A. (1993) *Gesture and Speech*. Transl. A. Bostock Berger. Cambridge (MA), MIT Press.
Lindstrøm, T.C. (2015) Agency 'in itself': a discussion of inanimate, animal and human agency. *Archaeological Dialogues* 22.2, 207–38.
Ling R. (1991) *Roman Painting*. Cambridge, Cambridge University Press.
Lintott, A. (1981) What Was the 'Imperium Romanum'? *Greece & Rome*, Second Series 28.1, 53-67.
Liu, J. (2016) Group membership, trust networks, and social capital: a critical analysis. In K. Verboven and C. Laes (eds) *Work, Labour, and Professions in the Roman World*, 203–26. Leiden, Brill.
Loopmans, M. (2007) Urban Governance, Neighbourhoods and Organised Residents. Resident Mobilisation and Urban Policies in Antwerp, Belgium. Unpublished PhD thesis, KU Leuven.
Lund, J. (2015) *A Study of the Circulation of Ceramics in Cyprus from the 3rd Century BC to the 3rd Century AD*. Aarhus, Aarhus University Press.
MacDonald, W.L. (1982) *The Architecture of the Roman Empire. I. An Introductory Study*. New Haven (CT), Yale University Press.
MacGregor, A. (1984) *Bone, Antler, Ivory and Horn. The Technology of Skeletal Remains since the Roman period*. London, Croom Helm.
Maiuri, A. (1947) *La Casa di Loreio Tiburtino e La Villa di Diomede*. Rome, Libreria dello Stato.
Malafouris, L. (2008) At the potter's wheel: an argument for material agency. In C. Knappett and L. Malafouris (eds) *Material Agency. Towards a Non-Anthropocentric Perspective*, 19–36. New York, Springer.
Malafouris, L. (2013) *How Things Shape the Mind. A Theory of Material Engagement*. Cambridge (MA), MIT Press.
Maran, J. and P.W. Stockhammer (eds) (2012) *Materiality and Social Practice. Transformative Capacities of Intercultural Encounters*. Oxford, Oxbow Books.
Marston, S.A., J.P. Jones and K. Woodward (2005) Human geography without scale. *Transactions of the Institute of British Geographers* 30.4, 416–32.
Masséglia, J. (2013) Phrygians in relief: trends in self-representation. In P. Thonemann (ed.) *Roman Phrygia. Culture and Society*, 95–123. Cambridge, Cambridge University Press.
Matthewman, S. (2011) *Technology and Social Theory*. Basingstoke, Palgrave Macmillan.
Mattingly, D. (2004) Being Roman: expressing identity in a provincial setting. *Journal of Roman Archaeology* 17, 5–25.
Mattingly, D. (2006) *An Imperial Possession. Britain in the Roman Empire*. London, Allen Lane.
Mattingly, D. (2007) Supplying Rome and the Empire: some conclusions. In E. Papi (ed.) *Supplying Rome and the Empire. The Proceedings of an International Seminar Held at Siena-Certosa di Pontignano on May 2-4, 2004, on Rome, the Provinces, Production and Distribution*, 219–27. Portsmouth, Journal of Roman Archaeology Supplementary Series 69.
Mattingly, D. (2011) *Imperialism, Power and Identity*. Princeton (NJ), Princeton University Press.
Mawer, F. (1995) *Evidence for Christianity in Roman Britain. The Small Finds*. Oxford, Archaeopress.
May, R. (1991) Les jeux de table en Grèce et à Rome. In R. May (ed.) *Jouer dans l'Antiquité*, 166–89. Marseilles, Musées Nationaux.

McGuire, R.H. (2002) *A Marxist Archaeology*. Clinton Corners, Percheron Press/Eliot Werner Publications.
McGuire, R.H. (2008) *Archaeology as Political Action*. Berkeley (CA), University of California Press.
Meskell, L. (2001) Archaeologies of identity. In I. Hodder (ed.) *Archaeological Theory Today*, 187–213. Cambridge, Polity.
Metzler, J and C. Gaing (2009) *Goeblange-Nospelt. Une nécropole aristocratique trévire*. Luxembourg, Musée National d'histoire et d'art.
Meyer, E.A. (2009) Writing paraphernalia, tablets, and muses in Campanian wall painting. *American Journal of Archaeology* 113, 569–97.
Miettinen, R. (1999) The riddle of things: activity theory and actor-network theory as approaches to studying innovations. *Mind, Culture, and Activity* 6.3, 170–95.
Miller, D. (1985) *Artefacts as Categories. A Study of Ceramic Variability in India*. Cambridge, Cambridge University Press.
Miller, D. (ed.) (2005) *Materiality*. Durham (NC), Duke University Press.
Miller, H.M.L. (2009) *Archaeological Approaches to Technology*. Walnut Creek (CA), Left Coast Press.
Millett, M. (1979a) An approach to the functional interpretation of pottery. In M. Millett (ed.) *Pottery and the Archaeologist*, 35–48. London, Institute of Archaeology.
Millett, M. (1979b) The dating of Farnham (Alice Holt) pottery. *Britannia* 10, 121–37.
Millett, M. (1983a) A Comparative Study of Some Contemporaneous Pottery Assemblages from Roman Britain. Unpublished DPhil thesis, University of Oxford.
Millett, M. (1983b) Excavations at Cowdery's Down, Basingstoke, 1978-81. *Archaeological Journal* 140, 151–279.
Millett, M. (1986) An early Roman cemetery at Alton, Hampshire. *Proceedings of the Hampshire Field Club and Archaeological Society* 42, 43–88.
Millett, M. (1987a) A question of time? Aspects of the future of pottery studies. *Bulletin of the University of London Institute of Archaeology* 24, 99–108.
Millett, M. (1987b) The Romano-British pottery. In D.H. Heslop (ed.) *The Excavation of an Iron Age Settlement at Thorpe Thewles Cleveland, 1980-1982*, 73–6. London, Council for British Archaeology.
Millett, M. (1990) *The Romanization of Britain. An Essay in Archaeological Interpretation*. Cambridge, Cambridge University Press.
Millett, M. (1991) Pottery: population or supply pattern? The Ager Tarraconensis approach. In G. Barker and J. Lloyd (eds) *Roman Landscapes. Archaeological Survey in the Mediterranean*, 18–26. London, British School at Rome.
Millett, M. (1993) A cemetery in an age of transition: King Harry Lane reconsidered. In M. Struck (ed.) *Römerzeitliche Graber als Quellen zu Religion, Bevölkerungsstruktur und Sozialgeschichte*, 255–82. Mainz, Johannes Gutenberg-Universität.
Millett, M. (2015) Archaeological studies of the Hayton data. In P. Halkon, M. Millett and H. Woodhouse (eds) *Hayton, East Yorkshire. Archaeological Studies of the Iron Age and Roman landscapes*, 498–541. Leeds, Yorkshire Archaeological Report 7.
Millett, M. and D. Graham (1986) *Excavations on the Romano-British Small Town at Neatham, Hants. 1969-1979*. Winchester, Hampshire Field Club and Archaeological Society Monograph 3.
Millett, M. and D. Russell (1984) Excavation of an iron age and Romano-British site at Viables Farm, Basingstoke. *Proceedings of the Hampshire Field Club and Archaeological Society* 40, 49–60.
Mintz, S. (1985) *Sweetness and Power. The Place of Sugar in Modern History*. New York, Viking.
Misa, T.J. (1994) Retrieving socio-technical change from technological determinism. In M.R. Smith and L. Marx (eds) *Does Technology Drive History? The Dilemma of Technological Determinism*, 115–41. Cambridge (MA), MIT Press.
Mitchell, W.J.T. (1996) What do pictures *really* want? *October* 77, 71–82.
Mizoguchi, K. (2015) A future of archaeology. *Antiquity* 89.343, 12–22.

Mogetta, M. (2015) A new date for concrete in Rome. *Journal of Roman Studies* 105, 1–40.

Mol, A. (2002) *The Body Multiple. Ontology in Medical Practice*. Durham (NC), Duke University Press.

Mol, A.A. (2014) *The Connected Caribbean. A Socio-Material Network Approach to Patterns of Homogeneity and Diversity in the Pre-Colonial Period*. Leiden, Sidestone Press

Mol, E.M. (2013) The perception of Egypt in networks of being and becoming: a Thing Theory approach to Egyptianising objects in Roman domestic contexts. In A. Bokern, M. Bolder-Boos, S. Krmnicek, D. Mascheck and S. Page (eds) *TRAC 2012. Proceedings of the Twenty-Second Annual Theoretical Roman Archaeology Conference. Frankfurt am Main*, 117–32. Oxford, Oxbow Books.

Mol, E.M. (2015) Egypt in Material and Mind. The Use and Perception of Aegyptiaca in Roman Domestic Contexts of Pompeii. Unpublished PhD thesis, Leiden University.

Mol, E.M. (2016) La Casa di Octavius Quartio. In F. Poole (ed.) *Il Nilo a Pompei. Visioni d'Egitto nel mondo romano*, 135–63. Turin, Museo delle Antichità Egizie.

Mols, S.T.A.M and E.M. Moormann (2008) *La villa della farnesina. Le pitture*. Milan, Electa.

Morley, N. (2015) Globalization and the Roman economy. In M. Pitts and M.J. Versluys (eds) *Globalisation and the Roman World. World History, Connectivity and Material Culture*, 69–98. Cambridge, Cambridge University Press.

Morton, T. (2013) *Hyperobjects. Philosophy and Ecology after the End of the World*. Minneapolis (MN), University of Minnesota Press.

Moss, C. (1988) Roman Marble Tables. Unpublished PhD thesis, Princeton University.

Murphy, E.A. and J. Poblome (2012) Technical and social considerations of tools from Roman Period ceramic workshops at Sagalassos (southwest Turkey): not just tools of the trade? *Journal of Mediterranean Archaeology* 25.2, 197–217.

Murphy, E.A. and J. Poblome (2016) A late antique ceramic workshop complex: evidence for workshop organisation at Sagalassos (southwest Turkey). *Anatolian Studies* 66, 185–99.

Murphy, E.A. and J. Poblome (2017) From formal to technical styles: production challenges and economic implications of changing tableware styles in Roman Imperial to Late Antique manufacturing waste. *American Journal of Archaeology* 121.1, 61–84.

Müskens, S.W.G. (2017) *Egypt beyond Representation. Materials and Materiality of Aegyptiaca Romana*. Leiden, ALSU 35.

Neyt, B., D. Braekmans, J. Poblome, J. Elsen, M. Waelkens and P. Degryse (2012) Long-term clay raw material selection and use in the region of Classical/Hellenistic to Early Byzantine Sagalassos (SW Turkey). *Journal of Archaeological Science* 39, 1296–305.

Niblett, R. (1985) *Sheepen. An Early Roman Industrial site at Camulodunum*. London, Council for British Archaeology.

Noë, A. (2004) *Action in Perception*. Cambridge (MA), MIT Press

Noë, A. (2009) *Out of our Heads. Why You Are Not Your Brain, and Other Lessons from the Biology of Consciousness*. New York, Hill and Wang.

Norman, D. (2002) [1988]. *The Design of Everyday Things*. New York, Basic Books.

Oleson, J.P., C. Brandon, S.M. Cramer, R. Cucitore, E. Gotti and R.L. Hohlfelder (2004) The ROMACONS Project: a contribution to the historical and engineering analysis of hydraulic concrete in Roman maritime structures. *International Journal of Nautical Archaeology* 33.2, 199–229.

Olsen, B. (2010) *In Defense of Things. Archaeology and the Ontology of Objects*. Lanham, Rowman and Littlefield.

Olsen, B., M. Shanks, T. Webmoor and C. Witmore (2012) *Archaeology. The Discipline of Things*. Berkeley (CA), University of California Press.

Orlin, E.M. (2008) Octavian and Egyptian cults: redrawing the boundaries of Romanness. *The American Journal of Philology* 129.2, 231–53.

Ortner, S.B. (1984) Theory in anthropology since the sixties. *Comparative Studies in Society and History* 26.1, 126–66.

Osborne, R. (2012) Cultures of empire: Greece and Rome. *New Left Review* 77, 105–20.
Ottaviano, G. (2008) Infrastructure and economic geography: an overview of theory and evidence. *EIB Papers* 13.2, 8–35.
Özden, S. (2015) Perge batı nekropolisi dolgu tabakasında bulunan (Parsel 159) Sagalassos kırmızı astarlı keramikleri. Unpublished PhD thesis, Istanbul University.
Parássoglou, G.M. (1979) Some thoughts on the posture of the ancient Greeks and Romans when writing on papyrus rolls. *Scrittura e civiltà* 3, 5–21.
Parker, G. (2007) Obelisks still in exile: monuments made to measure? In L. Bricault, M.J. Versluys and P.G.P. Meyboom (eds) *Nile into Tiber. Egypt in the Roman World. Proceedings of the IIIrd International Conference of Isis Studies, Leiden, May 11–14 2005*, 209–22. Leiden, Brill.
Parkes, M.B. (2008) *Their Hands Before our Eyes. A Closer Look at Scribes.* Aldershot, Ashgate.
Peacock, D.P.S. (1982) *Pottery in the Roman World. An Ethnoarchaeological Approach.* London, Longman.
Pearce, J. (2004) Archaeology, writing tablets and literacy in Roman Britain. *Gallia* 61, 43–51.
Pearce, J. (2015) A 'civilised' death? The interpretation of provincial Roman grave good assemblages. In J.R. Brandt, M. Prusac and H. Roland (eds) *Death and Changing Rituals. Function and Meaning in Ancient Funerary Practice*, 223–47. Oxford, Oxbow Books.
Pensabene, P. (1993) *Elementi architettonici di Alessandria e di altri siti Egiziana.* Rome, L'Erma di Brettschneider.
Perring, D. (2011) London's military origins. *Journal of Roman Archaeology* 24, 249–67.
Perring, D. and M. Pitts (2013) *Alien Cities. Consumption and the Origins of Urbanism in Roman Britain.* London, Spoilheap Publications Monograph. 7.
Petts, D. (2003) *Christianity in Roman Britain.* Stroud, Tempus.
Pfuhl, E. and H. Möbius (1979) *Die ostgriechischen Grabreliefs.* Mainz: Philipp von Zabern.
Picon, M. (2002) A propos des sigillées, présigillées et imitations des sigillées: questions de "coûts" et de marchés. *SFECAG, Actes du congrès de Bayeux*, 345–56.
Pitts, M. (2005) Pots and pits. Drinking and deposition in late Iron Age south-east Britain. *Oxford Journal of Archaeology* 24, 143–61.
Pitts, M. (2007) The Emperor's new clothes? The utility of identity in Roman archaeology. *American Journal of Archaeology* 111.4, 693–713.
Pitts, M. (2010a) Re-thinking the southern British oppida: networks, kingdoms and material culture. *European Journal of Archaeology* 13, 32–63.
Pitts, M. (2010b) Artefact suites and social practice: an integrated approach to Roman provincial finds assemblages. *Facta* 4, 125–52.
Pitts, M. (2014) Reconsidering Britain's first urban communities. *Journal of Roman Archaeology* 27, 133–74.
Pitts, M. (2015) Globalisation, circulation and mass consumption in the Roman world. In M. Pitts and M.J. Versluys (eds) *Globalisation and the Roman World. World History, Connectivity and Material Culture*, 69–96. Cambridge, Cambridge University Press.
Pitts, M. and D. Perring (2006) The making of Britain's first urban landscapes: the case of Late Iron Age and Roman Essex. *Britannia* 37, 189–212.
Pitts, M and M.J. Versluys (eds) (2015a) *Globalisation and the Roman World. World History, Connectivity and Material Culture.* Cambridge, Cambridge University Press.
Pitts, M. and M.J. Versluys (2015b) Globalisation and the Roman world: perspectives and opportunities. In M. Pitts and M.J. Versluys (eds) *Globalisation and the Roman World. World History, Connectivity and Material Culture*, 3–31. Cambridge, Cambridge University Press.
Pitts, M. and M.J. Versluys (forthcoming) Object-scapes: flows of objects and their impacts on societies.
Platz-Horster, G. (1978) Grabbeigaben für ein junges Mädchen. In K. Vierneisel (ed.) *Römisches im Antikenmuseum*, 184–95. Berlin, Antikenmuseum.

Poblome, J. (1999) *Sagalassos Red Slip Ware. Typology and Chronology*. Studies in Eastern Mediterranean Archaeology 2. Turnhout, Brepols.
Poblome, J. (2013) Money makes pottery go round. In J. Poblome (ed.) *Exempli Gratia. Sagalassos, Marc Waelkens and Interdisciplinary Archaeology*, 81–95. Leuven, Leuven University Press.
Poblome, J. (2016) The potters of ancient Sagalassos revisited. In A. Wilson and M. Flohr (eds) *Urban Craftsmen and Traders in the Roman world*, 377–404. Oxford, Oxford University Press.
Poblome, J. and Fırat, N. (2011) Late Roman D: a matter of open(ing) or closed horizons? In M.A. Cau, P. Reynolds and M. Bonifay (eds) *LRFW 1. Late Roman Fine Wares. Solving Problems of Typology and Chronology. A Review of the Evidence, Debate and new Contexts*. Roman and Late Antique Mediterraean Pottery 1, 49–55. Oxford, Archaeopress.
Poblome, J., D. Braekmans, B. Mušič, M. van der Enden, B. Neyt, B. De Graeve and P. Degryse (2013) A pottery kiln underneath the Odeon of ancient Sagalassos: the excavation results, the table wares and their archaeometrical analysis. In H. Fenning and C. Römer-Strehl (eds) *Networks in the Hellenistic World according to the Pottery in the Eastern Mediterranean and Beyond*. BAR International Series 2539, 175–86. Oxford, Archaeopress.
Poblome, J., P. Degryse, D. Cottica and N. Fırat (2001) A new Early Byzantine production centre in western Asia Minor: a petrographical and geochemical study of red slip ware from Hierapolis, Perge and Sagalassos. *Rei Cretariae Romanae Fautorum Acta* 37, 119–26.
Polfer, M. (2000) Reconstructing funerary rituals: the evidence of ustrina and related archaeological structures. In J. Pearce, M. Millett and M. Struck (eds) *Burial, Society and Context in the Roman World*, 30–37. Oxford, Oxbow Books.
Pommier, E. (2003) *Winckelmann, inventeur de l'histoire de l'art*. Paris, Gallimard.
Poplin, F. (2004) Numération et orientation des dés antiques et médiévaux. *Bulletin de la Société nationale des antiquaires de France* 2004, 51–65.
Porter, J.I. (2006) *Classical Pasts. The Classical Traditions of Greece and Rome*. Princeton (NJ), Princeton University Press.
Poux, M. (2004) *L'Âge du vin. Rites de boisson, festins et libations en Gaule indépendante*. Montagnac, Éditions Monique Mergoil.
Preston, B. (2000) The function of things: a philosophical perspective on material culture. In P. Graves-Brown (ed.) *Matter, Materiality and Modern Culture*, 22–49. London, Routledge.
Preston, B. (2013) *A Philosophy of Material Culture. Action, Function and Mind*. London, Routledge.
Pröttel, P. (1988) Zur Chronologie der Zwiebelknopffibeln. *Jahrbuch des Römisch-Germanischen Zentralmuseum Mainz* 35, 347–72.
Prown, J.D. (1996) Material culture: can the farmer and the cowman still be friends? In W.D. Kingery (ed.) *Learning from Things. Method and Theory of Material Culture Studies*, 19–27. Washington D.C., Smithsonian Institution Press.
Purcell, N. (1995) Literate games: Roman urban society and the game of Alea. *Past and Present* 147, 3–37.
Purcell, N. (2001) The *ordo scribarum*: a study in the loss of memory. *Mélanges de l'école française de Rome* 113.2, 633–74.
Quenemoen, C.K. (2014) Columns and concrete: architecture from Nero to Hadrian. In R.B. Ulrich and C.K. Quenemoen (eds) *A Companion to Roman Architecture*, 63–81. Malden, Wiley-Blackwell.
Raja, R. (2012) *Urban Development and Regional Identity in the Eastern Roman Provinces, 50 BC–AD 250. Aphrodisias, Ephesos, Athens, Gerasa*. Copenhagen, Museum Tusculanum Press.
Rawson, B. (2003) *Children and Childhood in Roman Italy*. Oxford, Oxford University Press.
Read, D.W. (2007) *Artifact Classification. A Conceptual and Methodological Approach*. Walnut Creek (CA), Left Coast Press.
Reece, R. (1987) *Coinage in Roman Britain*. London, Seaby.

Ribeiro, A. (2016) Against object agency: a counterreaction to Sorensen's 'Hammers and nails'. *Archaeological Dialogues* 23.2, 229–35.
Rice, P. (1987) *Pottery Analysis. A Sourcebook*. Chicago, University of Chicago Press.
Richardson, J.S. (1986) *Hispaniae. Spain and the Development of Roman Imperialism 218-82 BC*. Cambridge, Cambridge University Press.
Richardson, J.S. (1994) The administration of the empire. In J.A. Crook, A.W. Lintott and E. Rawson (eds) *The Cambridge Ancient History, vol. IX. The Last Age of the Roman Republic*, 564–982. Cambridge, Cambridge University Press.
Richardson, J.S. (2008) *The Language of Empire. Rome and the Idea of Empire from the Third Century BC to the Second Century AD*. Cambridge, Cambridge University Press.
Riva, C. (2006) The Orientalizing period in Etruria: sophisticated communities. In C. Riva and N. Vella (eds) *Debating Orientalization. Multidisciplinary Approaches to Processes of Change in the Ancient Mediterranean*. London, Equinox.
Rizzo, G.E. (1939) *Le pitture della "Casa di Livia"*. Rome, Istituto poligrafico dello stato.
Robb J. (2004) The extended artefact and the monumental economy: a methodology for material agency. In E. DeMarrais, C. Gosden and C. Renfrew (eds) *Rethinking Materiality. The Engagement of Mind with the Material World*, 131–9. Cambridge, McDonald Institute.
Robb, J. (2010) Beyond agency. *World Archaeology* 42.4, 493–520.
Robb, J. (2013) Material culture, landscapes of action, and emergent causation: a new model for the origin of the European Neolithic. *Current Anthropology* 54, 657–83.
Roberts, P. (1997) Mass-production of Roman finewares. In I. Freestone and D. Gaimster (eds) *Pottery in the Making. Ceramic Traditions*, 188–93. Washington D.C., Smithsonian Institution Press.
Robertson, R. (1992) *Globalization. Social Theory and Global Culture*. London, Sage.
Rockwell, P. (1990) Stone-carving tools: a stone-carver's view. *Journal of Roman Archaeology* 3, 351–7.
Rogers, T.T., J.R. Hodges, M.A. Lambon Ralph and K. Patterson (2003) Object recognition under semantic impairment: the effects of conceptual regularities on perceptual decisions. *Language and Cognitive Processes* 18, 625–62.
Rosenthal, S.S. and W.C. Strange (2004) Evidence on the nature and sources of agglomeration economies. In J.V. Henderson and J.-F. Thisse (eds) *Handbook of Regional and Urban Economics 4*, 2119–71. Amsterdam, Elsevier.
Roth, R.E. (2007) *Styling Romanisation. Pottery and Society in Central Italy*. Cambridge, Cambridge University Press.
Rutledge, S.H. (2012) *Ancient Rome as a Museum. Power, Identity, and the Culture of Collecting*. Oxford, Oxford University Press.
Sackett, J.R. (1985) Style and ethnicity in the Kalahari: a reply to Weissner. *American Antiquity* 50, 154–9.
Sackett, J.R. (1990) Style and ethnicity in archaeology: the case for isochrestism. In M. Conkey and C. Hastorf (eds) *The Uses of Style in Archaeology*, 32–43. Cambridge, Cambridge University Press.
Saller, R.P. (2011) The Roman family as productive unit. In B. Rawson (ed.) *A Companion to Families in the Greek and Roman Worlds*, 116–28. Malden, Wiley-Blackwell.
Sas, K. and H. Thoen (eds) (2002) *Schone schijn. Romeinse juweelkunst in West-Europa/Brillance et prestige. La jouaillerie romaine en Europe occidentale*. Leuven, Peeters.
Saurma-Jeltsch, L.E. and A. Eisenbeiss (eds) (2010) *The Power of Things and the Flow of Cultural Transformations. Art and Culture between Europe and Asia*. Berlin, Deutscher Kunstverlag.
Schnapp, A. (2013) *World Antiquarianism. Comparative perspectives*. Los Angeles (CA), Getty Research Institute.
Schädler, U. (1995) XII scripta, alea, tabula: new evidence for the Roman history of backgammon. In A.J. de Voogt (ed.) *New Approaches to Board Games Research. Asian Origin and Future Perspectives*, 73–98. Leiden, International Institute for Asian Studies.

Schaltenbrandt Obrecht, V. (2012) *Stilus. Kulturhistorische, typologisch-chronologische und technologische Untersuchungen an römischen Schreibgriffeln von Augusta Raurica und weiteren Fundorten.* Augst, Museum Augusta Raurica.
Scheidel, W. (2007) In search of economic growth. *Journal of Roman Archaeology* 22, 46–70.
Scheidel, W. (2012) Approaching the Roman Economy. In W. Scheidel (ed.) *The Cambridge Companion to the Roman economy*, 1–21. Cambridge, Cambridge University Press.
Schendzielorz, S. (2006) *Feulen. Ein spätlatènezeitlich-frührömisches Gräberfeld in Luxemburg.* Luxembourg, Musée National d'histoire et d'art.
Schiffer, M. (2004) Studying technological change: a behavioral perspective. *World Archaeology* 36.4, 570–85.
Schmid, E. (1978) Beinerne Spielwürfel von Vindonissa. *Gesellschaft pro Vindonissa* 1978, 58–80.
Schneider, C. (1965) Inhumations rituelles d'époque gallo-romaine à Caudebec-lès-Elbeuf. *Annales de Normandie* 15.3, 437–47.
Scott, E. (1993a) Writing the Roman Empire. In E. Scott (ed.) *Theoretical Roman Archaeology. First Conference Proceedings*, 5–22. Aldershot, Avebury.
Scott, E. (1993b) Introduction: TRAC (Theoretical Roman Archaeology Conference) 1991. In E. Scott (ed.) *Theoretical Roman Archaeology. First Conference Proceedings*, 1–4. Aldershot, Avebury.
Sennett, R. (2008) *The Craftsman*. New Haven, Yale University Press.
Shanks, M. (2007) Symmetrical Archaeology. *World Archaeology*, 39.4, 589–96.
Shanks, M. (2008) Post-processual archaeology and after. In R.A. Bentley, H.D.G. Maschner and C. Chippindale (eds) *Handbook of Archaeological Theories*, 133–44. Walnut Creek (CA), AltaMira Press.
Shennan, S. (2008) Evolution in Archaeology. *Annual Review of Anthropology* 37, 75–91.
Siegel, J. (1985) Koines and koineization. *Language in Society* 14, 357–78.
Silver, J. (2014) Incremental infrastructures: material improvisation and social collaboration across post-colonial Accra. *Urban Geography* 35.6, 788–804.
Simondon, G. (2005) *L'individuation à la lumière des notions de forme et d'information*. Grenoble, Jérôme Millon.
Simone, A. (2010) Infrastructure, real economies and social transformation: assembling components for regional urban development in Africa. In E. Pieterse (ed.) *Urbanization Imperatives for Africa. Transcending Policy Inertia*, 28–45. Cape Town, African Centre for Cities.
Sinopoli, C. (2003) *The Political Economy of Craft Production*. Cambridge, Cambridge University Press.
Skibo, J.M and M.B. Schiffer (2008) *People and Things. A Behavioral Approach to Material Culture*. New York, Springer.
Small, J.P. (1997) *Wax Tablets of the Mind. Cognitive Studies of Memory and Literacy in Classical Antiquity*. London, Routledge.
Snape, M. (1994) The southwest gate, *intervallum* and fort ditches. In P. Bidwell and S. Speak (eds) *Excavations at South Shields Roman fort*, vol. 1, 107–44. Newcastle, Society of Antiquaries of Newcastle-upon-Tyne.
Snodgrass, A.M. (1996) *Homer and the Artists*. Cambridge, Cambridge University Press.
Sorek, S. (2010) *The Emperors' Needles. Egyptian Obelisks and Rome*. Liverpool, Liverpool University Press.
Sørensen, T.F. (2013) We have never been Latourian: archaeological ethics and the posthuman condition. *Norwegian Archaeological Review* 46, 1–18.
Spawforth, A.J.S. (2012) *Greece and the Augustan Cultural Revolution*. Cambridge, Cambridge University Press.
Spriggs, M. (2008) Ethnographic parallels and the denial of history. *World Archaeology* 40.4, 538–52.
Spriggs, M. and D. Miller (1979) Ambone-Lease: a study of contemporary pottery making and its archaeological relevance. In M. Millett (ed.) *Pottery and the Archaeologist*, 25–34. London, Institute of Archaeology.

St. Clair, A. (2003) *Carving as Craft. Palatine East and the Greco-Roman Bone and Ivory Carving Tradition*. Baltimore, John Hopkins University Press.
Stannard, C. (2013) Are Ebusan coins at Pompeii, and the Pompeian pseudo-mint, a sign of intensive contacts with the island of Ebusus? In A. Arévalo, D. Bernal and D. Cottica (eds) *Ebusus y Pompeya, ciudades marítimas. Testimonios monetales de una relación*, 125–55. Cádiz, Universidad de Cádiz.
Stock, W. (2010) Concepts and semantic relations in information science. *Journal of the American Society for Information Science and Technology* 61.10, 1951–69.
Storey, V.C. (1993) Understanding semantic relationships. *VLDB Journal* 2, 455–88.
Strang, V. (2014) Fluid consistencies: material relationality in human engagements with water. *Archaeological Dialogues* 21.2, 133–50.
Stroobants, F. (in press) Civic coinage in Roman Pisidia: seeking a balance between the local and imperial level. In B. Hürmüzlü and L. De Jong (eds) *The Impact of Empire. Memory and Interaction in Hellenistic and Roman Pisidia*. London, British Institute at Ankara.
Swetnam-Burland, M. (2010) Aegyptus redacta: the Egyptian Obelisk in the Augustan Campus Martius. *The Art Bulletin* 92.3, 135–53
Swift, E. (2000) *Regionality in Dress Accessories in the Late Roman West*. Montagnac, Éditions Monique Mergoil.
Swift, E. (2007) Decorated vessels: the function of decoration in Late Antiquity. In L. Lavan, E. Swift and T. Putzeys (eds) *Objects in Context, Objects in Use*. Late Antique Archaeology 5, 385–409. Leiden, Brill.
Swift, E. (2009) *Style and Function in Roman Decoration. Living with Objects and Interiors*. Burlington, Ashgate.
Swift, E. (2014) Design, function and use-wear in spoons: reconstructing everyday Roman social practice. *Journal of Roman Archaeology* 27, 203–37.
Swift, E. (2017) *Roman Artefacts and Society. Design, Behaviour and Experience*. Oxford, Oxford University Press.
Talloen, P. (2011) From pagan to Christian: religious iconography in material culture from Sagalassos. In L. Lavan and M. Mulryan (eds) *The Archaeology of Late Antique 'Paganism'*, 575–607. Leiden, Brill.
Talloen, P. and J. Poblome (2005) What were they thinking of? Relief decorated pottery from Sagalassos: a cognitive approach. *Mélanges de l'Ecole Française de Rome. Antiquité* 117.1, 55–81.
Taylor, P., M. Hoyler and R. Verbruggen (2010) External urban relational process: introducing central flow theory to complement central place theory. *Urban Studies* 47, 2803–18.
Taylor, P., B. Derudder, M. Hoyler and P. Ni (2013) New regional geographies of the world as practiced by leading advanced producer service firms in 2010. *Transactions of the Institute of British Geographers* 38.3, 497–511.
ter Keurs, P. (2014) Entanglement: reflections on people and objects. In T. Bampilis and P. ter Keurs (eds) *Social matter(s). Anthropological approaches to materiality*, 45–60. Zürich, Lit.
Theuws, F. (1999) Changing settlement patterns, burial grounds and the symbolic construction of ancestors and communities in the late Merovingian Southern Netherlands. In C. Fabech and J. Ringtved (eds) *Settlement and Landscape. Proceedings of a Conference in Århus, Denmark May 4-7 1998*, 337–49. Højbjerg, Jutland Archaeological Society.
Theuws, F. (2009) Grave goods, ethnicity, and the rhetoric of burial rites in Late Antique Northern Gaul. In T. Derks and N. Roymans (eds) *Ethnic Constructs in Antiquity. The Role of Power and Tradition*, 283–319. Amsterdam, Amsterdam University Press.
Thomas, J. (2015) The future of archaeological theory. *Antiquity* 89.348, 1287–96.
Thomas, N. (1991) *Entangled Objects. Exchange, Material Culture, and Colonialism in the Pacific*. Cambridge (MA), Harvard University Press.
Thonemann, P. (2011) *The Maeander Valley. A Historical Geography from Antiquity to Byzantium*. Cambridge, Cambridge University Press.

Thonemann, P. (ed.) (2013) *Roman Phrygia. Culture and Society*. Cambridge, Cambridge University Press.
Tilley, C. (2010) *Interpreting Landscapes. Geologies, Topographies, Identities*. Walnut Creek (CA), Left Coast Press.
Timby, J. (2000) The pottery. In M. Fulford and J. Timby (eds) *Late Iron Age and Roman Silchester. Excavations on the site of the Forum-Basilica 1977, 1980-86*, 180–312. London, Society for the Promotion of Roman Studies.
Tomlin, R.S.O. (2011) Writing and communication. In L. Allason-Jones (ed.) *Artefacts in Roman Britain. Their Purpose and Use*, 133–52. Cambridge, Cambridge University Press.
Toner, J. (1995) *Leisure and Ancient Rome*. Oxford, Polity.
Torelli, M. (1980) Innovazioni nelle tecniche edilizie romane tra il I sec. a.C. e il I sec. d.C. In *Tecnologia, economia e società nel mondo romano. Atti del Convegno di Como, 27-29 settembre 1979*, 139–62. Como, Banca popolare commercio e industria.
Treggiari, S. (1976) Jobs for women. *American Journal for Ancient History* 1, 76–104.
Trimble, J. (2011) *Women and Visual Replication in Roman Imperial Art and Culture*. Cambridge, Cambridge University Press.
Trombley, F. (1987) Korykos in Cilicia Trachis: the economy of a small coastal city in late Antiquity (Saec. V–VI). A précis. *The Ancient History Bulletin* 1.1, 16–23.
Tronchin, F.C. (2011) The Sculpture of the Casa di Octavius Quartio at Pompeii. In E. Poehler, M. Flohr and K. Cole (eds) *Pompeii. Art, Industry and Infrastructure*, 24–40. Oxford, Oxbow.
True, M. and K. Hamma (eds) (1994) *A Passion for Antiquities*. Malibu, Paul Getty Museum.
Tyers, P. (1996) *Roman Pottery in Britain*. London, Batsford.
Van Aerde, M. (2015) Egypt and the Augustan Cultural Revolution. An Interpretative Archaeological Overview. Unpublished PhD thesis, Leiden University.
van der Enden, M., J. Poblome and P. Bes (2014) From Hellenistic to Roman Imperial in Pisidian tableware: the genesis of Sagalassos red slip ware. In H. Meyza and K. Domzalski (eds) *Late Hellenistic to Mediaeval Fine Wares of the Aegean Coast of Anatolia. Their Production, Imitation and Use*. Travaux de l'Institut des Cultures Méditerranéennes et Orientales de l'Académie Polonaise des Sciences 1, 81–93. Warsaw, Neriton.
van der Leeuw, S.E. and R. Torrence (eds) (1989) *What's New? A Closer Look at the Process of Innovation*. London, Unwin Hyman.
van Dommelen, P. and N. Terrenato (2007) Introduction: local cultures and the expanding Roman Republic. In P. van Dommelen and N. Terrenato (eds) *Articulating Local Cultures. Power and Identity under the Expanding Roman Republic*, 7–12. Portsmouth, Journal of Roman Archaeology Supplementary Series 63.
Van Eck, C., M.J. Versluys and P. ter Keurs (2015) The biography of cultures: style, objects and agency. Proposal for an interdisciplinary approach. *Cahiers de l'École du Louvre* 7, 2–22.
van Nijf, O. (1997) *The Civic World of Professional Associations in the Roman East*. Amsterdam, J.C. Gieben.
Van Oyen, A. (2013) Towards a post-colonial artefact analysis. *Archaeological Dialogues* 20.1, 81–107.
Van Oyen, A. (2015) Actor-network theory's take on archaeological types: becoming, material agency and historical explanation. *Cambridge Archaeological Journal* 25.1, 63–78.
Van Oyen, A. (2016a) *How Things Make History. The Roman Empire and its Terra Sigillata Pottery*. Amsterdam, Amsterdam University Press.
Van Oyen, A. (2016b) Historicising material agency: from relations to relational constellations. *Journal of Archaeological Method and Theory* 23, 354–78.
Vandkilde, H. (2017) Bronzization: the Bronze Age as pre-modern globalization. In T. Hodos, A. Geurds, P. Lane, I. Lilley, M. Pitts, G. Shelach, M. Stark and M.J. Versluys (eds) *The Routledge Handbook of Archaeology and Globalisation*. London, Routledge.

Versluys, M.J. (2010) Understanding Egypt in Egypt and beyond. In *Isis on the Nile. Egyptian gods in Hellenistic and Roman Egypt. Proceedings of the IVth International Conference of Isis Studies, Liège, November 27-29, 2008, Michel Malaise in honorem*, 7–36. Leiden, Brill.

Versluys, M.J. (2013) Material culture and identity in the late Roman Republic (ca. 200 BC – ca. 20 BC). In J. de Rose Evans (ed.) *Blackwell Companion to the Archaeology of the Roman Republic*, 647–62. London, Blackwell.

Versluys, M.J. (2014) Understanding objects in motion: an *archaeological* dialogue on Romanization. *Archaeological Dialogues* 21, 1–20.

Versluys, M.J. (2015) Roman visual material culture as globalising koine. In M. Pitts and M.J. Versluys (eds) *Globalisation and the Roman World. World history, Connectivity and Material Culture*, 141–74. Cambridge, Cambridge University Press.

Versluys, M.J. (2017a) Egypt as part of the Roman *koine*: mnemohistory and the Iseum Campense in Rome. In S. Nagel, J.F. Quack and C. Witschel (eds) *Entangled Worlds. Religious Confluences between East and West in the Roman Empire*, 274–93. Tübingen, Mohr Siebeck.

Versluys, M.J. (2017b) Exploring Aegyptiaca and their material agency throughout global history. In T. Hodos, A. Geurds, P. Lane, I. Lilley, M. Pitts, G. Shelach, M. Stark and M.J. Versluys (eds) *The Routledge Handbook of Archaeology and Globalisation*, 74–89. London, Routledge.

Viveiros de Castro, E. (1998) Cosmological deixis and Amerindian perspectivism. *Journal of the Royal Anthropological Institute* 4.3, 469–88.

Vroom, J. (2007) The archaeology of Late Antique dining habits in the eastern Mediterranean: a preliminary study of the evidence. In L. Lavan, E. Swift and T. Putzeys (eds) *Objects in Context, Objects in Use*. Late Antique Archaeology 5, 313–61. Leiden, Brill.

Waagé, F.O. (1948) Hellenistic and Roman tableware of North Syria. In F.O. Waagé (ed.) *Antioch-on-the-Orontes IV, 1. Ceramics and Islamic coins*, 1–60. Princeton (NJ), Princeton University Press.

Wallace, L. (2014) *The Origins of Roman London*. Cambridge, Cambridge University Press.

Wallace-Hadrill, A. (1989) Rome's cultural revolution. *Journal of Roman Studies* 79, 157–64.

Wallace-Hadrill, A. (1994) *Houses and Society in Pompeii and Herculaneum*. Princeton (NJ), Princeton University Press.

Wallace-Hadrill, A. (2008) *Rome's Cultural Revolution*. Cambridge, Cambridge University Press.

Wardle, D. (ed. and trans.) (2006) *Cicero. On Divination, Book 1*. Oxford, Clarendon.

Ward-Perkins, J.B. (1981) *Roman Imperial Architecture*. Harmondsworth, Penguin.

Waters, C.N. et al. (2016) The Anthropocene is functionally and stratigraphically distinct from the Holocene. *Science* 351.6269, DOI: 10.1126/science.aad2622.

Webmoor, T. and C.L. Witmore (2008) Things are us! A commentary on human/things relations under the banner of a 'social' archaeology. *Norwegian Archaeological Review* 41.1, 53–70.

Webster, J. (1995) Interpretatio: Roman word power and the Celtic Gods. *Britannia* 26, 153–62.

Webster, J. (2001) Creolizing the Roman provinces. *American Journal of Archaeology* 105, 209–25.

Wells, P.S. (2012) *How Ancient Europeans Saw the World. Vision, Patterns, and the Shaping of the Mind in Prehistoric Times*. Princeton (NJ), Princeton University Press.

Wengrow, D. (2010) Commodity branding in archaeological and anthropological perspectives. In A. Bevan and D. Wengrow (eds) *Cultures of Commodity Branding*, 11–33. Walnut Creek (CA), Left Coast Press.

Wengrow, D. (2014) *The Origins of Monsters. Image and cognition in the First Age of Mechanical Reproduction*. Princeton (NJ), Princeton University Press.

Werner, J. (1950) Zur Entstehung der Reihengräberzivilisation. *Archaeologica Geographic* 1, 23–32.

Westermann, W.L. (1914a) Apprentice contracts and the apprentice system in Roman Egypt. *Classical Philology* 9.3, 295–315.

Westermann, W.L. (1914b) Vocational training in Antiquity. *The School Review* 22.9, 601–10.

Whiting, W. (1925) The Roman cemeteries at Ospringe: description of finds continued. *Archaeologia Cantiana* 37, 83–96.
Wiessner, P. (1983) Style and social information in Kalahari San projectile points. *American Antiquity* 48, 235–76.
Wiessner, P. (1989) Style and changing relations between the individual and society. In I. Hodder (ed.) *The Meaning of the Things. Material Culture and Symbolic Expression*, 56–63. London, Unwin Hyman.
Wightman, E.M. (1985) *Gallia Belgica*. London, Batsford.
Wilkinson, D. (2013) The Emperor's new body: personhood, ontology and the Inka sovereign. *Cambridge Archaeological Journal* 23.3, 417–32.
Willet, R. (2012) Red Slipped Complexity. The Socio-Cultural Context of the Concept and Use of Tableware in the Roman East. Unpublished PhD thesis, KU Leuven.
Willet, R. and J. Poblome (2015) The scale of Sagalassos red slip ware production: reconstructions of local need and production output of Roman imperial tableware. *Adalya* 18, 133–157.
Willis, S. (2005) The context of writing and written records in ink: the archaeology of samian inkwells in Roman Britain. *Archaeological Journal* 162, 96–145.
Willis, S. (2007) Sea, coast, estuary, land, and culture in Iron Age Britain. In C.C. Haselgrove and T. Moore (eds) *The Later Iron Age in Britain and Beyond*, 107–29. Oxford, Oxbow Books.
Willis, S. (2011) Samian ware and society in Roman Britain and beyond. *Britannia* 42, 167–242.
Wilson, A. (2006) The economic impact of technological advances in the Roman construction industry. In E. Lo Cascio (ed.) *Innovazione tecnica e progresso economico nel mondo romano*, 225–36. Bari, Edipuglia.
Wilson, A. (2009) Approaches to quantifying Roman trade. In A.K. Bowman and A. Wilson (eds) *Quantifying the Roman Economy. Methods and Problems*, 213–49. Oxford, Oxford University Press.
Wilson Jones, M. (2000) *Principles of Roman Architecture*. New Haven (CT), Yale University Press.
Winckelmann, J.J. (1764) *Geschichte der Kunst des Alterthums*. Dresden, Walther.
Witmore, C.L. (2007) Symmetrical archaeology: excerpts of a manifesto. *World Archaeology* 39.4, 546–62.
Wittgenstein, L. (2001) [1953] *Philosophische Untersuchungen*. Ed. J. Schulte, Wissenschaftliche Buchgesellschaft, Frankfurt.
Wölfflin, H. (1915) *Kunstgeschichtliche Grundbegriffe. Das Problem der Stilentwicklung in der neueren Kunst*. Munich, Bruckmann.
Woodward, I. (2007) *Understanding Material Culture*. London, Sage.
Woolf, G. (1995) The formation of Roman provincial cultures. In J. Metzler, M. Millett, N. Roymans and J. Slofstra (eds) *Integration in the Early Roman West. The Role of Culture and Ideology*, 9–18. Luxembourg, Musée National d'Histoire et d'Art.
Woolf, G. (1998) *Becoming Roman. The Origins of Provincial Civilization in Gaul*. Cambridge, Cambridge University Press.
Woolf, G. (2000) Literacy. In A.K. Bowman, P. Guernsey and D. Rathbone (eds) *The Cambridge Ancient History* XI, 875–97. Cambridge, Cambridge University Press.
Woolf, G. (2001) The Roman cultural revolution in Gaul. In N. Terrenato and S. Keay (eds) *Italy and the West. Comparative Issues in Romanization*, 173–86. Oxford, Oxbow.
Woolf, G. (2009) Literacy or literacies in Rome? In W.A. Johnson and H.N. Parker (eds) *Ancient Literacies. The Culture of Reading in Greece and Rome*, 46–68. Oxford, Oxford University Press.
Worrell, S. (2008) Roman Britain in 2007 II: finds reported under the Portable Antiquities Scheme. *Britannia* 39, 337–67.
Yu, N., G. de Roo, M. De Jong and S. Storm (2016) Does the expansion of a motorway network lead to economic agglomeration? Evidence from China. *Transport Policy* 45, 218–27.
Zanker, P. (1988) *The Power of Images in the Age of Augustus*. Ann Arbor (MI), University of Michigan Press.

Zanker, P. (2000) The city as a symbol: Rome and the creation of an urban image. In E. Fentress (ed.) *Romanization and the City. Creation, Transformations, and Failures*, 25–41. Portsmouth, Journal of Roman Archaeology Supplementary Series 38.

Zanker, P. (2008) *Roman Art*. Los Angeles (CA), Getty Publications.

Zerubavel, E. (1982) The standardization of time: a sociohistorical perspective. *American Journal of Sociology* 88.1, 1–23.

Zienkiewicz, J.D. (1986) *The Legionary Fortress Baths at Caerleon. Volume II. The Finds*. Cardiff, National Museum of Wales.

Zimmer, G. (1982) *Römische Berufsdarstellungen*. Berlin, Gebrüder Mann Verlag.